25 Bicycle Tours in Ohio's Western Reserve

WITHDRAWN

Historic Northeast Ohio from the Lake Erie Islands to the Pennsylvania Border

Sally Walters

Photographs by the Author

A 25 Bicycle Tours™ Book

Backcountry Publications
The Countryman Press, Inc.
Woodstock, Vermont

OK

An Invitation to the Reader—Although it is unlikely that the roads you cycle on these tours will change much with time, some road signs, landmarks, and other terms may. If you find that changes have occurred on these routes, please let us know so we may correct them in future editions. Address all correspondence to:

Editor
25 Bicycle Tours™ Series
Backcountry Publications
P.O. Box 175
Woodstock, VT 05091

Library of Congress Cataloging-in-Publication Data

Walters, Sally.
    25 bicycle tours in Ohio's Western Reserve : historic northeast
Ohio from the Lake Erie Islands to the Pennsylvania Border / Sally
Walters ; photographs by the author.
        p.   cm. — (A 25 bicycle tours book)
    ISBN 0-88150-166-2
    1. Bicycle touring—Ohio—Western Reserve—Guide-books.
    2. Western Reserve (Ohio)—Description and travel—Guide-books.
    I. Title. II. Title: Twenty-five bicycle tours in Ohio's Western
Reserve. III. Series.
GV1045.5.O33W478 1991
796.6′4′0977136—dc20   91-687
                                                      CIP

Published by Backcountry Publications
A division of The Countryman Press, Inc.
Woodstock, Vermont 05091

Printed in the United States of America
Typesetting by The Sant Bani Press
Text and cover design by Richard Widhu
Photos by the Author
Maps by Richard Widhu, © 1991 Backcountry Publications

To the memory of my father,
Oliver Perry Walters,
who was named for the hero
of the Battle of Lake Erie
and who was a hero in his own right.

Acknowledgments

This book would not have been possible without the capable assistance of William Knight, whose dedicated work in collecting material from chambers of commerce and other sources was invaluable. I also want to thank the staffs of the Western Reserve Historical Society, the Cleveland Metroparks System, and the Hiram College Library. I am grateful to Joan Delia Speight, whose support and encouragement throughout the writing of this book were greatly appreciated, and to Anne Reid and Bob Howard for their special contribution. Particular gratitude goes to my dearest friend, JoAnn Moore, whose vitality and warm good humor enlivened many a visit to B&Bs and the Lake Erie Islands. I extend my appreaciation to Carl Taylor of Backcountry Publications for his patience and flexibility, and to my editor Sarah Spiers for her enthusiasm and sound advice. Most of all, I thank my mother Anne Kach Walters, who gave me my first bicycle and my first book.

Publisher's notice: Cycling involves inherent risks, and readers planning to follow tours in this book should first read carefully the "safety" section of the introduction. Cyclists in urban areas should also be alert to the problem of crime. Tours in this book are in areas considered safe to ride in at the time of publication, but cyclists should follow sensible precautions (such as never cycling at night and traveling with one or more companions) and should be alert to changing patterns of crime in the city.

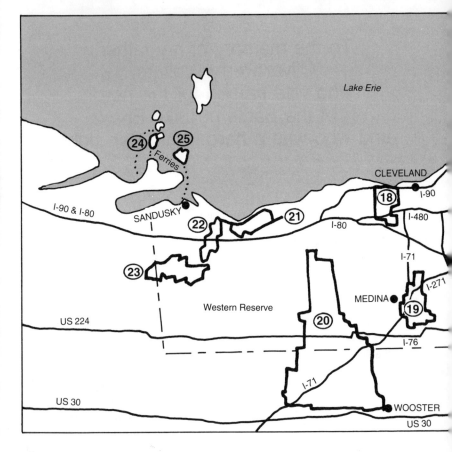

Contents

Introduction   6

Pennsylvania Borderland
  1. Town One, Range One (Mahoning County) 12
  2. Millionaire's Row—Then and Now (Trumbull County) 21
  3. Mosquito Creek Reservoir (Trumbull County) 31
  4. Architectural Sampler: A Two-Day Tour (Trumbull and
       Ashtabula Counties) 39
  5. Ashtabula's Covered Bridges (Ashtabula County) 51

Rural Heartland
  6. Lakeshore Vines and Wines (Lake and Ashtabula Counties) 60
  7. Lake County Loop 70
  8. Geauga Gems (Geauga County) 81
  9. Amish Country (Portage and Geauga Counties) 88
 10. Portage County Potpourri 97
 11. A Tale of Two Townships (Summit and Portage Counties) 106

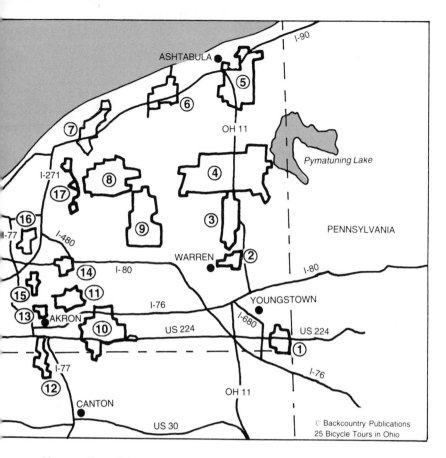

Map labels: ASHTABULA, I-90, ⑤, ⑥, OH 11, ⑦, Pymatuning Lake, I-271, ⑧, ④, ⑰, ③, PENNSYLVANIA, ⑯, I-480, I-77, ⑨, WARREN, ②, I-80, ⑭, I-80, ⑮, ⑪, I-76, YOUNGSTOWN, ⑬, AKRON, I-680, US 224, ⑩, US 224, ①, I-76, I-77, ⑫, OH 11, © Backcountry Publications, 25 Bicycle Tours in Ohio, CANTON, US 30

Metropolitan Fringe
12. Portage Lakes (Summit County)   116
13. Historic Akron (Summit County)   123
14. Hudson Triangle (Summit County)   131
15. CVNRA—South (Summit County)137
16. CVNRA—North (Summit and Cuyahoga Counties)   144
17. Emerald Necklace East—Chagrin Valley (Cuyahoga County)   152
18. Emerald Necklace West—Rocky River (Cuyahoga County)   162

West of the Cuyahoga
19. Medina Meander (Medina and Summit Counties)   174
20. Three-Day College Loop (Lorain, Ashland, Wayne, and
       Medina Counties)   183
21. Vermillion and the North Coast (Lorain and Erie Counties)   198
22. Firelands—Erie County   206
23. Firelands—Huron County   217
24. Lake Erie Islands: Kelleys Island   236

Appendix A: Cleveland Area Bike Shops Not Listed in Tours   245

Appendix B: Western Reserve Bibliography   246

Introduction

The Western Reserve

Ohio's Western Reserve is the most self-conscious region in the state, with a unique historical and cultural integrity. As with much of early American history, its origins go back to a royal charter from the English kings. The charter responsible for the Western Reserve was issued on April 23, 1662, by Charles II, granting the colony of Connecticut all the land

> bounded on the East by the Narragansett River . . . ; on the North by the line of the Massachusetts plantation, on the South by the sea; and in longitude . . . running East and West, that is to say, from the said Narragansett Bay in the East to the South sea on the West [the Pacific Ocean], with the islands thereto adjoining.

By the end of the Revolutionary War, the peculiar dimension of a colony some sixty-seven miles deep and three thousand miles wide posed major administrative problems. When the British ceded the Northwest Territories to the Americans at the end of the war, the young government was eager to stimulate settlement on these uncharted lands in order to hold them. The Indians, not having been party to the British and American treaty, needed to be convinced that the new nation had a right to expand westward, and an aggressive settlement policy was one way to establish a foothold.

By 1786, all the states except Connecticut had given up their western holdings. Driving a hard bargain, Connecticut agreed, on September 14, 1786, to cede her claims through Pennsylvania and west of Lake Erie to the Pacific. Only a 120-mile strip was reserved in the Ohio Territory (to become a state in 1803), beginning at the border of Pennsylvania between 41° and 42° 2′ north latitude, the projections of Connecticut's north and south boundaries. The Republic agreed, and the land became known as Connecticut's Western Reserve in Ohio or New Connecticut.

For several years, New Connecticut was seen as a colony of the original state; some envisioned it as a complete state in itself since, at well over three million acres, it was larger than Connecticut itself. The risks facing settlers were so great, however, that by 1795 only one sale had been made. The Connecticut General Assembly formed an eight-person committee, one from each county, charged with selling the land.

The proceeds were to be used as investment capital for a public school system. By September 2, 1795, the committee had sold the land for $1.2 million to fifty-seven speculators. The investments ranged from Sylvanus Griswold's $1,683 to Oliver Phelps' $168,185. No one paid cash, however. They gave bonds to the state treasurer and a mortgage against the property. It was their hope that the land they had never seen would sell for more than the thirty cents an acre, on average, they had promised to pay for it.

The investors formed the Connecticut Land Company, which hired a surveying team to measure off the Reserve into five-mile-square townships, beginning at the Pennsylvania line and extending westward to make up twenty-four vertical ranges. The townships were then broken into sections and classified as to value based on the reports of the surveyors. Shareholders drew lots for land parcels of varying quality scattered over the several townships.

The original title holders of the land became known as the lands' proprietors, most of whom hired agents to supervise the sale of the property to prospective settlers. As a result, most immigrants did not look over the land they hoped to buy but simply arrived with a purchased ticket in their pocket specifying their section of a particular township. The Reserve thus developed not in the rootless manner of much of the frontier but rather apportioned and settled with graph-paper exactitude.

To those who conceived this geometric distribution plan, it seemed an eminently just and tidily organized manner of land apportionment, encouraging settlement throughout the three million acres almost simultaneously. But no attention was given to the natural economic features of the land. The small settlements spread evenly throughout the Reserve were too isolated to make major improvements or build commercial enterprises. Given the lack of transportation through the vast stretches of wilderness between settlements, there was no market for produce either locally or back East. As a result, there was no way to accumulate capital to pay the proprietors back in Connecticut nor to pay taxes on the land to the state of Ohio. Descendants of the original proprietors found that, instead of inheriting profits from the initial investment, they were gaining unsold land encumbered with back taxes or settler/debtors who had no means of paying their mortgages. Oliver Phelps, the company's greatest investor, died in debtors' prison, leaving his family improverished.

After thirteen years, the Connecticut Land Company had paid back only half its commitment to Connecticut. In 1810, the state hired Yale graduate and U.S. Senator James Hillhouse as Commissioner of the School Fund to retrieve the state's money. Hillhouse undertook a study of the debt of each isolvent member of the Land Company. Through a brilliant fifteen-year program of on-site land inspection and ingenious financial counseling, Hillhouse brought solvency to the debtors and the beginning of stability to the Western Reserve economy by 1825. The wizardry of Hillhouse, plus the development of the Ohio Canal Begun in the same year, pulled the settlers of the Reserve out of poverty and into a prosperity worthy of its New England heritage. The introduction to each of the tours in this book provide details on many aspects of the Reserve's growth and development from a more personal and local perspective.

Today, the Western Reserve, which includes the cities of Cleveland, Akron, and Youngstown, is a major financial, industrial, and cultural center in the state. Visitors to the Reserve, however, are struck by the unmistakable New England ambience. "No other five-thousand square miles of territory in the United States, lying in a body outside New England," wrote B. A. Hinsdale, early president of Hiram College, "ever had, to begin with, so pure a New England population." New England names abound, and almost no community is without its village square. Even Cleveland, now the eighth largest city in the nation, retains its Public Square in the heart of its downtown. In the Western Reserve countryside, these village greens are usually surrounded by fine examples of New England architecture in numerous dwellings and churches. Intensely proud of their Western Reserve heritage, residents have made great efforts to preserve much of the past. Visitors will find numerous historical museums and re-created villages that ensure that the look and flavor of the pioneer past is not lost to later generations. For those interested in learning more about Western Reserve history and lore, a list of recommended reading is provided at the end of this book. The Western Reserve Historical Society at 10825 East Boulevard, Cleveland, 44106, has an expansive museum display and a twenty-five thousand-volume library.

The Tours

The Western Reserve includes the eleven northeastern Ohio counties of Trumbull, Ashtabula, Portage, Geauga, Lake, Summit, Cuyahoga, Medina, Lorain, Erie, and Huron, plus parts of Mahoning and Ashland counties. Bordered on the north by Lake Erie, it extends from the Pennsylvania line west to the Lake Erie Islands. The southern border of the Reserve, occasionally marked by a road called Base Line Road or Western Reserve Road, runs a few miles south of US 224.

Within its borders are attractions and interests for all ranges of tastes and interests. The Western Reserve contains some of the most densely populated and the most sparsely populated areas of Ohio. The terrain varies from the flat lake plains of Ashtabula County to the rugged hills and dales of the Cuyahoga drainage basin. The tours take you from rural wineries and picturesque covered bridges to busy college towns and bustling tourist centers. You might pedal next to the vast, glacially carved expanse of Lake Erie or along a placid, man-made canal or reservoir. You can stop for lunch in a peaceful county park or spend the night in a luxury bed and breakfast in the Cuyahoga Valley National Recreation Area. You may choose to spend a week on an island or only a day in the suburbs.

In picking a tour, two important considerations are length and degree of difficulty, information that is given at the beginning of each tour. Although most tours are in the fifteen- to forty-mile range, they run from a six-mile jaunt to a 108-mile excursion. All tours are loops, ending where they begin. Many include alternative route suggestions that reduce the total mileage. The degree of difficulty is based mainly on the height and steepness of hills and the surface quality of the road. Keep in mind, however, that the strength and direction of the wind are often more significant than hills in determining how much energy you'll have to expend. If a ride looks too long or strenuous, or you want to share the experience with a noncycling companion, most of the tours can also be completed by car.

It's best to read to the end of a tour before you undertake a particular ride. In addition to the difficulty rating in the introduction, the text relates specific information on especially grueling hills, open, windswept farmland, or slopes that provide effortless freewheeling. A pre-reading will also indicate whether to bring extra food, a bathing suit, or special equipment.

Directions are given for every turn, stop sign, or traffic signal. To avoid compounding errors and to eliminate the need for a cyclometer, you may want to calculate your mileage from one point to the next rather than from the beginning of the tour. Care has been taken to indicate whether a given road is signposted, but signs can change from year to year. Road names or numbers are given at unsignposted corners so you can confirm your position on a map or when a signpost appears farther along. The tours indicate interstates as "I-," federal highways as "US," and state highways as "OH." Because more roads are paved each year, you may occasionally find a paved road where directions indicate a gravel one.

Lunch or mid-tour rest stops are often suggested, and restaurants of note are included. Standard overnight accommodations are not mentioned except for the multi-day tours; however the bed and breakfast establishments on or near the routes are given for each tour, since many are not advertised and depend on word of mouth. Very few of the area's visitor's bureaus provide complete information on bed and breakfast accommodations. At the time of publication, this book provides the most thorough and up-to-date listing available for the entire Reserve.

For those who want to supplement the maps printed here, the best are those produced by each county's highway department. These can

be obtained by writing or calling the appropriate department. Some are free; others charge a dollar or two. Supplemental maps may denote a road name different from what is in the book. I have always used the name given on the signpost rather than that on a map.

Bicycling Safety

Although back roads or bypassed highways are chosen whenever possible, these tours have also been selected on the basis of historical, cultural, and general tourist interest. Automobile traffic thus sometimes exceeds what a bicyclist would consider ideal. The introduction to a tour will mention whether more heavily traveled roads are included or if it is not recommended for children or unskilled riders. However, alertness and good judgment are always needed, even on little-used back roads. Backcountry residents can drive rather fast; they expect little traffic and may be ill-prepared to encounter cyclists. Urban areas in the Reserve come with the delights and the dangers of urban center everywhere, thus cycling with a companion is recommended. Unfortunately, even suburban bike paths have been the scenes of assaults on females riding alone.

For short and easy tours such as those on the Lake Erie Islands, any bike, including the three-speed bikes available for rental, will suffice. Covering longer distances or hilly terrain is less difficult on a mountain bike or a lightweight bike with a wider choice of gears. Better made bikes increase efficiency and speed; they tackle hills more easily, and they generally have better brakes for safer descents. If you're unsure of your brakes, or any other bike part, have your bike checked by a competent mechanic. Bike parts and assistance can be found at the bike shops listed at the end of each tour. It's wise to call first to be sure the shop is open and has the parts or skills you need. For readers needing more information on equipment and safe cycling, I recommend Norman D. Ford's book, *Keep on Pedaling: The Complete Guide to Adult Bicycling* (The Countryman Press, Woodstock, Vermont).

Information Sources for Ohio Bicyclists

The Ohio Department of Transportation's Bicycle Transportation Administration offers a wealth of low-cost touring information. The *Ohio Bicycle Route Guide* includes a set of nineteen maps covering the entire state. Printed on waterproof paper and folded to fit in a handlebar bag, the whole set is available for five dollars. Make your check payable to ODOT and mail it to the Bicycle Transportation Administration, 25 South Front Street, Columbus, Ohio 43215. The Administration also provides an Ohio Bicycle Events Calendar and a list of over seventy Ohio bicycle clubs free of charge.

The *Ohio Bicycle User's Map* is a six-map set with fifteen thousand miles of "ride-tested" routes. The cost is $3.50, payable to the Ohio Bicycle User's Cartographic Society, 248 Highland Drive, Findlay, Ohio 45840. American Youth Hostels also supplies a series of maps for nine different trails throughout the state for five dollars per map. A list of routes can be obtained through Columbus Council AYH, P.O. Box 23111, Columbus, Ohio 43223.

An outstanding source of information for bicycling in Ohio is the former *BikeOhio* magazine, expanded into *Bike Midwest Magazine* beginning with its March 1991 issue. It now covers Indiana, Kentucky, Michigan, Pennsylvania, and West Virginia, as well as Ohio, and provides well-written articles along with a monthly calendar of cycling events and a thorough coverage of bike club news and activities. For subscription information, write to *Bike Midwest Magazine,* 2099 West Fifth Avenue, Suite C, Columbus, Ohio 43212, or call (614) 481–7723.

1

Town One, Range One

19 miles; moderate to difficult cycling
Frequent hills with some steep inclines
County map: Mahoning

In 1796, the Western Reserve of Connecticut was a vast, unsettled forest in the hands of New England investors who had bought shares in the Connecticut Land Company. When the company's surveying team reached the Ohio Territory on July 4, 1796, their objective was to survey the five thousand square miles of "New Connecticut" into five-mile-square townships. To do so it was necessary to resurvey the western Pennsylvania border, laid out ten years earlier by Andrew Ellicott and still referred to as the Ellicott line. The surveying party began at the north end of the Pennsylvania line on the morning of July 7, 1796, and reached the forty-first parallel just two weeks later. This parallel, which marks the southern border of Connecticut, would also form the southern border of its "Western Reserve." Two days later, Augustus Porter, deputy surveyor and second-in-command of the party, and third-ranking surveyor Seth Pease set a chestnut post at this point, marking it as the southeast corner of the Reserve. Their next task was to mark the town lines at five-mile increments from the forty-first parallel north to Lake Erie, and the range lines every five miles westward for 120 miles. The townships were numbered from south to north, while the ranges were numbered from east to west. The five-mile square at the southeast corner thus became Town One, Range One.

Turhand Kirtland of Wallingford, Connecticut, a major investor in the Connecticut Land Company, drew this township and portions of four others in the company's 1798 lottery, held to distribute the lands to the shareholders. Kirtland came west that year to take a look at his holdings, and by May 1799, Jonathan Fowler of Guilford, Connecticut, and his wife, Lydia Kirtland, Turhand's sister, had become the first permanent settlers of Town One, Range One. First called Fowler's, the township is said to have been christened Poland by Turhand Kirtland, whose sympathy for the subjugated Poles led him to declare, "Here will be a Poland that is free."

By 1804, the budding town had two gristmills, a sawmill, a tavern,

WESTERN RESERVE
BOUNDARY MARKER

SOUTHEAST CORNER OF THE
ORIGINAL WESTERN RESERVE
FIRST MARKER WAS PLACED ON
JULY 23ʀᴅ.1796 WHERE THIS
MONUMENT NOW STANDS.

RESTORATION BY
TROOP 46 B.S.A.
1977−1989

Connecticut Land Company surveyors marked the spot at which the southern border of Connecticut would extend into the Ohio Territory, thus marking the southern border of its "western reserve."

and, most significant for the area's history, the state's first blast furnace for smelting iron ore. With the discovery of vast iron ore deposits around Lake Superior, however, the local industrial focus eventually shifted to coal mining, steel refining, and shipping, centered in Youngstown, Pittsburgh, and Cleveland. The town of Poland, despite its industrial beginnings, thus never lost its original New England charm.

This tour begins in the parking lot of the Carbon Limestone Company, located on the Pennsylvania border at the junction of South Stateline Road and Felger Road. South Stateline Road can be reached from US 224 south of Youngstown via Stymie Road.

0.0   Turn LEFT out of the parking lot, going north on South Stateline Road.

On the south side of this small, limestone parking lot is a stone monument where once stood the surveying party's wooden post marking the southern boundary of the Western Reserve.

The surveying party could not have known that it was placing its marker above the Vanport limestone seam, whose high calcium content became important to the fledgling iron smelting operations that soon emerged in this area. In combination with iron ore and charcoal (later coal), limestone is loaded into a blast furnace where it serves as a fluxing agent, promoting the separation of the iron from its impurities. This present quarry is owned by Essroc Materials, Inc., which also uses the limestone for manufacturing cement products and crushed stone.

Stateline Road is patched and uneven here, as it parallels an unpaved truck access road within the quarry lands on the left. Immediately on the right is Pennsylvania, a hillocky area of former quarry land. You'll see former pits now filled with bright, greenish water, indicative of the lime content.

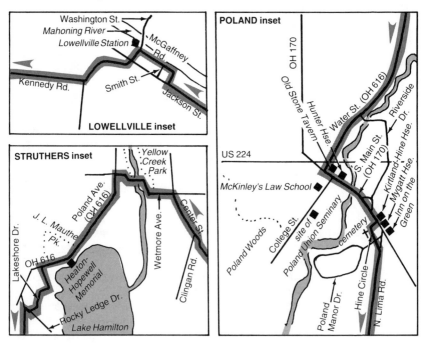

1.0   Continue STRAIGHT at the light at the intersection with the private access road.

At this intersection, you'll see a small landscaped area maintained by BFI Waste Systems. The Browning Ferris Industries lease old quarry properties and operate sanitary landfills here.

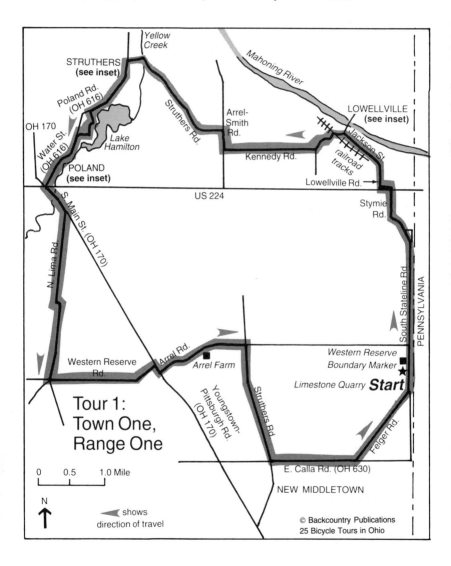

Tour 1:
Town One,
Range One

0   0.5   1.0 Mile

N

◄ shows direction of travel

© Backcountry Publications
25 Bicycle Tours in Ohio

1.7 At the Y-junction is a sign to the right reading "All Landfill Traffic;" take the LEFT arm, which is now called Stymie Road.

The massive stacks of cement blocks on your right are in Essroc's block division, where limestone is used to make cement. Stymie Road climbs uphill out of the valley of Burgess Run before making a short downhill to the Stop sign.

2.5 At the Stop sign, turn LEFT onto US 224.

US 224 runs two miles north of and parallel to the south border of the Western Reserve through its entire 120-mile expanse. Although long-distance traffic now uses I-76, this straight and well-maintained federal highway gets considerable traffic. Be prepared for the quick turn off the highway in one-tenth mile.

2.6 Turn RIGHT onto unmarked Lowellville Road.

Lowellville Road goes down a moderately steep hill. In a little over one-quarter mile the road curves to the left, crossing some uneven railroad tracks. Be prepared for them, for you are still on a significant downhill.

3.2 Lowellville Road continues as Jackson Street, where you'll see a "Do Not Enter" sign. Follow the main road as it makes a sharp turn to the RIGHT and becomes McGaffney Road. McGaffney makes two right-angle curves as it runs along the railroad (see village of Lowellville inset).

3.4 At the Stop sign, continue STRAIGHT on McGaffney Road, crossing Smith Street.

3.6 At the three-way Stop sign, turn LEFT onto Washington Street, over an area criss-crossed with railroad tracks.

To the right is the bridge over the Mahoning River leading to the village of Lowellville. On the northwest corner of the bridge, the preserved Lowellville train depot and the plethora of overlapping railroad tracks bespeak a more prosperous and dynamic industrial past. An extremely steep climb for half a mile over uneven train tracks is rewarded at the top with a classic view of a typical industrial village along the Mahoning. Once home of a bustling steel mill, this one-industry town declined when the Sharon Steel Plant closed in the early 1970s.

4.1 At the Y-junction, take the RIGHT arm, which is Kennedy Road.

5.4 At the Stop sign, turn RIGHT onto Struthers Road.

5.5 Turn LEFT to continue on unmarked Struthers Road (the road straight ahead is unmarked Arrel-Smith Road).

At this point, Struthers Road climbs gently and then, in nearly half a mile, begins a gentle downhill. The road is patched and generally uneven.

6.4   Continue STRAIGHT at the Stop sign and blinking red light, where Clingan Road comes in from the left; here Struthers Road becomes Center Street (see city of Struthers inset).

6.7   Go LEFT onto Wetmore Avenue, which is reached shortly after the blinking light signaling "Dangerous Intersection."
Wetmore Avenue is a steep downhill leading into the valley of the Yellow Creek. You are now in Yellow Creek Park, the municipal park of the city of Struthers.

After crossing Yellow Creek, Wetmore makes a steep climb out of the valley.

7.2   At the light, turn LEFT onto Poland Road (OH 616).
In half a mile, you'll see Lake Hamilton on the left and then the entrance to Mauthe Park. In this lakeside park is the Hopewell Memorial to Steelmaking, erected as a bicentennial project in 1976. Composed of a steel ingot with a time capsule enclosed, it is dedicated to the people who contributed to the local steel industry and to the Heaton brothers, who built the first blast furnace a quarter mile across Lake Hamilton.

In 1802, Dan, the most active of the five Heaton brothers, and his brother, James, discovered bog ore along Yellow Creek. Bog, or kidney, ore is found in lumps, because it is formed by the deposit of iron around organic vegetable formations. Noting the abundance of limestone and the seemingly endless supply of timber for making charcoal, the brothers built the Hopewell furnace in 1803, the year of Ohio's statehood. The "blast" for the furnace was provided by the rushing waters of Yellow Creek, which caused a current of air to pass through a conduit leading to the furnace. This first furnace was a complete ironware factory for the frontier, not only smelting the ore to obtain pig iron but also casting it into the ironware much in demand by the early settlers.

The Hopewell furnace was never a great success and was shut down at the start of the War of 1812. By then, however, its influence had spread throughout the area, and in the ensuing century, furnaces, forges, foundries, and rolling mills dotted the Mahoning Valley.

8.2   Turn LEFT onto Lakeshore Drive.
This brief jog off OH 616 takes you through a lakeview area of suburban, ranch-style homes.

8.3   Follow Lakeshore Drive as it makes a right-angle turn.

8.6   At the light, turn RIGHT onto Rocky Ledge, which leads to Poland Road (OH 616) where you turn LEFT.

In half a mile you'll enter the village of Poland, where Poland Road becomes Water Street and runs alongside Yellow Creek (see the village of Poland inset). Most of the houses on both sides of the street have historical markers indicating that they are century homes, built between the 1820s and the 1840s.

9.4   At the light, continue STRAIGHT through the intersection of US 224 and OH 616; at the blinking red light, make a LEFT onto South Main Street (OH 170).

It's best to walk your bike at this very busy intersection. Right after your turn, on the left, is the Old Stone Tavern at 121 South Main. Built by the first settler, Jonathan Fowler, in 1804, the stone masonry building with double chimneys remains unchanged since Fowler's day. A stagecoach stop between Pittsburgh and Cleveland, the tavern was operated from the 1840s to the 1860s as the Sparrow House and later served as a dining room. Today it is an antique store.

This part of South Main Street, from 121 to 331, is on the National Register of Historic Places.

9.5   Continue STRAIGHT at the light at the junction with unmarked College Street.

A right turn onto College Street will take you by a number of century-old homes. The mansard-roofed house on the right side of the street, now obscured behind a small commercial building, actually faced Main Street, although set far back from it. In this house, William McKinley, twenty-fifth president of the United States, studied law under Judge Charles E. Glidden. At the far end of this street, on the site of the present Middle School, once stood the Poland Union Seminary, opened as a private school in 1849. In 1852, William McKinley's family moved to Poland from nearby Niles so that the nine-year-old boy could begin school here. Ida Tarbell, the muck-raker journalist who became famous for writing a life of Lincoln and a history of the Standard Oil Company, was a teacher at the Poland Union Seminary in the early 1880s for five hundred dollars a year.

This end of College Street now provides access to Poland Woods, Ohio's first municipal forest. The 242-acre bird and wildlife sanctuary draws thousands to see the multitude of bluebells that blanket it each spring. Riding bicycles is prohibited in the woods.

Shortly after the light at College Street is the Town Hall on the right side of South Main. A modified Greek Revival home built in

1845, its lawn is so large and well kept it can be mistaken for the village green. Across the street at 307 South Main is the Greek Revival Hunter House. Built around 1830, it was acquired by the Poland Union Seminary in 1894 for use as a dormitory. Inside, the cast iron fireplace bears the name of students carved into its mantle. Although extensively remodeled by Judge Kennedy, who lived in what is now the Town Hall across the street, the hand-blown windowpanes, wainscoting, latches, and locks are all original. Immediately south of the Hunter House, nestled at the edge of Yellow Creek, is the Poland Public Library.

9.8   At the light at the intersection of Riverside Drive and South Main Street, continue STRAIGHT.

9.9   Before reaching the next light, turn RIGHT onto Hine Circle.
Hine Circle takes you behind the village green and in front of the Presbyterian Church. Next to the church is the old cemetery where Jonathan Fowler lies buried. Land for both the green and the cemetery were bequeathed to the town by proprietor Turhand Kirtland in 1804, shortly after the town was first settled. On the frontier, a "burying-ground" was one of the first necessities for any settlement. In front of the cemetery, an Ohio historical marker gives a lengthy list of the achievements of Judge Turhand Kirtland from the time of his residence in the Western Reserve in 1800 at the age of forty-five to his death in 1844. However, given the harsh conditions of the frontier, living until the age of eighty-nine may have been his greatest achievement of all.

The Kirtland-Hine house, the large, white, Greek Revival home facing the green, was built by George Kirtland, son of Turhand Kirtland, in 1845. The Mygatt House to the left, with more Gothic influence evident, was built in 1831 by Eli Mygatt upon his marriage to Turhand's daughter, Lois. Another son, Billius, built a fine Federal home in 1830 on the outskirts of town. Kirtland's most famous son, Jared Potter, did not come to Poland until 1823. He became one of the great naturalists of his time and before mid-century had moved to Lake County to pursue his career.

A bit further south, on the village green side of the street at 500 South Main, is The Inn on the Green, an impressive Italianate townhouse built in 1876. Now a bed and breakfast establishment, the inn maintains a turn-of-the-century ambience with its twelve-foot-high ceilings, five marble fireplaces, and original poplar floors. For reservations, call innkeepers Ginny and Steve Meloy at (216) 757–4688.

10.1   At the Stop sign, continue STRAIGHT, crossing Poland Manor Drive. At the Stop sign immediately following is a three-way inter-

section; take the road on the far right, which is unmarked North Lima Road.

12.1   At the six-way Stop sign, turn LEFT onto Western Reserve Road.
This road runs straight along the forty-first parallel, the southern boundary of the Western Reserve. Unlike the tangled wilderness that faced the original surveyors, Western Reserve Road is now dotted with picturesque farms interspersed with light woodland.

13.1   Follow the road as it turns to the LEFT and becomes unmarked Arrel Road.

13.5   At the Stop sign, turn RIGHT onto Youngstown-Pittsburgh Road (OH 170), then make an immediate LEFT back onto Arrel Road.
There is much more traffic on OH 170 than one would expect in this seemingly quiet corner of the Western Reserve. In about half a mile, you'll see the Arrel family farm, established in 1799 by John Arrel, a Pennsylvanian and one of Poland's first settlers.

14.8   At the four-way Stop sign, turn RIGHT onto Struthers Road.
Struthers Road begins here with a steep downhill and takes you out of the Western Reserve briefly into Springfield Township. In a little over a mile you'll reach the outskirts of New Middletown, where the paving improves. Unlike the towns in the Western Reserve, which were predominantly settled by New Englanders or New Yorkers, New Middletown is named for the Pennsylvania hometown of its original settlers.

16.3   At the Stop sign, turn LEFT onto OH 630. This is East Calla Road, but it is not posted.

17.4   Turn LEFT onto unpaved Felger Road; this turn appears suddenly as OH 630 begins a downhill.
Near the end of Felger Road, you'll see views of the derricks and cranes of the limestone industry looming behind the cattle in the surrounding fields.

18.6   At the Stop sign, turn LEFT onto South State Line Road; immediately turn LEFT into the parking lot by the commemorative marker.

Bicycle Repair Services

Deluxe Bicycle Shop, Inc., 1470 Churchill-Hubbard Road, Youngstown, OH 44505 (216) 759–2992.

Boardman Cycle Center, 6818 Market Street, Youngstown, OH 44512 (216) 758–6557.

Bike Nashbar Outlet, 4111 Simon Road, Youngstown, OH 44512 (216) 782–2244

Cycle Sales Co., 226 Boardman-Canfield Road, Youngstown, OH 44512 (216) 758–8090.

2

Millionaire's Row—Then and Now

17 miles; easy cycling
Generally rolling terrain with one moderate hill
County map: Trumbull

In the beginning of the nineteenth century the site of the first county seat of the entire Western Reserve, the city of Warren, appeared to be on its way to becoming the capital of the great Midwest. "It was," in the words of historian Harlan Hatcher, "a populous center of life when Cleveland was still a struggling and sickly village on the sand-choked Cuyahoga." From the start, Warren was the political and business center of the Reserve, with the Mahoning River providing links with Pittsburgh and the Ohio River.

As the nineteenth century progressed, primitive log cabins and farming gave way to mansions and manufacturing. Nestled in the Mahoning Valley, Warren, along with neighboring Youngstown, was in the heart of the steel belt, enjoying a prosperity that looked like it would never end. By the end of the 1970s, however, the steel belt had become the rust belt, and money for restoring old mansions was hard to come by. Some were demolished, some were lucky enough to be restored, and others still wait in architectural limbo.

This tour carries you from the site of former wealth in the city center to the homes of the *nouveau riche* in modern suburbia. Both areas provide fascinating cycling, from the history and architecture represented in the city to the open space and eclectic styles of the suburbs.

The tour starts at the Warren Public Library parking lot, on the corner of Mahoning and Monroe avenues. Mahoning can be reached via OH 45, which is accessed via the OH 82 bypass.

0.0   Turn RIGHT out of the library parking lot onto Monroe Street.
As you leave the parking lot, you'll see what may be the oldest home in the entire Western Reserve. Now used by the Trumbull County Historical Society (open Wednesdays and Sundays, 2 to 4 PM), the John Stark Edwards House was built for Edwards and his new bride in 1807. The house is constructed in the vernacular or colonial style, or what is locally known as Western Reserve style. Edwards was destined to live in his new home for only a short time. Elected the

Reserve's first representative to Congress in 1812, he died on a trip to Put-in-Bay, where his family had other land holdings, on January 29, 1813. He is buried in the pioneer cemetery visited at the end of this tour.

The Victorian-style house immediately to the right of the Edwards home is nearly a century younger than its neighbor, built in 1884 by local businessman, George W. Kneeland. Next to it, as you ride toward the intersection, is the 1840 Upton House, a simple Greek Revival home facing Mahoning Avenue. Harriet Taylor Upton, women's suffrage leader and Western Reserve historian, lived here during much of her girlhood. Daughter of Judge Ezra B. Taylor, she acted as his hostess during his thirteen years in Congress in Washington, D.C., and there met her husband George Upton, son of the chief justice of the Supreme Court. Ranked as one of the town's leading citizens, she was responsible for making Warren the headquarters of the National American Women's Suffrage Association.

On the right side of Monroe Street, facing Mahoning Avenue, the Valley Professional Building is an exceptional example of the board and batten Gothic Revival style, built about 1832. Because Gothic Revival homes required a larger lot than the contemporaneous Greek Revival and Italianate styles, they are seldom seen in urban areas.

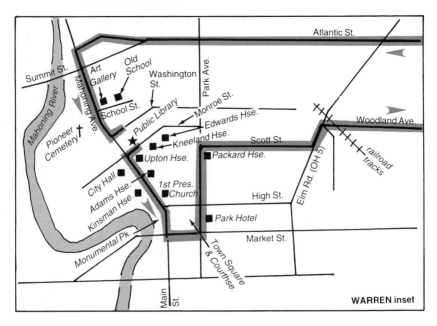

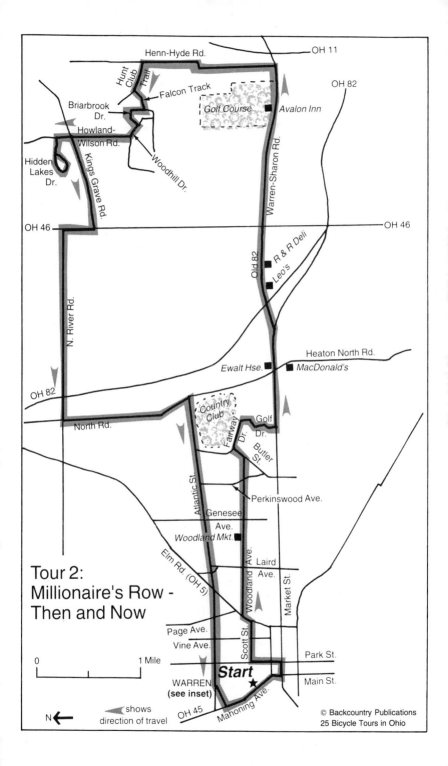

Henn-Hyde Rd.

OH 11

Hunt Club Trail

Falcon Track

OH 82

Golf Course

Avalon Inn

Briarbrook Dr.

Howland-Wilson Rd.

Woodhill Dr.

Hidden Lakes Dr.

Kings Grave Rd.

OH 46

OH 46

Warren-Sharon Rd.

N. River Rd.

Old 82

R & R Deli

Leo's

OH 82

Heaton North Rd.

Ewalt Hse.

MacDonald's

North Rd.

Country Club

Fairway Dr.

Golf Dr.

Butler St.

Atlantic St.

Perkinswood Ave.

Genesee Ave.

Woodland Mkt.

Elm Rd. (OH 5)

Woodland Ave.

Laird Ave.

Market St.

Tour 2:
Millionaire's Row -
Then and Now

Page Ave.

Vine Ave.

Scott St.

Park St.

0   1 Mile

Start

★

WARREN
(see inset)

OH 45

Mahoning Ave.

Main St.

N ←

shows
direction of travel

© Backcountry Publications
25 Bicycle Tours in Ohio

Three houses south on Mahoning from the Upton house is the 1839 Adams house, flanked on either side by houses in the Queen Anne style popular toward the end of the nineteenth century. The Webb home on the left was built in 1892; to the right is the 1894 Morgan House. Those interested in more historic and architectural details may want to purchase the small guidebook, *An Historic Walk along Mahoning Avenue,* at the Trumbull County Historical Society.

0.1   At the T-junction, turn LEFT onto Mahoning Avenue.

Take care making this left turn, for Mahoning is busy at any hour of the day. The view of Warren City Hall from this intersection is impressive. Built in 1871, this striking Italianate home belonged to Henry Bishop Perkins, youngest son of the renowned pioneer, General Simon Perkins. Henry was a state senator and longtime president of the Western Reserve Bank. Since 1931, the City Hall has been located here.

Immediately to the south of the City Hall on the same side of the street, you'll see the County Veteran's Services Office, formerly the Connecticut Land Company Office, constructed around 1820. This one-story Greek Revival building, minus its modern wing, is probably the oldest office building in the Western Reserve. General Perkins worked here, as did his son-in-law, Frederick Kinsman. Next to the diminutive office is the elegant Kinsman House, a dramatic Greek Revival home built in 1832. The land was a wedding present from General Simon Perkins, whose daughter Olive married Frederick Kinsman. When designer Isaac Ladd added the portico on a scale unusual for the Western Reserve, it was predictable that this part of Mahoning between Summit and High streets would become known as Millionaire's Row, or, officially, the Mahoning Avenue Historic District.

Nearest the town square on the left is the Gothic First Presbyterian Church, built in 1875. The first church on this site was constructed in 1832 by the second-oldest congregation in Warren.

0.2   At the light at the corner of High Street and Mahoning Avenue, continue STRAIGHT on Mahoning, with the court house and town square to your left. At the next light, at the corner of Main and Market streets, turn LEFT onto Market Street.

To your right, as you pause at the first stop light, is the Civil War memorial. The narrow strip of land bordering the Mahoning River is called Monumental Park, appropriately named since it contains memorials to every conflict from the Spanish-American to the Vietnam War. Another plaque marks the site of the first school house of the Western Reserve. The log cabin at the south end of the park is a replica of that 1801 school. If you're waiting at either of the lights on this side of the square, you might reflect on how reliable is the local claim that Stephen Foster was inspired to write "My Old Kentucky Home" while strolling along the Mahoning River.

Near the light on Main and Market was the spot along the river that Ephraim Quinby, who founded the town of Warren, built his log cabin. He named the town after Moses Warren, a Connecticut-born surveyor who helped lay out the Western Reserve. A year after Quinby's arrival, Governor St. Clair named all the Western Reserve Trumbull County for Governor Jonathan Trumbull of Connecticut. Warren, then the largest settlement in the Reserve, was designated the county seat.

After your left turn onto Market Street, you'll get a splendid view of the grandeur of the Trumbull County Courthouse. This 1895 Richardsonian Romanesque masterpiece replaced a former court-house built on this site in 1854 and destroyed by fire. That had replaced the outgrown 1815 building that was built when the out-door court sessions held between two corn cribs on Quinby's farm were no longer suitable. Richardson's design for the courthouse in nearby Pittsburgh is thought to have been the inspiration for the present building. The style was in favor not only due to its classical form but also because the absence of ornately carved, stone embel-lishments made it less expensive. The courthouse square, with its quaint gazebo, is typical of most Western Reserve towns. The tradi-tion of establishing a central village commons was brought here from New England, birthplace of most Western Reserve pioneers.

0.3   Turn LEFT at the light on the corner of East Market and Park streets. (Because this turn is prohibited for automobiles, it may be safest to dismount and make this turn as a pedestrian.)

The storefronts lining the south and east border of the square are fine examples of mid-nineteenth-century Victorian shopping blocks. The Park Hotel midway along Park Street is recently renovated. Built in a style now referred to as Queen Anne Commercial, it began as a hotel in 1888 when the inclusion of the onion dome would have pleased Victorian tastes. Victorian memorabilia found during the 1988 renovation are on display in the hotel lobby.

Those interested in a lunch or snack will find wonderful gourmet delights at Simply Delicious near the corner of Park and High streets. Takeout is available for those who want to picnic in the park or carry food with them.

0.5   At the light on the corner of North Park and High streets, continue STRAIGHT on North Park.

0.7   Turn RIGHT at the first light onto Scott Street.

On the southeast corner of Scott and Park is the Buckeye Club, formerly the home of automotive pioneer W. D. Packard, built in 1837 in the then-fashionable Greek Revival style. The Packard brothers set up a company in 1890 for manufacturing incandescent lamps and electrical products. As a result, Warren was one of the first cities in America to light with electricity. The business continues today as the Warren-based Packard Electric Division of General Motors, the world leader in automotive wiring. Toward the end of the century, Packard turned his genius toward improving the horseless carriage and formed the Ohio Automobile Company, which produced the first automobile with a steering wheel rather than the conventional tiller. Lacking local capital, he moved the business to Detroit to manufacture the Packard car, and by 1903 all operations in Warren ceased. In addition to this home, W. D.'s legacies to his hometown include the Packard Music Hall and Packard Park, both on Mahoning Avenue.

1.0   At the Stop sign at the T-junction with Elm Road, turn LEFT onto Elm. (Elm is OH 5 at this point and is heavily traveled, so make this turn with care.)

1.1   At the light, make a right onto Woodland Avenue. You'll immediately come to a Y-junction; take the LEFT arm of the Y across the railroad tracks.

1.6   Continue STRAIGHT at the light, crossing Laird Avenue.

In about a quarter mile, at the intersection of Woodland and Kenilworth, you'll see the locally famous Woodland Market, a gourmet's dream, with an outstanding bakery on the premises. Known for its choice varieties of cheeses, good wines, and fresh fish and poultry, the Woodland Market draws customers from all over northeast Ohio. A hungry cyclist will find portable delights at the deli counter.

2.0   Continue STRAIGHT through the light, crossing Genesee Street.

2.4   Go STRAIGHT at the Stop sign, crossing Perkinswood Avenue.

2.6   At the four-way Stop sign, make a LEFT onto Butler Street.

2.7   Butler ends at the traffic triangle; follow to the RIGHT onto Fairway Drive.

3.0   At the T-junction, make a RIGHT onto Golf Drive.

As you ride away from the city center, you'll see the tall, narrow homes on small urban lots change to large, low residences on more commodious properties.

Just preceding and following the last World War, the streetcar made it possible for those with the money to move further away from the city center, where they could build one-story homes on larger lots and still get to work on time. The architectural styles popularized by the Eclectic Movement toward the end of the nineteenth century began to dominate developments like this one around the country club. The modern geometrical design of 231 Golf Drive, near the intersection with Crescent Drive, is a striking contrast to the eclecticism of its neighbors.

3.3 Turn LEFT at the T-junction onto East Market Street.

This road, known almost universally to locals as "Old 82" was the main thoroughfare through Warren before the OH 82 bypass was built. It still gets a lot of traffic, since it is one of only three roads that cross Mosquito Creek to the eastern suburbs. The left turn should be made with care; once on East Market, you'll find the road heavily traveled, but comfortably wide.

3.8 At the light at the intersection of Heaton North Road and East Market, continue STRAIGHT on East Market Street.

This is a very busy intersection with a very long red light. The MacDonald's to the right on North Road, complete with glass-sided elevator, was billed as "the most beautiful MacDonald's in the world" upon its completion in 1989. On the northeast corner of this intersection is the Ewalt House, built in 1820. Like the Edwards house, its style is Western Reserve. When you cross North Road, you'll be entering Howland Township, and this is probably the township's oldest home.

For the next ten miles, you're officially in the township that the easterner John Howland purchased for $24,000 from the Connecticut Land Company. The area east of North Road, which you are now entering, was mainly farmland until the last two decades.

4.1 On the downhill after Heaton North Road, bear LEFT to follow "Old 82" as it crosses the westbound lane of "New 82"; the Yield sign at this point serves as a reminder that the westbound traffic is not going to stop for you. Once across the westbound lane, bear RIGHT to continue on "Old 82," which officially changes its name from East Market to Warren-Sharon Road.

Those who have not been tempted by earlier eateries may be interested in the impeccably authentic Italian food at Leo's Ristorante on your right. Pasta comes in forms here that even ethnic food lovers have not heard of before, with sauces that make the standard marinara sauce look like plebian fare. Another temptation between this restaurant and Howland Plaza is the R&R Gourmet Village and Delicatessen, which serves superb German food at little tables inside or outside or packs it all up to go. You can take your edibles to the Howland Township Park, a half mile left down Clifton Drive, found just west of the deli.

5.2   At the light, continue STRAIGHT up the hill on the Warren-Sharon Road as it intersects OH 46.

A mile past the light, you'll see the Avalon Inn to your left and the Avalon Golf Course on your right. Behind the Inn is the Avalon *Lakes* Golf Course, rated among the top twenty-five golf resorts in the country by *Golf Digest*. In operation since 1969, the Avalon has 144 rooms for the many golfers, cross-country skiers, and conventioneers who come here regularly.

6.6   Just before the bridge over OH 11, turn LEFT onto Henn-Hyde Road.

The pond with the little covered bridge and cascade a mile along this road on the right is often frequented by families of Canada geese, as is the one on your left a few hundred yards further.

7.7   Turn LEFT onto Hunt Club Trail.

This area, not developed until late 1988, provides an interesting contrast to the type of architecture seen in the city. In addition to the ranch, you'll see samples of neo-colonial and neo-French architecture.

8.0   Turn LEFT on Falcon Track.

8.2   At the Stop sign, turn RIGHT onto the unmarked Briarbrook Drive.

This turn puts you in a somewhat older development called Sherwood Greens, the very similar houses being almost all in the neo-colonial style, and constructed in the late 1970s and early 1980s.

8.5   Turn RIGHT at the Stop sign as Briarbrook forms a T-junction with Woodhill Drive.

8.6   At the Stop sign, the road forms a very broad Y-junction with the unmarked Howland-Wilson Road; continue STRAIGHT, which puts you on the right arm of the Y.

9.1   Continue STRAIGHT at the Stop sign, crossing the unmarked King-Graves Road.

9.3   At the "Hill" sign before the downhill on Howland Wilson Road, make a LEFT turn onto the unmarked Hidden Lakes Drive; at the immediate Y-junction, continue STRAIGHT on the right arm of the Y.

This area forms the "Millionaire's Row" of modern Trumbull County. It completes the nearly two hundred years of architectural history on this tour, with excellent examples of what are termed Modern and neoeclectic styles. On this wealthy roundabout are examples of the Shed, neo-Mediterranean, neo-French, neo-Tudor, and neo-Classical Revival styles. Even an architectural "neo-Phyte" will probably be able to guess which house fits which style.

10.0   At the Stop sign, turn RIGHT and retrace your route out of the Hidden Lakes development.

10.1   Turn RIGHT at the Stop sign and return along Howland-Wilson Road.

10.2   At the Stop sign, turn RIGHT onto the unmarked King-Graves Road.

11.0   At the Stop sign, make a RIGHT onto OH 46.

11.3   Make a cautious LEFT turn from this busy highway onto the unmarked North River Road.
This wooded and farmed area contiguous to the city resembles what all Howland was like before the encroachment of the suburbs.

13.1   At the light, turn LEFT onto North Road. (Maps say Heaton North, but the signs say only "North Road.")

14.3   Turn RIGHT at the light onto Atlantic Street.

15.4   Continue STRAIGHT, crossing Genesee Avenue.

15.8   Ride STRAIGHT at the light, crossing Laird Avenue.

16.0   Continue STRAIGHT across Elm Road, which is OH 5 at this point.

16.2   Go STRAIGHT at the light, crossing Paige Avenue.

16.5   At the light, continue STRAIGHT across Vine Avenue.

16.7   Ride STRAIGHT at the light to cross North Park Street.
Returning now to the older residences of the city center, and back a hundred years in architectural history, you'll find a Queen Anne house on the northwest corner of this intersection. This was the dominant style of domestic architecture from about 1880 to 1900.

16.8   At the Y-junction, take the RIGHT arm of the Y, staying on Atlantic Street.

17.1   At the Stop sign, turn LEFT onto Mahoning Avenue.

17.2   Go STRAIGHT at the light, crossing Summit Street; note that the right lane is only for those turning right.
Summit is the northern limit of "Millionaire's Row." On the corner of School Street is the Gillmer House, now the home of the Trumbull

Art Gallery. This Italianate residence, built in the 1850s, was the first house in Warren to feature indoor electric lights, and the original lights, bordering the ceilings in the main floor room, still function. Behind the Gillmer House, on the corner of School and Prospect, is the oldest schoolhouse remaining in Warren, built in 1871. Just north of the Trumbull Art Gallery is the Twin Maples Bed & Breakfast Guest House. Built in 1906, it was formerly the home of E. F. Moulton, superintendent of the Warren Schools before the turn of the century. For reservations for a room and full breakfast, call (216) 399–7768.

A few yards further on your right is an historical marker indicating the driveway of the Trumbull Red Cross Chapter House, which leads to the Pioneer Cemetery on the banks of the Mahoning River. This burial site of the earliest pioneers of the Western Reserve was used primarily from 1804 to 1848. Just left of the entrance on the far side of the cemetery is the stone for John Stark Edwards, buried with his two sons, aged four and six, who died within a month of each other in 1814. The children passed away less than two years after their father.

17.6   Go STRAIGHT at the light across Perkins Street and make an immediate LEFT onto Washington Street. An immediate RIGHT brings you back to the Warren Public Library where you began your tour.

In addition to the spacious library, this building holds a fine local history collection and the Sutliff Museum, which houses the nineteenth-century furnishings of the Sutliff family. In his will, Judge Sutliff, first Trumbull County resident elected to the State Supreme Court, left money for the youth of Warren. The money was used to help fund the first library building.

Bicycle Repair Services

Thumm's Bicycle Shop, 330 West Market Street, Warren, OH 44481 (216) 392–6288.

Deluxe Bicycle Shop, Inc., 3635 Elm Road NE, Warren, OH 44483 (216) 372–2666.

Paceline Bicycle Shop, 168 Niles-Cortland Road, Warren, OH 44484 (216) 856–5083.

Bicycle Shop, 1053 Youngstown-Niles Road, Niles, OH 44446 (216) 652–0412.

3

Mosquito Creek Reservoir

24 miles; easy cycling
Mainly flat terrain
County map: Trumbull

There are some 60,000 lakes, ponds, and reservoirs in Ohio totaling 200,000 acres of water, of which only 6,700 acres are natural. Ever since the 1830s, man-made lakes have been augmenting nature's water allocations to Ohio. Over a century later, with the passage of the first federal flood control legislation in 1936, the Army Corps of Engineers added twenty-five more lakes to the state. The corps refers to these as multipurpose lakes, artificial bodies of water created to control floodwaters as well as provide municipal water supplies, augment stream flow to maintain water quality and navigability, and supply recreational and wildlife management areas.

Mosquito Creek Reservoir is a good example of bureaucratic cooperation between state government and the corps. The reservoir and much of its surrounding land are leased by the corps to the Ohio Department of Natural Resources as Mosquito Lake State Park. With nearly twelve thousand acres and forty miles of shoreline, it is now one of the most heavily used parks in the state.

Mosquito Reservoir, operated and maintained by the corps, functions in conjunction with other reservoirs in the Mahoning, Beaver, and Ohio river valleys in an integrated system of flood control and stream augmentation. The Mosquito Creek Lake Project, completed in 1944, controls the drainage of a ninety-seven-square-mile area by means of a dam built at the reservoir's south end. The dam controls the amount of water flowing south into the Mahoning Valley and eventually to the Ohio River. Mosquito Reservoir is unique, however, because it has an uncontrolled natural spillway at the north end as well. When the reservoir reaches 904 feet above sea level, it also drains north into the Grand River and Lake Erie. It is thus the only reservoir to drain into two different watersheds.

The fact that the reservoir sits in a floodplain makes it attractive to cyclists who prefer the ease of pedaling a level route. There are virtually no inclines on the whole, twenty-four-mile oblong around Mosquito

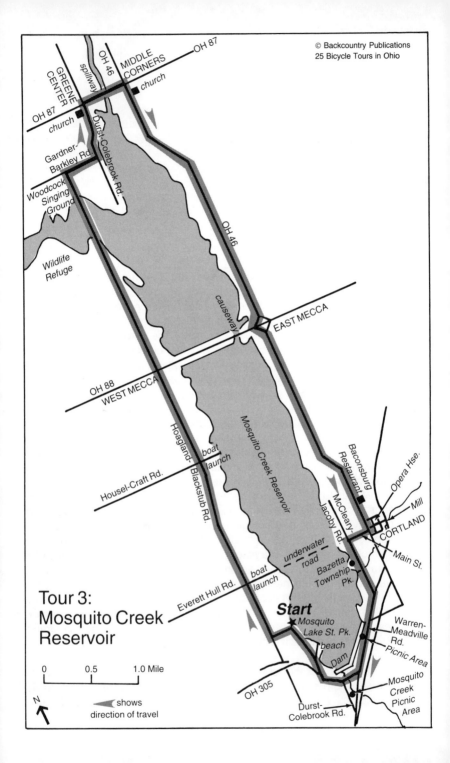

© Backcountry Publications
25 Bicycle Tours in Ohio

OH 87

MIDDLE CORNERS

OH 87

GREENE CENTER

spillway

OH 46

church

church

OH 87

Gardner-Barkley Rd.

Durst-Colebrook Rd.

Woodcock Singing Ground

Wildlife Refuge

OH 46

causeway

EAST MECCA

OH 88

WEST MECCA

Hoagland-Blackstub Rd.

boat launch

Housel-Craft Rd.

Mosquito Creek Reservoir

Baconsburg Restaurant

Opera Hse.

Mill

McCleary-Jacoby Rd.

CORTLAND

Main St.

underwater road

boat launch

Everett Hull Rd.

Bazetta Township Pk.

Start

Tour 3:
Mosquito Creek
Reservoir

Mosquito Lake St. Pk.

beach

Dam

Warren-Meadville Rd.

Picnic Area

Mosquito Creek Picnic Area

0   0.5   1.0 Mile

N

◄ shows
direction of travel

OH 305

Durst-Colebrook Rd.

Creek Reservoir, and a convenient causeway cutting across the middle of the lake allows you to reduce the trip to about fifteen miles. Located in a bypassed rural area, the roads would be traffic-free were it not for the two million state park visitors. Even this traffic is largely confined to the southern end of the lake where the beach and campgrounds are located.

The tour begins at the visitor parking lot of the campground entrance to Mosquito Lake State Park, at the lower west side of Mosquito Creek Reservoir. This entrance is on Hoagland-Blackstub Road, which can be reached from OH 5 northeast of the city of Warren or from OH 11 east of Warren and north of Youngstown. OH 11 can be reached via I-80.

0.0   Turn RIGHT out of the park entrance and proceed north on Hoagland-Blackstub Road.

The road at this point has no berm and can have quite a bit of traffic at "recreation rush hour." Across from the park entrance is the Bazetta Mall, actually a small convenience store carrying groceries, camping and fishing supplies, and a very convenient air pump.

In a little over three-quarters of a mile, you'll reach an intersection with Everett-Hull Road called Klondike Corners (reportedly named during the Klondike gold rush of 1897). A sign on the right indicates "Open Water Ahead." A half-mile ride to the right brings you to another sign warning "road ends in water," where you'll see the pavement disappear out of sight and into the reservoir. This road formerly carried residents of west Bazetta Township into the town center, now the city of Cortland. Directly across the lake is the slight incline of Cortland's West Main Street, which, before the construction of the reservoir, formed a continuous and busy thoroughfare through what is now over a mile of water. Despite the advantages of the reservoir, it is a continual hindrance to those on the west side of Bazetta, who must now make a nearly five-mile detour around the bottom of the lake to reach the town's churches, schools, and stores. The road does provide a fine boat ramp, however, and is convenient for anglers looking for the best walleye spots, which are said to be toward the center of the lake at this point.

One-tenth mile past the Everett-Hull Road intersection is the entrance to the Trumbull County Expo Center and Fairgrounds on the left. On the north side of the fairgrounds is a small, restored village. The 1848 Bazetta Christian Church is here, along with the tiny Orangeville jail.

A little over two miles from the fairgrounds is another boat launch site at the intersection with Housel-Craft Road. This road also continued east under the water as far as the now-vanished Durst-Colebrook Road, which ran along the west side of Mosquito Creek.

4.8   At the Stop sign, continue STRAIGHT, crossing OH 88.

This junction is called West Mecca, known as Power's Corners long before the reservoir split Mecca Township completely in two. Little remains of the village except for a remnant of the village green next to the West Mecca United Methodist Church on the northwest corner and an even smaller portion of it on the southwest corner, with the ubiquitous war memorial.

A major proprietor of the Connecticut Land Company, Judge Turhand Kirtland was the original owner of the northern half of Mecca Township. He made easy land purchasing terms for potential settlers, requiring that they pay only the interest. Still, no settlers arrived until 1811, discouraged by Indians who told them the water was tainted with oil. Although some settlers collected the oil or sold a few gallons as a machinery lubricant, most residents were disturbed by it because it lowered the property value.

By the late 1850s, however, news that a large profit was being made from oil wells drilled in western Pennsylvania cast a different light on Mecca's "nuisance oil." In 1859, a blacksmith named William Jeffrey drilled a well on his land southwest of Power's Corners and started pumping a thick oil with a consistency somewhat like glycerine. Soon a strip of land a half-mile wide and three-miles long was dotted with seventy-five oil rigs, and Mecca, named for the holy city in Arabia, seemed to be living up to its name.

By 1860, an estimated seven hundred wells had been drilled, and a new town of Dixie, later called Oil Diggings, was alive with speculators. Building lot prices soared, and some 150 buildings were constructed in that first year.

The "pay formation" for all this speculation was the Berea sandstone, which was about one hundred-feet thick in the Mecca area. The Ohio Historical Society reports that "when the oil in these fields first came in, it reportedly flowed so profusely that tanks could not be constructed fast enough, so hastily dug open pits were used for temporary storage." Given the limited understanding of geology at the time, knowledge of the relation of oil to these subsurface formations was scant. As it turned out, only the top ten to fifteen feet of the Berea Sand in this field contained oil. This fact, combined with the beginning of the Civil War and a subsequent labor shortage, quickly brought drilling to an end, and eventually Oil Diggings became a ghost town.

To the right at the West Mecca intersection is the causeway that carries OH 88 across the reservoir to East Mecca. A popular fishing spot, the causeway has pit toilets, parking areas, and stairways leading along the sides of the causeway for better fishing access. Swimming is prohibited. A detour to the right here will take you, in two miles, to East Mecca where you can pick up the route at mileage point 16.3, eliminating eleven and a half miles around the north end of the lake.

Hoagland-Blackstub Road has considerably less traffic north of OH 88. In about three and a half miles, on the left, is the parking lot for the State Game Refuge Area. Signs for the next few miles designate the area as the Mosquito Creek Waterfowl Management area, maintained by the Ohio Department of Natural Resources. The refuge occupies a large area at the northwest corner of the reservoir and is excellent for birdwatching. In addition to attracting Canada geese, hawks, egrets, eagles, herons, and numerous ducks, the refuge is home to the massasauga rattlesnake, common in these wetlands but an endangered species statewide.

In about three-quarters of a mile, in open grassland on the left, is an ODNR sign announcing "Woodcock Singing Ground: courtship flights March 15 to May 15; best time sunset to dark." Woodcocks are almost never seen except by those fortunate enough to observe their courtship flight in the early spring. Referred to in birding manuals as "spectacular aerial displays," these flights are made by the male to attract the attention of his *inamorata* and to give a "claws-off" warning to possible rivals. Announcing his performance with a nasal *"peent,"* he spirals aloft, circling higher and faster, his stiff wing tips making a loud whistling sound. At a height of some three hundred feet, he emits a sharp whistle and then pitches to the ground. He may repeat this several times if the object of his affection remains unduly aloof.

8.7   At the Stop sign and T-junction, turn RIGHT onto unmarked Gard-ner-Barkley Road.

9.3   The road curves to the LEFT and becomes unmarked Durst-Col-ebrook Road. Durst-Colebrook also extends to the right, where it dead-ends in swampland.

10.4   At the Stop sign, turn RIGHT onto OH 87.

This small community is Greene Center, named for one of the town's two proprietors. The other was Samuel Parkman, whose name was given to a Geauga County township visited in tour #8. The comely, Gothic Greene Community Foursquare Church, which originated as a Methodist church in 1877, and the 1877 Town Hall on the opposite corner have earned Greene Center a spot on the National Register of Historic Places. The extensive "lawn" next to these two buildings constitutes the village green.

In half a mile you'll cross the northern outlet of the reservoir, a natural spillway in times of high water.

Everett-Hull Road, which once carried residents of west Bazetta Township into the town center in Cortland, now lies under Mosquito Creek Reservoir.

11.1   At the Stop sign, turn RIGHT onto OH 46.

At this intersection, called Middle Corners, there is again evidence of a village green. The Greene Church of the Nazarene on the southeast corner was originally a Disciples of Christ church, built in 1851. In five miles on the left is an attractive, Gothic-style farmhouse, followed by a small, pre–World War I cemetery on the right.

16.1   At the Stop sign, follow the East Mecca traffic circle around to the RIGHT.

If you chose to cross the lake via the causeway, you'll pick up the tour here. East Mecca has a grocery store on the northeast corner, an ice cream stand on the southeast corner, and the popular Enzo's Pizzeria, which also serves breakfast, on the southwest corner.

State park lands begin again near the Bazetta town line but remain undeveloped at this point. The Baconsburg Family Restaurant on the left as you enter Cortland recalls the city's original epithet, named for Enos Bacon who opened a store here in 1829. The name of Cortland was officially selected in 1859, but both names were used through the turn of the century.

20.2   At the three-way Stop sign, turn RIGHT onto West Main Street.

A left turn here onto East Main Street takes you into the city of Cortland. A subsequent left turn onto Park Avenue leads to the 1841 Opera House, now home to the Cortland Historical Society. A little further east on Main Street, on Walnut Creek, is the Old Mill, originally the Bacon family mill, now a twenty-room furniture store.

The ride downhill toward the lake on West Main Street is the only grade on this whole trip. In half a mile you'll reach another "Road Ends in Water" sign, a match to its partner directly west of this point. To the right is the Hillside Cemetery. The adjacent parking area is for the use of fishermen and boat owners. Swimming is not permitted.

20.7   At the barrier, turn LEFT onto unmarked McCleary-Jacoby Road.

21.9   At the Stop sign, bear RIGHT onto Warren-Meadville Road.

In a little over one-quarter mile is the Bazetta Township Park, with tennis courts and restrooms.

22.2   Stay on Warren-Meadville Road as it becomes OH 305.

The road to the right, where OH 305 comes in from left, leads to another boat launch site. In half a mile is the entrance to the Lakeview Picnic Area, where you can find water and restrooms. The picnic area is well situated to afford excellent views across the water of the dam and its spillway. This picnic site is actually part of the dam construction. A rolled, earthfill embankment, the dam is 5,650-feet long at the top and forty-seven feet above the creekbed.

22.8   As Warren-Meadville Road goes straight ahead, bear RIGHT to stay on OH 305 next to the lake.

In one-quarter mile, you'll cross the bridge that carries OH 305 over the outlet facilities, which are built through the dam leading to the controlled spillway on the left side of OH 305. Just past the bridge on the left is a road leading to the Tailwater Access Area and the Mosquito Creek Picnic Area, where restrooms and water are available. This unmarked road is Durst-Colebrook Road, which you traveled on briefly at the north end of the lake.

23.7   Turn RIGHT into the entrance to Mosquito Lake State Park; at the immediate Y-junction, bear LEFT.

The right arm of the Y leads to the six hundred-foot swimming beach. Continuing along the left arm of the Y will take you by the park's marina facilities, with space for 251 boats.

24.2   Continue STRAIGHT at the "Do Not Enter" sign, which will take you back to the visitors' parking lot beyond the campground's "Checkpoint Charlie."

In addition to its 234 campsites, many with lake views, the camping area provides an amphitheater for programs and a three-mile self guided nature trail.

Bicycle Repair Services

Pedal Power Sports, 218-B South High Street, Cortland, OH 44410 (216) 638–6789.

4

Architectural Sampler: A Two-Day Tour

68 miles; easy to moderate cycling
Generally flat with some hills
County maps: Trumbull, Ashtabula

After the retreat of the last glacier, the area now comprising Pymatuning Reservoir was left sculpted into rolling terrain with dozens of kettlehole lakes. The Indians loved it for the abundant wildlife attracted by the rich wetlands, but the area was nearly impassable when the surveyors in Moses Cleaveland's party were ascertaining the western boundary of Pennsylvania. Eighteen-year-old Milton Holley, a leader of one of the surveying parties, recorded in his diary on July 11, 1796, that they were surveying "through the most abominable swamp in the world. . . ." Despite the 1933 dam that impounded the Pymatuning Reservoir, enough remnants of the original swamp remain to attract many forms of wildlife, including the rare bald eagle.

For those interested in historic architecture, the towns in southern Ashtabula County and along northern Trumbull County's highway 87 offer some magnificently restored dwellings, as well as others sadly in need of a sympathetic owner. The oldest houses on this ride are those in what is locally called "Western Reserve" style, also referred to as colonial or simply vernacular; that is, anything reflecting local tastes and limited building resources. Next, chronologically, are those in the English Adam style, often referred to in America as the Federal style. The dominant historic architecture in the rural Western Reserve is Greek Revival, popular in America from about 1825 to 1860, although you'll see several examples built after that period. Also represented are homes in the Gothic Revival and Italianate styles, built from around 1840 to 1885. Finally, there are the eclectic-looking houses in the Queen Anne style, popular from about 1880 to 1900.

The earnest bicyclist and/or noncamper may prefer to do this tour in one day. I suggest it as a two-day trip because of its length, its occasional hills, and the camping and bed and breakfast opportunities near beautiful Pymatuning State Park.

This tour starts in the village of Mesopotamia, which was placed on the National Register of Historic Places in 1975. Those wishing to do the tour in two days can leave their car at a parking area near the village green. Check with Mr. Ken Schaden of the End of the Commons General Store to insure a safe parking place, out of the way of customers. He can be reached at (216) 693–4295. Those wishing to do the tour in one day may choose to start here or at the Pymatuning Lake campgrounds at the eastern end of this tour. Mesopotamia is at the intersection of OH 87 and OH 534. Pymatuning Reservoir is just east of OH 7. Either can be

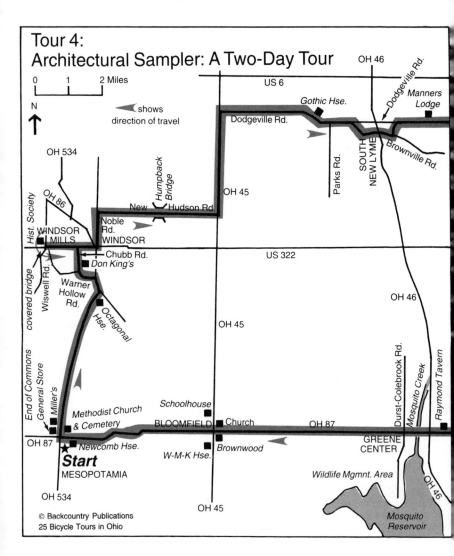

reached from OH 11, which is accessible from both I-80 and I-90.

0.0   Leave from the south end of the commons, between the Amish hitching post and the Civil War memorial in the circular village green. Ride north along the east side of the commons, on OH 534.

Mesopotamia, which means "between two rivers," is located between the Cuyahoga and the Grand rivers. The center of Meso-

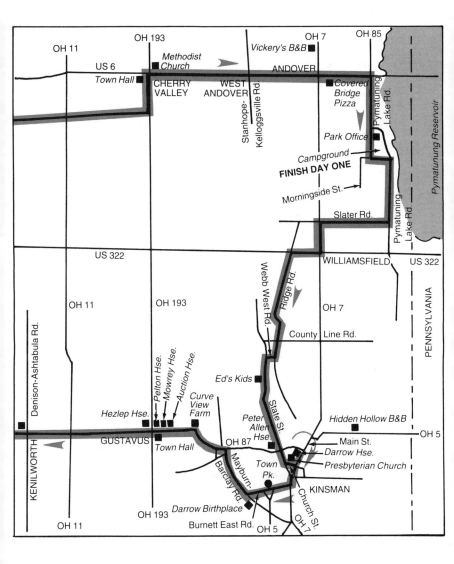

potamia is atypical for a Western Reserve village in that its town "square" is an extremely long and narrow rectangle. The town also has an accompanying village green at the south end, where the Civil War memorial stands.

For those preparing for a long bike ride, it is hard to imagine a better send-off than the End of the Commons General Store. Known as Northeast Ohio's largest pre-packaged bulk food store, it has been in continuous operation since 1840. Relics of its past are displayed, including the old post office, cash registers, and a working player piano. With fifteen hundred Amish in the local community, the store also supplies Amish hats and bonnets, candles and kerosene lamps, horse and buggy supplies, and other such necessities. Tourists beware: All businesses in this community are closed on Sunday, and there is very little on this route in the way of nourishment for the next thirty miles.

Surrounding the commons are thirty century homes (one hundred years old or more), the oldest dating from 1816. At the southeast corner of the intersection, facing OH 534, is the notable Gothic Revival cottage known as Newcomb House. The Mesopotamia Historical Museum and Meeting House facing the east side of the green was built in 1846. Note the double front doors, one side for men, the other for women. Next to this building is the 1830 Greco-Gothic Mesopotamia United Methodist Church, behind which is the beautifully maintained Fairview Cemetery. Established in 1818, the cemetery is famous for its unique tombstones carved into natural forms, such as bears and seashells, by the nineteenth-century local artisan, Howard Brigden. Across the green from the church, facing west, is Miller's Harness and Leather Shop in a fine 1850 Greek Revival home.

0.2   At the north end of the commons, continue STRAIGHT on OH 534.
Many plain but prosperous Amish homes dot the countryside along OH 534. The road has no berm, but it is lightly used for a state highway. Just before your next turn to the left is the remarkable Hegley-Pelen House, the largest octagon house in Ashtabula County. Built around 1860, each of the eight sides is eighteen-feet long. Each floor has four square and four triangular rooms, and the central hall has a stairway winding up to the cupola. Popularized by phrenologist Orson Fowler in the mid-nineteenth century, the design was said to promote the good health of the residents. Fowler claimed that one of the benefits was the increased ventilation aided by the ubiquitous cupola.

4.3   Turn LEFT onto unmarked Warner Hollow Road; the road will be

gravel for about 1.5 mile. (Those wishing to cut about 3 miles from this tour can continue STRAIGHT and rejoin the tour at mileage point 8.0 in the village of Windsor.)

The road is flat for half a mile, then climbs until the next intersection.

5.0   Turn RIGHT onto unmarked Chubb Road.

You will see three flags flying in the distance as you make this turn, and soon you'll see several large, plaster figures of animals beyond the pond. Shortly, you'll come to the entrance of this estate, marked by a large wrought iron gateway and a sign saying "The Kings." This is the home of Don King, manager for boxing champion, Mike Tyson, whose own residence is sequestered in the surrounding countryside.

5.7   Turn LEFT onto US 322.

6.7   Turn LEFT onto Wiswell Road. After seeing the bridge and the church, retrace your route east on US 322 to the town of Windsor.

Just a few hundred feet from this intersection you'll see the 1867 Wiswell Road Covered Bridge, open to foot traffic only. Just across from this intersection is the Christ Episcopal Church, built between 1832 and 1834 with a combination of Greek and Gothic elements. Use of the Gothic style in the Western Reserve was very rare this early. The church now houses the Windsor Mills Historical Society and is open Sundays from 1 to 4 PM from Memorial Day to October.

8.0   Turn LEFT at the blinking yellow light, following the sign for OH 86; at the immediate Y-junction, bear RIGHT to take the unmarked Noble Road.

Those who omitted the trip to Windsor Mills can pick up the tour at this point.

Windsor has a town "triangle" rather than a square, with the ubiquitous war memorial. The town was named in honor of the proprietor and the first two settlers, all of whom came from Windsor, Connecticut.

9.0   Bear RIGHT, following the arrow and covered bridge sign onto unmarked New Hudson Road.

Like many of the roads on this tour, New Hudson is the ideal bicycling road: flat, straight, well paved, and nearly traffic free. In about two miles, you'll cross a Roman, or "humpback," bridge built in 1906 to test concrete. As of this writing, it continues to pass the test.

12.5   At the Stop sign, turn LEFT onto OH 45.

A major route to downtown Warren, this road has a bit more traffic than New Hudson Road; however, it's very flat and straight, and you're on it for fewer than three miles.

15.3 **At the sign pointing to New Lyme Baptist Church, turn RIGHT onto Dodgeville Road.**

You now traverse ten miles of quiet, untraveled road. About three miles down the road, at the intersection of Parks and Dodgeville roads is a carefully landscaped, restored Gothic home.

19.0 **At the Y-junction, follow the road around to the RIGHT — Brownville Road (unposted) — avoiding the left arm, which is the continuation of Dodgeville Road.**

There are several large, midcentury, Italianate homes in tiny South New Lyme.

19.7 **Go STRAIGHT at the Stop sign, crossing OH 46.**

20.1 **At the No Outlet sign, where the road turns to gravel, follow the paved road around to the LEFT.**

20.4 **At the Stop sign, turn RIGHT onto unmarked Dodgeville Road.**

The signs for "Manners" refers to the large evergreen nursery through which you are riding. In about half a mile is Charlie Manners Pine Tree Lodge, open to visitors on weekends year-round. Call (216) 294–2444 for program and hours.

25.4 **At the Stop sign, turn LEFT onto OH 193.**

26.4 **At the blinking red light and Stop sign, turn RIGHT onto US 6.**

US 6, the Grand Army of the Republic Highway, is surprisingly busy because it leads to the causeway that crosses the Pymatuning Reservoir into Pennsylvania. This hamlet of Cherry Valley has a unique village green sliced into four small squares, one on each corner of an intersection. The 1886 Town Hall is on the southwest corner, and the vaguely Gothic United Methodist Church is on the northeast one.

In about two and a half miles you'll reach the village of West Andover, where there is a good example of a Gothic board and batten house. The Stanhope-Kelloggsville Road, which runs north-south through the village, is another route richly rewarding for those in search of nineteenth-century rural architecture. As you approach Andover, you'll see that the old part of town is west of the square, with many fine Italianate homes.

31.3 **At the Stop sign in front of the Andover town square, follow the Grand Army of the Republic Highway to the RIGHT around the Andover Township Park; on the east side of the park, the road becomes OH 85.**

If you continue further around the square and turn right onto OH 7 North, you'll reach Vickery's Bed and Breakfast, a one hundred-year-old home on one hundred acres complete with pond and accompanying paddleboat. Call Robert and Ruth Vickery at (216) 293–6875 for reservations.

This town was named after Andover, Connecticut, birthplace of many of the original immigrants. Clarence Darrow, the renowned criminal lawyer, practiced law here before moving on to Chicago. You'll visit his birthplace and childhood home later in this tour.

On East Main Street, on your right a little beyond the square, is the Covered Bridge Restaurant. Actually half of a real covered bridge built in 1862, the restaurant has an extensive menu including salads, soups, chili, spaghetti, and sub sandwiches, in addition to extraordinarily good pizza on white or whole wheat crust. The other half of the bridge is home to another restaurant in North Kingsville.

32.8 At the light, turn RIGHT onto Pymatuning Lake Road.

Continuing straight on OH 85 will take you to Pennsylvania, where the state's fish commission operates a fish hatchery near Linesville. There is a waterfowl museum nearby with a viewing area that allows you to see a bald eagle nesting area. At the Pymatuning spillway, carp compete with ducks for bits of bread tossed by visitors. The fish are so abundant that the ducks walk on them to catch the handouts.

A half mile down this road brings you to the public beach, with a bathhouse, showers, lockers, and a snack bar.

34.3 At the sign to the park office, turn LEFT into the campsite area.

This is the halfway point of the tour and a good place to stop for the night. The park's campground, the second largest in the state, has electric hook-ups, heated wash houses, and a laundry and camp commissary. For those who prefer more substantial shelter, very well-maintained four- and six-person cabins furnished with linen, towels, and cooking and eating utensils can be reserved up to a year in advance. There is a second public beach in the cabin area. During the summer, interpretive programs are conducted, and boats are available for rental. The park office at this turn has maps and brochures. For more information and reservations, call the park manager at (216) 293–6030.

35.7 At the Stop sign by the boat livery, continue STRAIGHT, avoiding the right onto Morningside Street; this route is the continuation of Pymatuning Lake Road.

This section of Pymatuning Lake Road has several private camp-grounds and small resorts.

37.3 At this point, Pymatuning Lake Road goes to the left with a sign to US 322; ride STRAIGHT on Slater Road, with the sign directing you to OH 7.

39.4 **Turn LEFT at the Stop sign onto OH 7.**

40.2 **At the light in Williamsfield, turn RIGHT onto US 322.**
This township was bought by Connecticut-born General Joseph Williams.

41.2 **Turn LEFT onto Ridge Road. (Some maps may call this route Old Salt Road, but the sign reads "Ridge Road.")**
Ridge Road is a well-paved rural road with no traffic and fine views overlooking the valley of Pymatuning Creek.

43.6 **Ride STRAIGHT at the Stop sign, crossing unmarked County Line Road.**

44.2 **Turn RIGHT after a downhill onto unmarked Webb West Road.**

44.4 **At the Stop sign, turn LEFT onto unmarked State Street. (Some maps may call this Kinsman Road.)**
State Street continues like Ridge Road, with little traffic and good views into the valley to your right. In half a mile is Ed's Kids, a pygmy goat farm.
Just before the Stop sign at the intersection with OH 87 is the famed Peter Allen House on your right, easy to miss because of the large maples in front. Built in 1821, it has been called "a masterpiece of early architecture in Trumbull County . . . not surpassed in refinement of detail by any other house in the Western Reserve."

46.8 **At the Stop sign, continue STRAIGHT on State Street, crossing OH 87.**

47.2 **Make a LEFT onto Church Street.**
The Kinsman Presbyterian Church was built by Willie Smith, who also built the Peter Allen House. Built around 1832 in a blend of Gothic and classical forms, this church, like the one in Windsor Mills, is considered Greco-Gothic and said to have been modeled on the Old North Church in New Haven, Connecticut. Across the street is the Kinsman Public Library.

47.4 **Turn LEFT onto Main Street for .25 mile to see the Clarence Darrow Octagon House; then continue back south on Main Street toward the center of town.**
Clarence Darrow moved to this eight-sided home with his family in 1859 when he was two years old. He spent only one year in law school before becoming a member of the Ohio Bar Association. His cases became topics for household conversation even before his famous defense of John Scopes, who had defied a Tennessee law prohibiting the teaching of evolution.
Two miles north on OH 5, you'll come to the Hidden Hollow Bed

and Breakfast. Call Rita White at (216) 876–8686 for reservations.

48.0   Follow around the square to the RIGHT.

The large building to your right is Kinsman Optical, formerly a stagecoach stop built in 1825. The bandstand in the village square was built in 1915; before that time, the square was a baseball diamond, which Darrow speaks of in his novel, Farmington (1904), based on the village of Kinsman during the 1850s and 1860s. There are several restaurants and food stores in this area.

48.1   At the Stop sign, go LEFT on State Street, the west side of the square; ride out of town on OH 5 and 7.

48.3   Turn RIGHT between the two gas stations, leaving OH 7 and following OH 5.

48.8   At the Y-junction, OH 5 goes off to the left; ride on the smaller, RIGHT fork—Burnett East Road.

The Kinsman Township Park on your right is dedicated to Clarence Darrow. It has covered picnic tables and a baseball diamond.

49.6   Turn LEFT onto Mayburn-Barclay Road for a couple hundred yards, where you'll see a house on your right with a dormer window. This was the birthplace of Clarence Darrow. Retrace your route, continuing STRAIGHT on Mayburn-Barclay Road.

51.0   At the Stop sign, go LEFT onto OH 87.

OH 87 is quite straight and flat, with minimal traffic for nearly twenty miles. As the road bends to the left in about a mile, you'll see Hartman's Curve-View Farm, built in 1820. In two miles on your right is the Gustavus Auction House, a Greek Revival building. Next to it is a colonial or Western Reserve house, the Charles Mowrey House, circa 1846. Next comes the 1890 Town Hall, a curious building with a hip roof and modified mansard tower. Across from the Town Hall is the 1840 Greek Revival Lysander-Pelton House.

53.2   Go STRAIGHT at the Stop sign marking the intersection with OH 193.

The entire town center of Gustavus is on the National Register of Historic Places. The village green, like that in Mesopotamia, is rectangular and is surrounded by historic buildings. A good map of all the structures of historic significance in Gustavus Township is posted next to the fireplace in the picnic shelter on the village green. On the west side of the green is the Shopkeeper's House (1840), the Fraternal Hall (1870), and the Gustavus Federated Church (1856). All these are basically Greek Revival, some with a slight Gothic influence. On the east side is the colonial-style Parsonage (1830). As

Octagonal houses, such as the Hegley-Pelen House in Windsor, were more popular in Ashtabula County than in any other part of Ohio.

you head west on OH 87, off the northwest corner of the square is the outstanding Greek Revival Hezlep House (1832), made of Gustavus brick, formerly home of the Maple Lawn Inn. The 1928 Schoolhouse on the left is on the site of the first centralized school in the nation.

The road climbs gently as you leave Gustavus, but not enough to tire you if there is no headwind. About three and a half miles from Gustavus, at the intersection of Denison-Ashtabula Road, is the hamlet of Kenilworth. On the northwest corner stands the 1830 Liberty G. Raymond Tavern, a beautiful Greco-Gothic building that was a popular stagecoach stop. It was also a stop on the underground railroad, the hidden compartment under the stairs serving as a hiding place for slaves.

57.3   At the Stop sign, go STRAIGHT through the intersection with OH 46.

As you cross Mosquito Creek, the large Mosquito Reservoir is to your left. Normally draining to the south, when the lake reaches 904 feet above sea level the flow reverses and the lake drains through the natural spillway at this end.

58.1   At the Stop sign, go STRAIGHT at the intersection with Durst-Colebrook Road.

The tiny village of Greene Center boasts a village green that is actually a square, an 1877 Greek Revival Town Hall south of the green beyond the picnic shelter, and the impressive Gothic Greene Community Foursquare Church.

For the next five miles you'll be riding along the north border of the Mosquito Creek Wildlife Waterfowl Management Area. The most common resident is the Canada goose, who shares the area with a number of hawk species, the African cattle egret, bald and golden eagles, herons, and a variety of ducks. It is also home to the Eastern massasauga, a poisonous rattlesnake.

63.2   Ride STRAIGHT at the intersection of OH 45 in Bloomfield.

Like Gustavus, Kinsman, and Mesopotamia, Bloomfield, organized in 1816, has a number of notable historic dwellings. On the east side of the rectangular village green is the Greek Revival Church, so Greek, in fact, that its tower is in the form of a miniature Parthenon. A quarter mile north of the square is the old Greek Revival Schoolhouse, now enlarged and converted into an apartment house. Across from the green, facing OH 45 is the remarkable dwelling called Brownwood, a masterpiece of Federal or Adamesque architecture built in 1819. Just across the highway was another home, built in 1834 by Ephraim Brown of Brownwood, which was destroyed by an explosion in the 1970s. It was a mirror image of the central part of Brownwood. Just south of the now empty lot, up a curving gravel drive, is the Wing-McAdoo-Kennedy House, a charming 1846 Gothic cottage said to have been built by Brown for his daughter. Like the tavern at Kenilworth, this, too, was a stop on the underground railroad, where slaves hid in a capacious cupboard in the kitchen.

68.0   Swing right after the Mesopotamia circular village green. This turn will put you in front of the End of the Commons General Store.

Bicycle Repair Services

Pedal Power & Sports, 218-B South High Street, Cortland, OH 44410 (216) 638–6789.

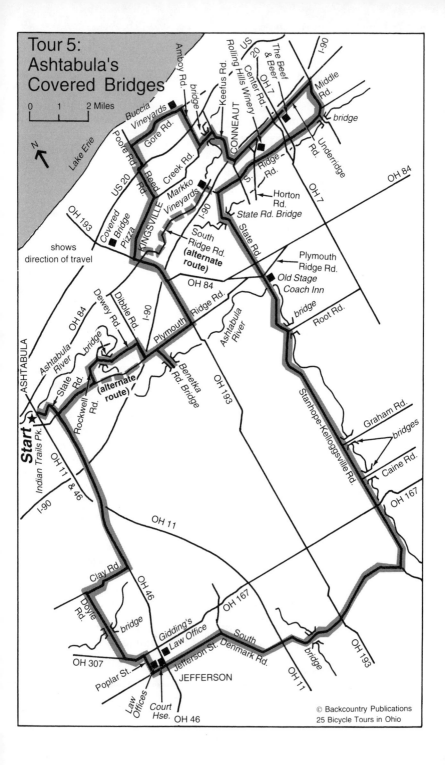

Tour 5:
Ashtabula's
Covered Bridges

0   1   2 Miles

N

Lake Erie

Amboy Rd.

bridge

Keefus Rd.

Rolling Hills Winery

US 20

Center Rd.

OH 7

The Beef & Beer

I-90

Middle Rd.

bridge

Buccia Vineyards

Gore Rd.

CONNEAUT

Underridge Rd.

Poore Rd.

Reed Rd.

Creek Rd.

US 20

Ridge Rd.

US

Horton Rd.

OH 7

OH 84

OH 193

Covered Bridge Pizza

KINGSVILLE

Markko Vineyards

I-90

State Rd. Bridge

shows direction of travel

South Ridge Rd. (alternate route)

OH 84

Plymouth Ridge Rd.

Old Stage Coach Inn

State Rd.

bridge

Root Rd.

OH 84

Dewey Rd.

Dibble Rd.

I-90

Plymouth Ridge Rd.

Ashtabula River

Ashtabula River

bridge

State Rd.

Rockwell Rd.

(alternate route)

Benetka Rd. Bridge

OH 193

Stanhope-Kelloggsville Rd.

ASHTABULA

Start

Indian Trails Pk.

OH 11 & 46

I-90

OH 11

Graham Rd.

bridges

Caine Rd.

OH 167

Clay Rd.

OH 46

Doyle Rd.

bridge

OH 167

Gidding's Law Office

South

Denmark Rd.

OH 307

Poplar St.

Jefferson St.

JEFFERSON

bridge

OH 193

OH 11

Law Offices

Court Hse.

OH 46

© Backcountry Publications
25 Bicycle Tours in Ohio

5

Ashtabula's Covered Bridges

54 miles; easy to strenuous cycling
Rolling hills with some flat stretches; about 15 miles of unpaved road
County map: Ashtabula

Early pioneers in the Western Reserve usually sought a riverside site that would provide water and a form of transport in the roadless frontier. When road building began, however, rivers became the greatest obstacles to wheel and rail travel. Until the Revolutionary War, fords and ferries were the standard river crossings. When bridges were built, they were generally low to the water and supported by closely spaced pilings, prime targets for ice and flood damage. Those constructed with stone had the best chance of withstanding the ravages of time and weather, but building them was a slow and immensely laborious task. The solution lay in the construction of wooden bridges designed to sustain long spans with a minimum number of pilings and to weather well.

The basics of truss bridge construction had been known since the sixteenth century from the writings of Italian architect Andreas Palladio. In 1792, Timothy Palmer was the first American to use the truss design in Connecticut. By 1805, the first cover had been added to a wooden bridge, and it was successful in substantially reducing deterioration to the bridge surface. Whatever succeeded in Connecticut was sure to appear in the Western Reserve, and by mid-nineteenth century there were over forty covered bridges in Ashtabula County alone.

Seventeen covered bridges remain in the Western Reserve, and fourteen are in Ashtabula County. The county has not only worked hard to preserve its covered bridges but has actually built two new ones in the 1980s. Details on the construction of the new bridges and the preservation of the old are available from the County Engineer's Office, Old Courthouse Building, Jefferson, Ohio 44047.

This tour takes in ten of Ashtabula's covered bridges and visits three wineries. With so much to see and with fifty-four miles to cover, some on hilly or unpaved roadways, even conditioned cyclists will find this a challenging ride. Given the camping and overnight accommodations available in the Conneaut area, the tour can easily be adapted for a two-day trip. For those wishing to condense the route, suggested shortcuts are included in the route directions. The tour begins just south of the junction of OH 11/46 and OH 84 at Indian Trails Park, which forms the southeast corner of the city of Ashtabula. OH 11 can be reached via I-90. The mileage starts at the park's south entrance, which has no identifying sign. There are two yellow posts marking this entrance.

0.0   Turn RIGHT out of the park onto unmarked State Road.

Indian Trails Park forms a narrow border along both sides of the Ashtabula River, which would have been named the Mary Esther River after Moses Cleaveland's daughter had the Western Reserve's chief surveyor had his way. Ashtabula and the city of Conneaut fourteen miles to the northeast were the first two settlements in the Western Reserve, established by members of Cleaveland's party of Connecticut Land Company surveyors. The Indian names, Ashtabula and Conneaut, both mean something akin to "fish river." The river was the boundary between the eastern tribes—the Iroquois—and certain Algonquin tribes to the west. The park has facilities for picnicking, fishing, and primitive camping for tents and trailers.

The route begins with a steepish climb up to Plymouth Ridge Road, which follows the ridge of a former Lake Erie shoreline.

1.5   At the four-way Stop sign, continue STRAIGHT on State Road, crossing Plymouth Road.

In half a mile is an overpass across I-90, followed shortly by another over OH 11. At this point, State Road becomes OH 46.

5.3   Turn RIGHT onto Clay Road.

6.6   Turn LEFT onto Doyle Road; there is no road sign, but there is a sign reading "Bridge one mile ahead."

Doyle immediately becomes unpaved. You'll reach Doyle Road Bridge over Mill Creek in a little over a mile. The bridge was built in 1868 by a carpenter from Vermont who reportedly copied it from a bridge in his hometown. It has a lattice truss, patented in 1820 by Ithiel Town. The Town lattice is the most common style of truss bridge surviving in Ashtabula County and was favored by carpenters because it was easy to construct from heavy planks. In its 1988 restoration, the bridge acquired an attractive Burr arch on each interior wall to increase the load capacity of the bridge. Developed in 1804, the Burr arch was designed to reinforce the basic truss and might be constructed along with the original structure or, as in this case, added later. The narrow, window-like openings on each side of the bridge permit those on the bridge to see if traffic is approaching.

8.8   At the Stop sign, turn LEFT onto unmarked OH 307.

9.3   Turn RIGHT onto Poplar Street, following the sign to the County Fairgrounds.

Since 1984, Ashtabula County has sponsored a Covered Bridge Festival during the second weekend in October. A parade is held in downtown Jefferson, the county seat, with farm events, lots of food, and square dancing at the nearby fairgrounds. Information on the festival can be obtained by calling (216) 567–9090.

9.8   At the Stop sign, go LEFT onto West Jefferson Street.

10.4   Go STRAIGHT at the Stop sign onto East Jefferson Street, crossing Chestnut Street (OH 46).

Historian Harriet Taylor Upton called Jefferson "a facsimile of many New England towns, . . . the Concord of the West." The traditional village green, however, has been cut into quarters by this intersection. The County Court House was built in 1850 and was remodeled substantially in 1891. To the west of the courthouse is Lawyer's Row, built some time after 1850. If you turn left for a block and a half onto Chestnut Street, you'll see Joshua Giddings' law office at 108 Chestnut Street. Built in 1823, this diminutive, Federal-style building was in keeping with the tradition of early nineteenth-century doctors and lawyers who built offices next to, but detached from, their homes.

Famous in the history of the abolitionist movement, this office at one time served both Joshua R. Giddings and his friend and colleague, Benjamin F. Wade. Both were elected to Congress and spent their careers as outspoken opponents of slavery. Wade was elected president of the Senate during the Johnson administration and, as such, would have become president of the United States had one more senator voted for the impeachment of Andrew Johnson. Giddings' office still houses his desk, law library, and the first safe brought to Ashtabula County. The office is open weekends from June through August, from 1 to 4 PM.

On the same street, behind the courthouse, is the 1870 probate court building, built by Levi T. Scofield who designed the famous Soldiers' and Sailors' Monument in Cleveland.

Gideon Granger, postmaster general under President Thomas Jefferson, was the first proprietor of Jefferson township, which he named in the president's honor. Another well-known Jeffersonian from this township was William Dean Howells, editor, novelist, and first president of the American Academy of Arts and Letters.

10.6   At the light, continue STRAIGHT on East Jefferson, crossing over Market Street.

12.1   Turn RIGHT onto South Denmark Road, following the covered bridge sign.

In a little under three miles, you'll reach the South Denmark Road Bridge, to the right of the bypass bridge that was built in 1975 to lighten the traffic on the historic bridge. Both are open to traffic. Built over Mill Creek in 1890, it is said by some to have been constructed from a former bridge on the same spot. Like the Doyle Road Bridge, this one is of Town lattice construction.

16.1   At the Stop sign, continue STRAIGHT on South Denmark Road, crossing unposted OH 193.

South Denmark Road continues to be a beautiful, well-paved, and mostly flat route, with just enough dips and curves to make for exquisite bicycling conditions.

18.4   At the Stop sign, turn LEFT onto Stanhope-Kelloggsville Road, which is not posted.

Flat and well-paved, with shade trees on either side, the Stanhope-Kelloggsville Road is known for its historic rural architecture.

20.3   At the Stop sign, continue STRAIGHT on Stanhope-Kelloggsville Road, crossing OH 167.

In just under a mile, unpaved Caine Road is to your right. A quarter mile detour will take you to the Caine Road Covered Bridge, one of the two added by Ashtabula County Engineer, John Smolen. Spanning the west branch of the Ashtabula River, the bridge was built in 1986 using a Pratt truss construction, standard for most modern highway bridges but rarely used for wooden bridges. The bridge is ninety-six-feet long and replaced a former steel truss bridge.

A quarter mile past the Caine Road junction, on the same side of the road, is a covered bridge sign pointing down Graham Road. Again, a quarter mile detour with take you to the Graham Road Bridge, which was moved to this site from its location over the east branch of the Ashtabula River. It was built from the remains of a former covered bridge that was washed more than a mile downstream during the devastating flood of 1913. Of Town lattice construction, it is ninety-seven-feet long and has a slight hump in the west end of the roof line due to a builder's error. Moved to the south side of the road in 1971, adjacent to but not spanning the river, the bridge is now under the care of the Ashtabula County Metropolitan Parks Commission. A grill is provided and steps lead up to the bridge interior. At the end of the bridge overlooking the river, a picnic table is conveniently placed in the bridge's interior.

The road continues flat, providing a comfortable ride through pleasant countryside. Three and a half miles after Graham Road, you'll come to the Root Road Covered Bridge at the junction of Stanhope-Kelloggsville Road with Root Road. Traversing the east branch of the Ashtabula River, this 114-foot bridge was built in 1868 with a Town lattice truss. In danger of collapse in 1963, it was reinforced with guide wires to counteract its south-leaning tendencies. The entire bridge was rehabilitated in 1982–1983 by raising the bridge eighteen inches and adding new abutment piers, laminated girders, new flooring, siding, and gables.

26.7   At the Stop sign, continue STRAIGHT, crossing over Plymouth Ridge Road.

At the southeast corner of this intersection is the Old Stagecoach Inn, built in 1824. In private hands and not in good repair, it is still a delightful example of Federal architecture, although the incongruous "carport" is a much later addition. The last stagecoach stopped here in 1852 just as the railroad began operation. Now no more than a crossroads, Kelloggsville was once alive with mills and distilleries established by Caleb Blodgett, who came here from Vermont in 1810. Blodgett built the inn as well as the road you've been riding on for the last eight miles.

27.1   At the Stop sign, continue STRAIGHT on what is now called State Road, crossing over OH 84.

The road goes downhill and begins curving as it nears Conneaut Creek, where the State Road Bridge was constructed in 1983. The bridge cost some two to three times that of a steel bridge. County Engineer John Smolen selected this site because the existing steel bridge was deteriorating and unsafe, and it is known that there was a covered bridge on this site prior to 1897. The bridge was built in five months using the Town lattice truss and required ninety-seven thousand board feet of southern pine and oak. Constructed on land, it was moved onto its abutment piers by the county highway department and dedicated in November 1983. This dedication was the forerunner of the annual Covered Bridge Festival.

Half a mile past the bridge you'll cross into Conneaut Township, and the road becomes unpaved.

29.5   At the Stop sign, turn RIGHT onto unpaved South Ridge Road (unposted).

To visit Markko Vineyards, turn left instead of right and ride through the underpass.

Markko Vineyards opened in 1968 and produced its first vintage in 1972. With the well-drained soil of the lake ridges and its proximity to Lake Erie, the area proved agreeable to the French imports. Markko now has over ten acres of chardonnay, white riesling, and cabernet sauvignon and produces only dry, French-style wines. The winery is open from 11 AM to 6 PM, Mondays through Saturdays, and offers fruit, bread, and cheese to accompany wine samples.

After your visit, retrace your route back under the highway and continue east on South Ridge Road.

(You can reduce this tour to approximately thirty-eight miles by continuing west on South Ridge Road after visiting the Markko Vineyards. You then pick up the tour in Kingsville at OH 193 [mileage mark 43.7]. You will miss two wineries and two covered bridges; but you'll also avoid several miles of dirt road.)

A mile and a half from the intersection of State Road and South Ridge Road is the Rolling Hills Winery, owned and operated by Ray and Jenny Palagyi. The small but attractive sampling room is at the rear of their ranch-style home and is open from 4 to 7 PM on Fridays, noon to 6 PM on Saturdays, and other times by appointment.

After Rolling Hills, continue west on South Ridge Road, which remains unpaved.

(The cyclist can also elect to shorten the route by five miles at this intersection by turning left onto Horton Road and rejoining the tour on Underridge Road, a half mile past mileage point 36.1.)

32.1   At the Stop sign, go STRAIGHT on South Ridge Road, crossing OH 7.

In just under a mile and a half you'll see a covered bridge sign to the right, pointing to unposted Middle Road. To visit the bridge, go down a short, steep, unpaved hill for a tenth of a mile to Conneaut Creek. Built in 1868, this bridge was constructed using the Howe truss. William Howe developed this truss in 1840, improving on an 1830 design by Colonel Stephen Long that consisted of wooden planks erected in a series of boxed X's. Howe took this idea and substituted wrought-iron rods for the upright plank between each of the X's. Turnbuckles on these tie-rods allowed the bridge to be adjusted whenever it began to sag. Howe's design met with immediate success, and thousands were built by bridge companies throughout the country.

On January 6, 1984, a timber snapped on this bridge, collapsing the bridge eighteen inches at one end. To keep it from crashing into Conneaut Creek and into oblivion, volunteers, supervised by county employees, did restoration work for four months. On October 14, 1984, the bridge was rededicated at the first Ashtabula Covered Bridge Festival.

33.7   From South Ridge Road, turn LEFT, away from the bridge sign, onto unmarked Middle Road.

Continuing unpaved, Middle Road goes up the ridge for about half a mile, then rolls down the north side.

34.7   Turn LEFT onto unmarked Underridge Road.

This road is wonderfully flat and resumes paving for a short time in a little under a mile.

36.0   At the Stop sign, go STRAIGHT on Underridge Road, crossing OH 7.

Just before crossing the intersection, you may be surprised to see a large sign for "The Beef and Beer" up a hill on your left. Those requiring more fuel for the remaining miles will appreciate the comprehensive menu and good service at this classic highway travel stop.

36.1   Continue STRAIGHT on Underridge Road, crossing Center Road.

After Center Road, the road reverts to dirt again.

37.8   Turn RIGHT at the T-junction onto Keefus Road.

Keefus carries you immediately over I-90. Don't let the macadam paving fool you into expecting smooth sailing; it disappears in a few hundred yards.

39.1   Turn LEFT onto unpaved Creek Road.

You'll have an immediate downhill to Conneaut Creek, where you'll cross the Creek Road Bridge in just under a mile. The bridge is built high over the creek in the familiar Town lattice style and is believed to be well over a century old. A steel and concrete support was added in the center of the span in 1982, and new siding was provided in 1983.

39.4   At the Stop sign, turn RIGHT onto unmarked Amboy Road. (To eliminate about three miles, continue straight on Creek Road, which becomes paved shortly, and rejoin the tour at Reed Road [mileage point 43.9].)

For those spending the night in or near Conneaut, there is Conneaut Cottage, with weekend or weekly rentals (216–757–0694), and a bed and breakfast available at the Buccia Winery (see below). Campers can stay at Evergreen Lake Park on Center Street (216–599–8802) or at The Big D Campgrounds (216–224–1668) near Kingsville.

40.0   At the light, continue STRAIGHT on Amboy Road, crossing US 20.

40.6   At the Stop sign, turn LEFT onto Gore Road.

Both Amboy and Gore are completely flat, but Gore returns to a dirt surface in a few hundred feet. Just past the railroad tracks you'll come to Buccia Vineyards, established by Alfred and Joanna Bucci in 1975. In addition to tours and wine samples, the Buccis provide salami, cheese, and homemade bread plates for a small charge.

They maintain a country craft store in their hospitality room and provide sleeping accommodations complete with a loft waterbed and a hot tub. Call 216–593–5976 for more information. The winery is open every day but Sunday.

Shortly after the vineyards, the road becomes paved again.

42.3   At the Stop sign and T-junction, turn LEFT onto Poore Road.

43.0   Turn RIGHT onto US 20 at the Stop sign, then make an immediate LEFT onto Reed Road.

43.9   At the Stop sign, turn RIGHT onto Creek Road.
The Big D Campground is near this intersection.

45.9   At the Stop sign, turn LEFT onto OH 193.
A right turn here will bring you to the Covered Bridge Pizza Parlor in about half a mile. Opened in 1975, the restaurant is in half of the former Forman Road Bridge in Eagleville, which washed out in 1972. Originally built in 1862, it was 126 feet long and weighed some 55 tons. Only original material went into the restaurant's interior, while new roofing and siding reinforced the outside. Inside, beneath the original roof trusses, Ashtabulans sit in wooden booths or at tavern tables and study the original exterior walls, looking for initials carved when they were kids. The other half of the bridge serves as a similar pizza diner in Andover (see tour 4).

46.0   At the light, continue STRAIGHT onto what becomes OH 84 East/ OH 193 South; when OH 84 goes off to the left, stay on OH 193.

48.4   Turn RIGHT onto Plymouth Ridge Road.
In one and a quarter miles, a strenuous, half-mile detour onto unpaved Benetka Road takes you to the Benetka Road Covered Bridge. The steep gravel road goes downhill to the Ashtabula River, where the bridge poses for photographers who find it equally appealing both from upstream or downstream. Built at the turn of the century, this beautiful Town lattice bridge was completely rehabilitated in 1985 with new laminated arches, floor system, siding, ends, and roof.

50.1   Turn RIGHT just past the overpass onto Dibble Road.
(You can continue straight on Plymouth Ridge Road and save a little over two miles, about a mile and a half of which is a difficult and hilly gravel surface.)

50.5   Turn LEFT onto unmarked and unpaved Dewey Road.
Riding on Dewey is not for the fainthearted; the rollercoaster terrain would be a challenge even if it were paved. You'll reach the Olin Bridge after a little over a mile of rugged riding. Built between 1873

and 1875, the bridge is named for the family who owned the adjoining property. Another Town lattice construction, it was refurbished in 1981, receiving a new shingle roof, siding, gables, and guardrails. The west end of the bridge accesses an Ashtabula River swimming hole.

Leaving the river valley requires more hill climbing. After another mile and a half, the road makes a right-angle turn to the left and becomes Rockwell Road.

52.6   At the Stop sign, turn RIGHT onto unmarked Plymouth Creek Road.

53.9   At the Stop Sign, turn RIGHT onto State Road.
You'll have one last curving and demanding downhill back into the valley of the Ashtabula.

54.4   Turn RIGHT into the parking area for Indian Trails Park.
In Ashtabula, Michael Cahill's Bed and Breakfast is in a fine 1887 Victorian home at 1106 Walnut Boulevard (216–964–7449). Just down the street is the Great Lakes Marine and Coast Guard Museum, which is open from Memorial Day through October on Friday through Sunday and on holidays from 1 to 5 PM.

Bicycle Repair Services
B. J. Baker Bicycle Sales and Service, 4722 Foster Avenue, Ashtabula, Ohio 44004 (216) 997–3486.

6

Lakeshore Vines and Wines

34 miles; easy to moderate cycling
Flat lake plain and rolling hills; about 5 miles of unpaved road
County maps: Lake, Ashtabula

In 1860, Ohio led the nation in wine production, with vineyards blanketing the slopes along the Ohio River. It was not until the turn of the last century, however, that the Lake Erie region began to be recognized for its ideal grape-growing conditions. The tempering effect of Lake Erie on the climate of northern Ohio considerably prolongs the growing season, with an average of 193 frost-free days along the Lake County shore. Fewer than forty miles inland, central Portage County can count on only 133 days without frost.

In addition, the soil of the lake plain is overlaid with parallel, sandy ridges that provide the drainage lacking in the clay soil of the adjacent land. This good fortune is due to the action of the last glacier, which sculpted Lake Erie and then retreated haltingly, leaving a sandy shoreline at every pause in its withdrawal north.

Lying above the surrounding, swampy lake plain, these former shorelines attracted the earliest settlements and determined road patterns. In Lake County, US 20 follows the north ridge closest to the lake, Middle Ridge Road runs atop the next, and OH 84 is South Ridge Road. Although only a few feet higher than the flat lake plain, these ridges provide for excellent sun exposure and good drainage, optimum conditions for the vintner. The area around the city of Geneva accounts for forty-five percent of Ohio's grape production.

For several decades, the vinegrowers of Ashtabula and Lake counties sold their produce to major wineries. But in the late sixties and early seventies, small home wineries began to appear, most selling their products only from their own winery, some combining the winery with a restaurant. Detailed information on all aspects of Ohio wine production, including a five dollar "Tasting Kit," is available from the Ohio Wine Producers Association, 822 North Tote Road, Austinburg, Ohio 44010, or by calling 1-800-227-6972.

This tour visits four wineries, all of which offer snack foods or full meals. All provide tastings as well, although beware of combining exertion and sunshine with alcohol. It's best to stay alert for the whole trip, which includes two covered bridges, a state park with a swimming beach on Lake Erie, several beautiful county parks, and a visit to the architecturally and historically rich village of Madison. If you choose, you can cap off your ride with the fine cuisine at the Old Tavern, which has been serving tourists and travelers since 1798.

The tour begins in the main parking lot of Geneva State Park at the intersection of Lake and Padanarum roads off US 20, about 10 miles west of Ashtabula and 60 miles east of Cleveland.

0.0   Turn RIGHT out of the park office lot onto the park road.

Turning left out of the parking lot will take you to the newly constructed small boat harbor, beautifully situated on the shores of the land-hungry Lake Erie. Further east along this shore is the swimming beach, where you will see evidence of several attempts at erosion control by the U.S. Army Corps of Engineers. To the west of the boat harbor are twelve cabins and a ninety-one site campground. Reservations can be made by calling (216) 466–8400. Anglers find the park's two creeks and three miles of shoreline good for catching trout, Chinook coho salmon, walleye, and smallmouth bass.

0.1   At the four-way Stop sign at the intersection of the park road and Lake Road, continue STRAIGHT across Lake Road onto Padanarum Road.

This perfectly straight road goes south through flat, uncultivated farmland. Trucks are prohibited, and very little other traffic will disturb your speedy trip toward the city of Geneva.

2.2   Turn LEFT onto unpaved North Avenue.

North Avenue continues flat along the lake plain; the paving resumes in a little over a mile.

3.8   At the Stop sign, turn RIGHT onto North Broadway (OH 534).

4.2   At the light, continue STRAIGHT on Broadway, crossing US 20.

Geneva is probably named for another lakeside town in upstate New York from which many of its pioneers came. Some speculate, however, that it was named by its proprietor, Gideon Granger, for Geneva, Switzerland, the home of Albert Gallatin who was a colleague of Granger's in Thomas Jefferson's cabinet. Either way, it was settled by a party of New Yorkers around 1805, which may account for the absence of the traditional New England common.

Geneva was well known in the nineteenth and early twentieth centuries as the home of Platt R. Spencer, promoter of the embellished script now known as Spencerian penmanship.

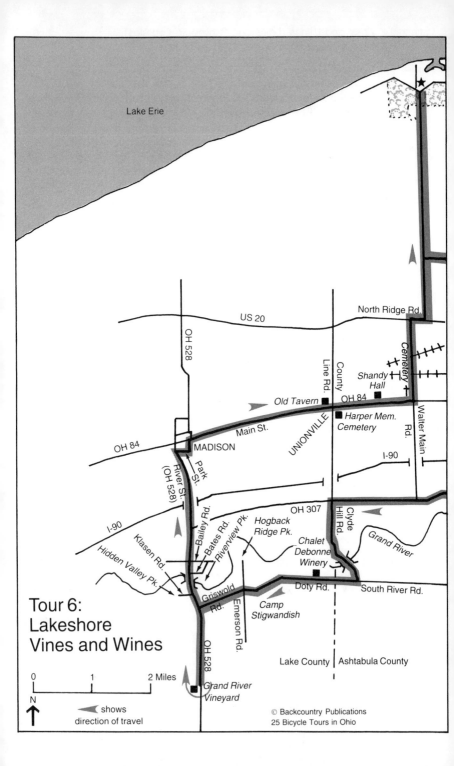

Lake Erie

North Ridge Rd.

US 20

OH 528

Line Rd.

County

Cemetery

Shandy Hall

Old Tavern   OH 84

Main St.   UNIONVILLE   Harper Mem. Cemetery

Walter Main Rd.

OH 84   MADISON

River St. (OH 528)

Park St.

I-90

OH 307

I-90

Clyde Hill Rd.

Grand River

Bailey Rd.

Bates Rd.

Hogback Ridge Pk.

Riverview Pk.

Chalet Debonne Winery

Klasen Rd.

Hidden Valley Pk.

Griswold Rd.

Emerson Rd.

Doty Rd.   South River Rd.

Camp Stigwandish

Lake County | Ashtabula County

Tour 6:
Lakeshore
Vines and Wines

0   1   2 Miles

N

Grand River Vineyard

shows
direction of travel

© Backcountry Publications
25 Bicycle Tours in Ohio

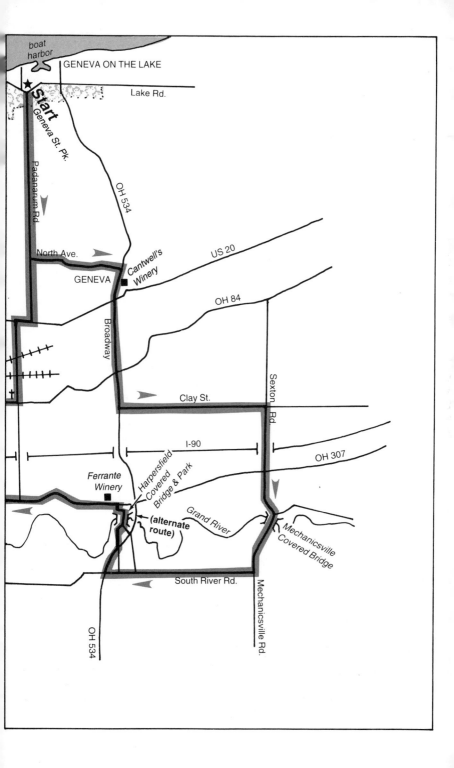

Half a mile from the turn onto Broadway is Cantwell's Old Mill Winery at 403 South Broadway. The building now looks more like a tavern than a mill or a winery, but a turn into the parking lot reveals a home wine operation in a back outbuilding. Sandwiches and snacks are available inside, as well as wine, and the place is open long hours, including Sunday.

5.4   At the light, continue STRAIGHT on OH 534, crossing OH 84.

At this point, you leave the flat lake plain and climb the gentle incline of the south ridge. This ridge was once the shoreline of what geologists call Lake Whittlesey, a precursor of the considerably smaller Lake Erie.

5.9   Turn LEFT onto Clay Street.

Clay Street continues the pattern of perfectly straight roads, running through attractive rural landscape that, in about a mile, becomes overlaid with vineyards on either side of the road.

8.3   Turn RIGHT onto Sexton Road.

9.3   At the Stop sign, continue STRAIGHT over OH 307.

10.1 Turn RIGHT onto Mechanicsville Covered Bridge, continuing on what is now called Mechanicsville Road.

At 156 feet, the Mechanicsville Covered Bridge is the longest single span bridge in Ashtabula County. Built in 1867, it is one of the oldest of Ashtabula County's fourteen covered bridges and is unique in the county in that it combines the Howe truss with a Burr arch. The Howe truss, designed by William Howe in 1840, incorporates an iron tie-rod into the standard wooden truss, which allows for adjustments as the bridge sags. The arch, patented by Theodore Burr in 1804, is designed to strengthen the truss. The Mechanicsville Covered Bridge overlooks the location of the county's first mill, built in 1801. This was also the original site of the Ashtabula Institute of Science and Industry, established in 1831. A manual training school and business college, its aim was to provide young men with practical experience in milling and other manual labor and with the business expertise to run such enterprises. In 1835, the school was moved to Austinburg and called the Grand River Institute.

11.0 Turn RIGHT onto unpaved South River Road.

13.2 Turn RIGHT at the Stop sign onto OH 534.

13.5 Turn LEFT onto Harpersfield Road, following the covered bridge sign. The road goes gently downhill, crossing an irrigation ditch to the filtration plant on the left, then makes a right turn leading to the entrance of Harpersfield Covered Bridge Park.

This park is one of the most beautifully situated parks in the entire Western Reserve. It affords easy access to the water and spectacular views of the 236-foot bridge, crossing the river in two spans. Like the Mechanicsville bridge, it is of Howe construction, but without the added arch. The north end of the bridge was washed out by the flood of 1913, and a 140-foot steel section was added. The park, maintained by the Ashtabula Metropolitan Park Commission, provides picnic and recreation facilities.

14.1   Turn LEFT onto Harpersfield Covered Bridge. (If the bridge is closed, bear right on the unpaved and unmarked road, which is State Road; turn left onto OH 534, crossing the bridge over the Grand River and getting unique views of the covered bridge; turn left onto OH 307.)

The park continues on this side of the bridge with restrooms and a concession stand.

14.5   At the Stop sign, turn LEFT onto OH 307.

In a quarter mile is the Ferrante Winery and Restaurant, overlooking acres of vineyards. Ferrante's also has a gift shop.

OH 307 is busier than most of the other roads on this tour, particularly in the grape harvest season. On a warm afternoon in late summer and fall, however, any discomfort due to traffic is outweighed by the delicious fragrance of ripe grapes filling the air for miles.

17.4   Turn LEFT onto unpaved and unmarked Clyde Hill Road just before the sign for entering Lake County.

You'll cross the Grand River for the third time in seven miles, the acres of vineyards evidence that the Grand has a most-favored-river status among grape growers.

18.6   Turn RIGHT onto South River Road.

Upon entering Lake County, South River changes to Doty Road. You have just left Ashtabula, Ohio's largest county, and entered the state's smallest. Shortly, on your left, you'll see the Swiss-style headquarters of the Chalet Debonné Vineyards nestled against a vine-covered hillside. The Debevcs made family wine for three generations before turning the place into a business in 1970. Wines are served accompanied by Ohio cheese, sausage, paté, and hot homemade breads.

Continuing west on Doty Road, to the northwest you can see the twin stacks of the Perry Nuclear Power Plant, a rather incongruous sight as you ride through the bucolic beauty of the vineyards, lush with the odor of sun-ripened grapes.

To your right is the north perimeter of the Boy Scouts' Camp

Stigwandish, named for a famous Seneca Indian chief. Known for his wisdom and nobility and his friendship with whites, Stigwandish is best known today as something of a prototypical teetotaler. In his pre-abstainer days, he threw a tomahawk at his squaw in a drunken rage. It lodged instead in the head of the papoose on her back, his own child, and he avoided "fire water" ever after.

20.4   Follow the road to the LEFT as it becomes Emerson Road; make an immediate RIGHT turn onto Griswold Road.
A right turn for a quarter mile onto Emerson will bring you to Hogback Ridge Reserve, the first of three nearly contiguous metro-parks along this part of the Grand River. A secluded park known for its spring wildflowers, Hogback Ridge has picnic facilities, including restrooms and drinking water.

21.2   At the Stop sign, turn LEFT onto OH 528, Chardon-Madison Road.
Continue for about one and a quarter mile and look for an unobtrusive sign on your right pointing to the Grand River Vineyard. Proprietor Bill Worthy, a former banker, has grown grapes here since 1972. Worthy plants most of his vineyards with French hybrids, that is, French vines that were grafted onto sturdy American rootstock.
The winery, opened in 1978, is a rustic, L-shaped building with one wing as an open pavilion where visitors can watch the crushing and pressing of grapes. The tasting room, which also serves cheese and cracker plates, has an attractive antique bar. A third larger room that opens onto a patio is used during the summer and fall for dinner theater. Reservations can be made by calling (216) 298–9838.

22.5   Turn RIGHT out of the winery entrance onto OH 528 and retrace your route back to the intersection with Griswold Road; continue STRAIGHT on OH 528.
About a mile and a half north of the Grand River Vineyard is the Klasen Road entrance to Hidden Valley Metropark. Located on the banks of the Grand River at a point where the river has cut a deep, narrow valley into the surrounding sedimentary rock, the park is sheltered by a magnificent sheer cliff face. Picnic shelters are available, as are restrooms and drinking water.
In another mile and a half, you can visit Riverview Park on the north side of the river by turning right onto Bates Road. Bailey Road, another right turn in half a mile, leads to the park, which has picnic facilities, including restrooms and drinking water.
As you near the village of Madison, OH 528 becomes known as River Street. Madison is famous for its carefully restored homes, one of which is at 367 River Street. This home is considered a "transi-

tional" Greek Revival house, the peculiar columns and multi-angled brackets illustrating the shift from the purity of the Greek elements. At 232 River Street is another home that mixes styles, in this case, the addition of Tudor window moldings on an otherwise Italianate house. Back to the right side of the street, at 143 River, is an 1876 Victorian home, of which architectural historian Richard Campen says, "no more flamboyant expression of high Victorian design or more exuberant use of the lathe and jigsaw can be found in northeastern Ohio."

26.1   Turn RIGHT onto Park Street.

The township of Madison, organized in 1811, was named for the incumbent president, James Madison. It is now the Western Reserve's largest township, located in the state's smallest county. The village of Madison became incorporated in 1868 and is listed on the National Register of Historic Places.

The Western Reserve Fine Arts Building on the south side of the common was built in the Greek Revival style in 1828 and moved to this site in 1840 for use by the town. In 1867 it was enlarged to its

present size and used as the Town Hall. An old jail cell still remains. It was later used as the post office, and then housed the Madison Historical Society.

26.2   Turn LEFT, continuing around the common.

On the east side of the common is the 1861 Behm-Oberly House, noted for the distinctive fretwork trimming the porch roof. It is now a sportswear store. Next door, on the corner of Park and Main, is the former Madison Savings and Loan Building, an 1875 Victorian commercial building that served as a bank for ninety-four years. The vault is still visible in the basement. The Main Street Deli, across the street, is a fine choice for a quick lunch or snack.

26.3   Turn RIGHT onto East Main Street.

26.4   At the light, continue STRAIGHT on East Main Street, which is now OH 84 since OH 528 goes off to the left.

The Greco-Federal home at 21-25-29 East Main Street was built in 1830 and was formerly the Paige Hotel. Later, the east wing was a Notary Public Office, while the west wing housed a milliner's and dressmaker's shop. In the rear, a livery rented horses and carriages. The Madison Historical Society Gift Shoppe and Museum is next door.

Back on the lake plain now, the route is virtually flat for the rest of the tour. In under two miles you'll enter Unionville, so named because it is at the junction of two townships, Madison and Harpersfield. About a quarter of a mile after entering the village, on the left is the 1817 Connecticut Land Company Office, thought to have been built by Abraham Tappan, a surveyor for the company.

The Old Tavern stands on the northwest corner of the intersection of OH 84 and County Line Road. The original twelve-foot by fourteen-foot log cabin was built in 1798 and served as a rest stop for pioneer families headed west. Enlarged to its present two-story saltbox shape in 1818, it acquired its classical porch in 1820. The second-story ballroom, added around the same time, is still used for large groups. Formerly known as the New England House, it is said to have been a station on the Underground Railroad and was placed on the National Register of Historic Places in 1973. Guests can roam the public rooms filled with antiques and gifts and can eat in one of several cozy dining rooms. The Old Tavern serves excellent country-style fare, accompanied by crunchy corn fritters with syrup and sweet and spicy tomato jam, all made on the premises. Reservations can be made by calling 1–800–7–TAVERN.

28.8   Continue STRAIGHT at the light on OH 84.

On the southeast corner of the intersection is the Unionville United

Church of Christ, a Greek Revival building built in the 1840s. Behind it is the Alexander Harper Memorial Cemetery. During the Revolution, Captain Harper was captured by the British and imprisoned for nearly three years in Quebec. After his release in 1783, he returned to Harpersfield, New York, which he had helped found in 1770. Never one to gather moss, he moved to the Western Reserve in 1798 to found Harpersfield, Ohio. Two months after his arrival, he contracted malaria and died on September 10. Buried in a hollowed log, he lies in the Unionville Cemetery in the oldest marked grave of a white man in the Western Reserve.

A mile from the cemetery, on your left, is a modest sign to Shandy Hall, the Harper family home, run by the Western Reserve Historical Society. Built in 1815, this saltbox-style frame house is one of the oldest in the Western Reserve. Despite the modest exterior, its seventeen rooms are what might be called "pioneer luxurious," furnished with nineteenth-century antiques belonging to the Harper family whose members lived here until 1935. A piano, brought by oxcart, is believed to have been the first in the Reserve. A thirty-two-foot by sixteen-foot banquet room was added some ten years after the house was built and decorated with rare, block print French wallpaper bought from a bankrupt Buffalo hotel. The original kitchen with fireplace is still in the basement. The library has rare editions, including a copy of Thomas Stern's fanciful novel *Tristram Shandy,* for which the house was named. The home is open May through October, Tuesday through Saturday from 10 AM to 5 PM, and Sundays and holidays from 1 PM to 5 PM. Admission is $2.50 for adults, $1.50 for seniors and children.

29.1   Turn LEFT onto unpaved Walter Main Road.

Another cemetery for Harper family members is just around the corner on the left. The paving picks up in less than half a mile as you cross into Geneva Township. You'll have two sets of rugged railroad tracks to cross on this stretch.

30.2   Turn RIGHT onto OH 20, which is North Ridge Road.

30.6   Turn LEFT onto Padanarum Road.

33.7   At the Stop sign, go STRAIGHT into the park, crossing Lake Road.

33.9   Turn LEFT into the parking lot.

Bicycle Repair Services

Green's Cyclery, 6214 North Ridge West (OH 20), Madison, Ohio (216–428–6770).

7

Lake County Loop

35 miles; moderate to strenuous
Mostly hilly terrain with some Great Lakes plain
County map: Lake

"The pigmy of the Buckeye State," said Harriet Taylor Upton of Lake County in her worthy, if wordy, fourteen-hundred page work, *The History of the Western Reserve.* Created from Geauga County in 1840, this smallest of Ohio counties retains much of the beauty of the Geauga hills with the added bonus of over thirty miles of attractive Lake Erie shore-line. The warmest and most biologically productive of the Great Lakes, Erie has a mitigating effect on the harsh winter climate of northeastern Ohio. While neighbors in Geauga County, the heart of the snowbelt, haul out their toboggans and skis, Lake County fruit growers and nursery operators prepare for the next growing season, which is considerably longer than is expected at this latitude.

In addition to the warming influence of the lake, the clayey loam, interspersed with ridges of sand and gravel, makes the county well adapted to fruit culture, especially grape growing. The early surveyors of the Western Reserve gave a more favorable report on the soil quality of this area than on any other section of the Reserve. As a result, the

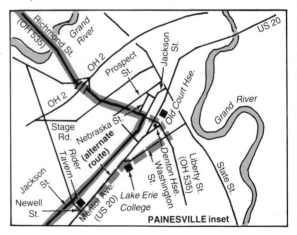

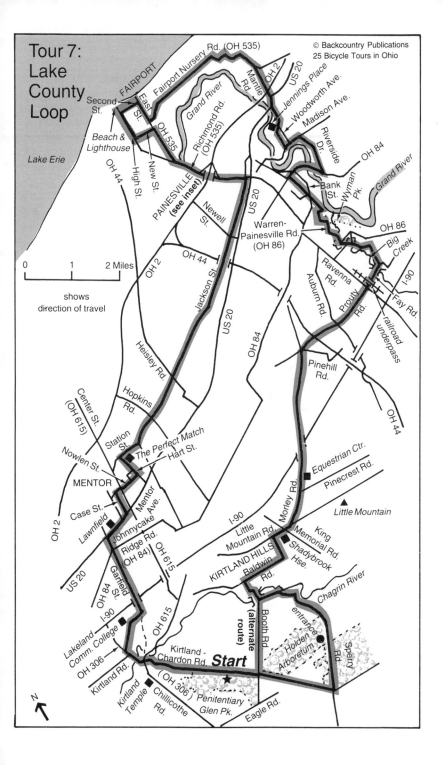

Tour 7:
Lake
County
Loop

© Backcountry Publications
25 Bicycle Tours in Ohio

Lake Erie

shows
direction of travel

0   1   2 Miles

FAIRPORT

Second St.

Beach &
Lighthouse

Fairport Nursery Rd. (OH 535)

Grand River

Mantle Rd.

OH 2

US 20

Jennings Place

Woodworth Ave.

Madison Ave.

Riverside Dr.

OH 84

Grand River

East St.

OH 535

New St.

High St.

OH 44

Richmond Rd. (OH 535)

PAINESVILLE
(see inset)

Newell St.

Bank St.

Wyman Pk.

OH 86

Big Creek

Warren-
Painesville Rd.
(OH 86)

US 20

OH 2

OH 44

Jackson St.

US 20

OH 84

Ravenna Rd.

Prouty Rd.

Fay Rd.

railroad underpass

I-90

Auburn Rd.

Pinehill Rd.

OH 44

Heisley Rd.

Hopkins Rd.

Center St.
(OH 615)

Station St.

The Perfect Match

Hart St.

Nowlen St.

MENTOR

Case St.

Lawnfield

Mentor Ave.

Johnnycake Ridge Rd. (OH 84)

OH 615

OH 2

US 20

OH 84

Garfield St.

I-90

Lakeland
Comm. College

OH 306

Kirtland Rd.

Kirtland
Temple

Chillicothe Rd.

OH 306

I-90

Little Mountain Rd.

Morley Rd.

Equestrian Ctr.

Pinecrest Rd.

Little Mountain

King Memorial Rd.

Shadybrook Hse.

KIRTLAND HILLS

Baldwin Rd.

Chagrin River

(alternate route)

Booth Rd.

entrance

Holden
Arboretum

Sperry Rd.

Kirtland-
Chardon Rd.

Start

Penitentiary
Glen Pk.

Eagle Rd.

N

Connecticut Land Company designated the townships of the area "equalizers," acreage to be given to those with land holdings known to be of poor quality. Today, thirty-one hundred of those prime acres are put to good use in the Holden Arboretum, the largest arboretum in the country.

This glacially carved terrain provides some challenging hills for bicyclists, although the northern half of the route includes nearly fifteen practically effortless miles along the flat lake plain. Because descendants of settlers who came here grew wealthy from the land and, later, from the industry of the area, this route is particularly rich in architectural history, especially in the county seat of Painesville. The Mentor home of Lake County's most famous son, President James A. Garfield, is included along this route, as are the campuses of Lake Erie College and Lakeland Community College. A stop at Fairport affords the opportunity for a swim in Lake Erie, and several parks provide pleasant picnicking and fishing spots. There are opportunities to dine or buy groceries in the cities of Mentor and Painesville and in the village of Fairport.

The tour leaves from the parking lot of Penitentiary Glen Park on Kirtland-Chardon Road off OH 306 in the town of Kirtland. OH 306 is accessible from I-90 east of Cleveland.

0.0 **Turn RIGHT out of the parking lot of Penitentiary Glen Park onto Kirtland-Chardon Road.**

Penitentiary Glen is the newest of the eighteen parks that make up the Lake Metroparks District and is the site of the district administrative headquarters. The Program Center here maintains a large exhibit area and a nature gift shop and provides restrooms and a drinking fountain. A nationally acclaimed Wildlife Rehabilitation Center is on the premises, along with an amphitheater and the Lake Shore Live Steamers Railroad, a miniature steam train operated for children during special events.

A deep shale and sandstone gorge splits the park into two parts, revealing four separate rock layers from the Mississippian to Devonian periods. Only guided hikes are permitted in the gorge; once in the gorge, the hiker has a hard time getting out again, hence the name.

0.1 **At the Stop sign, continue STRAIGHT on Kirtland-Chardon Road, crossing Booth Road.**

(Those who wish to avoid the unpaved Sperry Road can save almost three miles by turning left here onto Booth Road and picking up the tour at the 4.3 mile point.)

1.5 **At the four-way Stop sign, turn LEFT onto unpaved Sperry Road, following the sign to the Holden Arboretum.**

In about a mile you'll come upon the arboretum entrance on your left, just past the duck and geese ponds. Unless you're an especially fast cyclist, you should probably save a visit through the arboretum until you have enough time to justify your admission fee. Indeed, one could spend an entire day here and not see all of the horticultural collections, including the maple, the nut tree, and the conifer collections plus numerous display gardens. There are twenty miles of trails from self-guided walks (one with an audio guide and family activity pack) to rugged ravine hikes. The attractive Visitor's Center has interpretive displays, a gift shop, and a six thousand-volume library.

After a mile and a half of this occasionally hilly dirt road, Sperry becomes paved as you leave Kirtland and enter Kirtland Hills. The latter has a topography to justify the name change. In a little over a mile, you'll come to a long, winding downhill with sharp curves that can be difficult to maneuver. The road deposits you on the beautiful Chagrin River Valley floor, with the river so near the road it is often used by locals and passers-by for pleasure wading.

4.3 At the Yield sign, turn RIGHT, crossing the bridge over the east branch of the Chagrin River onto Booth Road.

4.7 At the Stop sign, turn RIGHT onto Baldwin Road.
Directly across from this intersection is Lake Metroparks' Red Brick Schoolhouse Children's Nature Park. The beautifully restored District No. 2 schoolhouse and its twelve surrounding acres are reserved for nature study classes for children aged three to twelve.

Baldwin begins with a very steep and curving uphill, followed by a sharp turn to the left after a mile of climbing.

5.9 At the Stop sign, turn RIGHT onto Little Mountain Road.

6.2 At the four-way Stop sign, continue STRAIGHT on Little Mountain Road, crossing King Memorial Road.
A tenth of a mile to the right at 8610 King Memorial Road is the Lake County History Center in beautifully situated Shadybrook House. The Lake County Historical Society maintains a museum and library here and hosts educational and recreational programs. The spacious grounds are also home to the Chincapin Equestrian Center, and the annual Little Mountain Folk Festival is held here in July.

6.4 At the Y-junction, bear LEFT onto Morley Road, avoiding the dirt continuation of Little Mountain Road.
Little Mountain, about a mile east of here, was a legendary sacred hill for the local Indians. A beautiful, pine-topped peak with superb sandstone rock formations, it was probably the first spot in the Western Reserve to be developed as a recreational area. The Little

Mountain Hotel opened for the children and grandchildren of the first pioneers in 1831, followed by a homeopathic water cure spa with a large bathing house and gymnasium in 1855. In the twentieth century it became a private summer home retreat for the urban wealthy.

At this intersection, you'll cross from Kirtland into Concord Township, named for the famous site of the Revolutionary War battle.

6.9   At the Y-junction, continue STRAIGHT on Morley Road by bearing LEFT, avoiding Pinecrest Road.

In about a quarter mile you'll see the four hundred-acre George M. Humphrey Lake Erie College Equestrian Center. Competitive horse shows are scheduled regularly here, where Lake Erie College students work toward a degree in equestrian studies.

9.4   At the Stop sign and red blinking light, turn RIGHT onto Prouty Road, avoiding Pinehill Road on the extreme right. Note the sign warning "Dangerous Intersection."

This right turn takes you immediately down a steep hill to Kellogg Creek, a tributary of the Grand River, and back up an even steeper incline.

10.2   At the Stop sign, continue STRAIGHT on Prouty Road, crossing Auburn Road.

11.1   At the Stop sign, go STRAIGHT onto Fay Road, crossing over Ravenna Road.

Crossing through the concrete, tubular, B&O Railroad underpass, you'll descend another steep and winding downhill to the valley of Big Creek, another Grand River tributary. After the bridge, Fay Road makes a sharp turn to the left and follows closely along the shady and picturesque creek valley.

12.4   At the three-way intersection, take the middle, level road that is the continuation of Fay (unmarked).

12.7   At the Stop sign, turn LEFT onto the unmarked Warren-Painesville Road (OH 86).

In less than half a mile is the Helen Hazen Wyman Park, the first park established in the Lake Metroparks District. Located at the junction of Big Creek and Grand River, it is favored by anglers. Drinking water, restrooms, and picnic shelters are available here.

After the park, OH 86 starts to wind slowly uphill until it enters Painesville.

13.8   At the Stop sign and red blinking light, you are at a five-way

intersection; follow the sign for OH 84 East and OH 86 North.
Beware of the uneven railroad tracks after this intersection.

14.2   At the light, follow OH 84 to the RIGHT.

14.3   At the light at the intersection of OH 84 and Bank Street, go STRAIGHT on OH 84.
The downhill ride takes you to the bridge over the Grand River.

15.0   At the light, turn LEFT onto Riverside Drive.

15.7   At the Stop sign, turn LEFT onto Madison Avenue.

16.1   Turn RIGHT onto Casement Avenue just before the cemetery; in one-tenth of a mile is a Stop sign where Casement merges with Woodworth Avenue.
Note the imposing Italianate home on the left about a quarter mile after the merge with Woodworth. This Tuscan villa overlooking the Grand River was home to Frances Jennings Casement and her Civil War hero husband, General J. S. Casement. Mrs. Casement was the first president of the Ohio Women's Suffrage Association and hosted suffragist leaders such as Susan B. Anthony and Elizabeth Cady Stanton here at "The Jennings Place."

16.8   At the Stop sign, go EAST on US 20, North Ridge Road.

16.9   As US 20 goes off to the right, continue STRAIGHT onto Mantle Road.

17.6   At the T-junction, turn LEFT onto Fairport Nursery Road (OH 535).

20.1   At the blinking red light, turn RIGHT onto East Street.

20.4   At the Stop sign, turn LEFT onto Second Street.
Fairport's village green is unusual in that it is rimmed with modest private residences rather than with commercial buildings as in most Western Reserve towns of some size. Fairport, again quoting Mrs. Upton, has the "finest natural harbor on the south shore of Lake Erie." Laid out in 1812, the village enjoyed a brief period of affluence after the completion of the Erie Canal and boasted four hotels by 1845. It experienced another flurry of activity with the rise of the iron and steel industry, which accounts for the abundance of railroad tracks leading toward the harbor. In 1909 over 350 vessels entered and cleared the well-favored harbor with a tonnage of over one million. Today, it has returned to its original New England quietude. It now appeals to bathers, with a fine beach off the corner of Second and High streets, and to marine buffs, who visit the prominent Fairport Marine Museum lodged in the 1871 lighthouse and

keeper's residence. The original lighthouse, built in 1825, was designed by renowned architect Jonathan Goldsmith. The present lighthouse, built of Berea sandstone, is on the National Registry of Historic Places. Attached to the lightkeeper's dwelling is a fully equipped pilot house from the carrier *Frontenac*. The museum is open weekends and holidays during the summer from 1 PM to 6 PM. Admission is charged.

20.8   Turn LEFT onto High Street.

20.9   At the blinking yellow light, continue STRAIGHT on High Street.

21.3   Turn LEFT onto New Street, which is unmarked; it is the first street after Seventh Street.
New Street has preserved its brick surface, a rare sight these days and a little awkward for the narrow tires of present-day touring bikes.

21.4   At the Stop sign, go STRAIGHT on New Street, crossing Vine Street.

21.5   At the Stop sign, turn RIGHT onto East Street.

22.2   At the light, go LEFT on OH 535 (south).

22.8   Continue STRAIGHT at the light, on OH 535 South.

23.0   At the light, avoid the entrances for OH 20 and OH 2 and continue STRAIGHT on OH 535.

23.1   Continue STRAIGHT at the light on OH 535, crossing Stage Road; at this point, OH 535 is called Richmond Road.

23.3   At the light, continue STRAIGHT on Richmond, crossing Prospect Street.

23.6   Turn RIGHT at the light onto West Jackson Street.
This turn allows the bicyclist to avoid the traffic of the courthouse square district of Painesville. Those with an interest in architecture, however, will find central Painesville richly rewarding. There are nearly a dozen homes and buildings attributed to Jonathan Goldsmith, the finest builder-architect of the early Western Reserve. In addition to his work, you will find the Town Hall, formerly the old courthouse, a Greek Revival edifice built in 1840, and the present courthouse, a stately building erected in 1907.
Jonathan Goldsmith, a twenty-seven-year-old carpenter and joiner, came to the young settlement in 1811 and soon gained a wide reputation for his estimable workmanship. Among his best work in Painesville is the 1816 Denton House at 55 Mentor Avenue (believed to be the first house by Goldsmith in the Western Reserve);

the 1828 Hitchcock House, which has been divided and placed in two locations, 96 Nebraska Street and 254 South State Street; and the 1836 Morley House at 231 North State Street.

The finest remaining example of Goldsmith's work is the Dr. John Mathews House, built in 1829 and now moved to 309 West Washington Street on the campus of Lake Erie College. To see the Lake Erie College grounds, continue straight on Richmond instead of turning right on Jackson. Cross over OH 20 (Mentor Avenue) and take the third right onto West Washington Street. In addition to the Mathews House, the "College Hall," built in 1859 by the architectural firm of Heard and Porter, is a fine Italianate building now used as the administration building. Charles Heard was Goldsmith's apprentice and married his eldest daughter. The Kilcawley Building at 391 West Washington Street houses the Indian Museum of Lake County, with exhibits on prehistoric Ohio from 10,000 BC to AD 1650. On this detour you can also see the Rider Tavern at 792 Mentor Avenue, an early stagecoach stop on the road from Cleveland to Buffalo. Although the tavern's original portion was built in 1818, Jonathan Goldsmith added the second story and the stately portico in 1832. Restored as a pub and restaurant, Rider's is known for its generous Sunday brunches.

Rejoin Jackson Street by turning right onto Newell Street, then left onto Jackson.

24.3   **At the light, continue STRAIGHT on Jackson, crossing West Eagle Street.**

24.6   **Go STRAIGHT on Jackson at the light, crossing Newell Street.**

25.0   **At the light at the entrances to OH 44, continue STRAIGHT on Jackson, crossing OH 44 via an overpass.**

Running parallel to busy US 20, Jackson Street is a peaceful, flat, straight route from Painesville to Mentor.

27.3   **At the light, go STRAIGHT on Jackson, crossing Heisley Road.**

28.0   **Continue STRAIGHT on Jackson at the light, crossing Hopkins Road.**

28.6   **At the Stop sign, bear RIGHT at the Y onto Station Road, which is not posted.**

The building on your left was Mentor's oldest factory. Built in 1868 by the Hart Nut and Washer Manufacturing Company, it was subsequently a barrel factory and cider mill, a knitting mill, and finally the Columbia Match Company in 1938. The match factory continued until the 1970s when it was converted into an office complex. One entire wing was gutted of all but the walls and beams to house the

Perfect Match, a restaurant that uses the ductwork and wiring of the old factory as part of its interior design. Plants, skylights, a fireplace, and a patio combine to make this unique restaurant cozy in a factory setting.

29.0 Turn LEFT onto Hart Street, which comes into Station Street where the Gatsby Restaurant is located.

29.1 At the broad Y, take the LEFT arm, staying on Hart.

29.2 At the Stop sign, turn RIGHT onto Nowlen.

29.4 At the Stop sign, go STRAIGHT on Nowlen, crossing Center Street (OH 615).

There is no light at this intersection, and Center Street can be frustratingly busy. Cross with caution.

29.5 Turn LEFT onto Case Street at the Stop sign.

29.7 At the Stop sign, go STRAIGHT on Case, crossing Prospect.

29.9 Turn RIGHT at the Stop sign onto Mentor Avenue (US 20).

30.2 At the light, continue STRAIGHT on US 20, crossing over Sharon-Lee Drive.

In less than a quarter mile you'll see Lawnfield on your right, the home of James A. Garfield while he was campaigning for president in 1880. The home became famous as the site of the country's first "front porch campaign," during which Garfield received delegations at his home rather than range out among the electorate.

Garfield bought the estate in 1876, which he referred to as a "dilapidated farmhouse on 119 acres." After Garfield's death, donations to his widow poured in, and she added a stone Queen Anne wing to the original frame structure that included a library with a noteworthy collection. Also on the property is a reconstruction of the log cabin originally located in Orange Township where Garfield was born.

30.5 At the light, turn LEFT onto Garfield Street.

30.8 At the light, go STRAIGHT on Garfield, crossing Johnnycake Ridge.

Garfield begins a gentle uphill at this point, the first real climb since approaching Fairport some fifteen miles back.

31.9 At the Y, bear RIGHT onto the road with the sign "Welcome to Lakeland Community College," avoiding Garfield which ends in a dirt path.

In a little over a quarter mile on the left is the sprawling Moore

Mansion, a curious mixture of architectural styles built at the turn of the century, a similarly curious period in architectural history.

32.0   At the Stop sign, bear RIGHT around the traffic circle and turn RIGHT immediately.

32.3   At this Stop sign, placed here to regulate parking lot traffic, continue STRAIGHT, toward the clock tower.

Lakeland Community College was founded in 1969 and currently enrolls close to ten thousand students from Lake and neighboring counties. The attractive campus is well known as the training camp for the Cleveland Browns. Training sessions are open to the public. Call (216) 696–5555 for the training schedule, which usually begins toward the end of July.

32.5   Turn RIGHT opposite the clock tower, heading toward the main entrance of the college off OH 306.

32.7   Turn LEFT at the light onto OH 306.

32.8   Continue STRAIGHT at the light on OH 306, where Kirtland Road comes in on the right.

33.4   Turn LEFT onto Kirtland-Chardon Road just to the right of the Whitney Store Museum. Continue STRAIGHT across the intersection with OH 615 to the left and OH 306 to the right, following Kirtland-Chardon Road as it goes downhill.

This crossroad was central to the history of the Mormon church during a difficult time in its formative period from 1831 to 1838. Joseph Smith, founder of the Mormon church, arrived in Kirtland from Palmyra, New York, to build a new religious community. Newel Whitney was one of his first converts, and this store became a commissary for the Church of Jesus Christ of Latter-Day Saints, as Smith's followers officially called themselves. Free tours of the store and surrounding buildings are conducted daily from 9 AM to 9 PM. Some proselytizing may be included.

In 1833, the growing community began building a temple, the first Mormon house of worship. Smith claimed to have been given the exact details of the building in a divine revelation and chose the sight just south of the store at the crest of the hill on what is now OH 306, the historic Chillicothe Road. Dedicated in a frenzied ceremony that lasted for two days in 1836, the building reveals Smith's vision in a mixture of Federal and Gothic influences in a blend not seen before or since.

In Ohio, as in other states, Smith met bitter opposition to his sect, some of it fueled by scandalous reports concerning the practice of polygamy. The pressure increased when it was learned that a

The Fairport lighthouse, built in 1871 by renowned architect Jonathan Goldsmith, is now a Marine Museum.

bank of questionable legality that Smith had founded was not able to back up its paper with silver. The object of numerous legal suits, Smith was arrested seven times and had to flee the state in 1838 to escape mob violence. He died in Carthage, Illinois, attacked by a mob while in jail awaiting trial for treason.

35.4   Turn RIGHT into the parking lot of Penitentiary Glen Park.

Bicycle Repair Services
Mentor Schwinn, 7802 Munson Avenue, Mentor, Ohio 44060 (216) 257-2170.
REM Cycle, 8529 Mentor Avenue, Mentor, Ohio 44060 (216) 255-6294.
City Cyclery, 670 Mentor Avenue, Painesville, Ohio 44077 (216) 352-0042.

8
Geauga Gems

37 miles; moderate to strenuous
Undulating to hilly terrain
County map: Geauga

Created in 1806, Geauga was the second county in the Western Reserve, and its rolling hills were the early settlers' nightmare. Although the highlands made good dairy country and the forests yielded more maple syrup than any other county in the state, the undulating terrain made the transport of produce hazardous and isolation a way of life.

In 1873, James A. Garfield, congressman and later president, addressed a meeting of the Geauga County Historical Society. "On this Western Reserve," he told the descendants of those hardy early settlers, "are townships more thoroughly New England in character and spirit than most of the towns of New England today. Cut off from the metropolitan life, . . . they have preserved here in the wilderness the characteristics of New England as it was when they left it." Fewer and fewer people, however, were willing to pay the price to maintain that character and spirit. At the time of Garfield's address, the county population had gone from a high of 17,827 in 1850 to 14,100 and was still declining. Not one settlement was showing signs of becoming a city.

There are still no cities in Geauga County, yet its population has grown faster than that of any other county in the Western Reserve in the last thirty years. Ease of transportation and disenchantment with the inner city have induced increasing numbers to make their money in the city and spend it, lavishly in many cases, in the Geauga highlands. Horse breeding and pond-building are *de rigueur* for the present-day Geaugan, who might also work to keep alive the pioneer industries of cheesemaking and maple syrup production. Indeed, Geauga appears to have the best of both worlds—an abundance of farm markets next to small, chic shopping plazas; ample pasturage for raising horses and a trendy polo field in nearby Chagrin Falls.

To add to the appeal, the county has the fourth largest Amish population in the world. Quaint, old-world customs contrast comfortably with upwardly mobile consumerism, and representatives of both apparently agree on the importance of the horse. The blacksmith's trade is not a relic of the past in these parts.

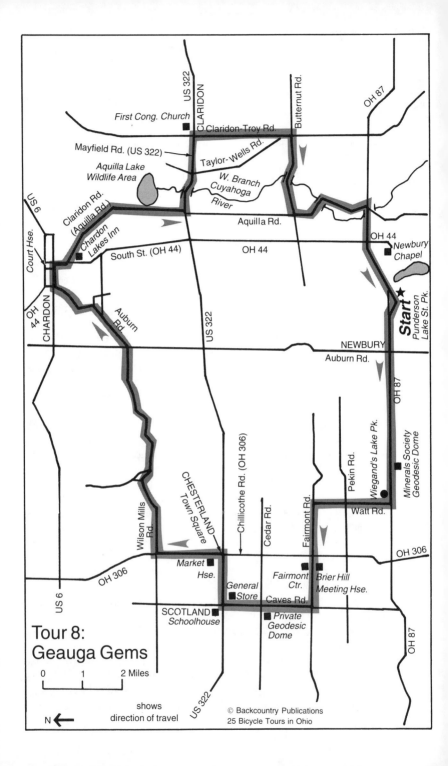

First Cong. Church

US 322

CLARIDON

Butternut Rd.

OH 87

Claridon-Troy Rd.

Mayfield Rd. (US 322)

Taylor-Wells Rd.

Aquilla Lake
Wildlife Area

W. Branch
Cuyahoga
River

US 6

Claridon Rd.
(Aquilla Rd.)

Aquilla Rd.

OH 44

Chardon
Lakes Inn

Newbury
Chapel

Court Hse.

South St. (OH 44)

OH 44

OH 44

CHARDON

Auburn
Rd.

US 322

Start

Punderson
Lake St. Pk.

NEWBURY

Auburn Rd.

OH 87

Minerals Society
Geodesic Dome

CHESTERLAND
Town Square

Chillicothe Rd. (OH 306)

Cedar Rd.

Fairmont Rd.

Pekin Rd.

Wiegand's Lake Pk.

Watt Rd.

Wilson Mills
Rd.

OH 306

OH 306

Market
Hse.

Fairmont
Ctr.

Brier Hill
Meeting Hse.

US 6

General
Store

Caves Rd.

SCOTLAND
Schoolhouse

Private
Geodesic
Dome

OH 87

Tour 8:
Geauga Gems

0   1   2 Miles

N ←

shows
direction of travel

US 322

© Backcountry Publications
25 Bicycle Tours in Ohio

This tour begins in Punderson Lake State Park on OH 87, 1.5 mile west of the junction of OH 87 and OH 44. OH 44 is accessible from I-90 east of Cleveland. The odometer reading begins in the parking lot nearest the highway (the one for the tennis courts and the Sports Chalet). For those staying or eating at the park lodge or staying in the cabins, it is one mile of gentle uphill from the lodge to the highway.

0.0   Leave the parking lot and turn RIGHT onto the park road.

With the largest and deepest of Ohio's glacial lakes, Punderson is best known as a winter sports park. The Sports Chalet, a heated, indoor facility unique in the Ohio State Park system, is used for tennis in the summer and serves as a warming house for ice skating, sledding, tobogganing, and snowmobiling in winter.

Punderson Lake State Park began as a small resort. It now has its own golf course, and a boat rental concession operates at the north end of the ninety-acre lake. The Manor House, a Tudor-style lodge, offers luxury accommodations, and its restaurant and lounge are open to the public. Evening entertainment is available in Punde's Pub.

This stylish park grew out of the little settlement established by Lemuel Punderson in 1808, first pioneer of Newbury Township. An ambitious land agent, Punderson built a dam at the south end of what he called his "big pond" and placed a grist mill there. Using the by-products to distill liquor, he soon had the means to build a small estate next to the lake now named for him. Throughout the rest of the century, the Punderson place was a popular gathering spot, and his descendants held elegant reunions at the old estate. In 1929, construction began on the Manor House; the Parks Division remodeled it for public use in 1956 and has since renovated it in 1979 and 1982. For those who prefer more rustic accommodations, a spacious campground is located on the site of a former Indian village, and twenty-six deluxe cabins are also available. For further information on all the park facilities, call the park office at (216) 564–2279.

0.3   At the Stop sign, turn LEFT onto OH 87.

1.6   At the light, go STRAIGHT through the intersection with Auburn Road.

Many of the settlers who first laid out the village green on the southwest corner of this intersection were from Glastonbury, Connecticut. In 1817, residents found "New"-bury an appropriate contraction to commemorate their roots. Newbury Township is typical of the Geauga environs, with country taverns, century homes, pasturage, ponds, antique shops, company corporate headquarters, and a brickworks, all scattered comfortably throughout its twenty-five square miles.

About two and a half miles along undulating OH 87, look for an immense, aluminum-framed geodesic dome in a valley to your left. Built of thirteen miles of aluminum tubing, this commanding construction hovers over the curvilinear headquarters of the American Society for Minerals, a lobbying group that maintains research and instructional facilities here. A large mineral garden surrounds the central fountain. Grounds are open to visitors until 10 PM, but there are no public facilities and picnicking here is discouraged.

A mile further is Wiegand's Lake Park, a private campground on another of the county's plentiful lakes.

5.0   Turn RIGHT onto Watt Road just after Wiegand's; be prepared to make this turn in the middle of a downhill run.

6.1   At the Stop sign, go STRAIGHT across Pekin Road.

6.7   At the Stop sign, turn LEFT onto unmarked Fairmont Road.

8.0   At the light, go STRAIGHT, crossing the unmarked Chillicothe Road (OH 306).

The Brier Hill Meeting House on the southwest corner of this intersection was built as a church in 1851. It is now a community center and museum. Across the street, the Fairmont Center for Creative and Performing Arts hosts youth theater performances and other cultural presentations.

9.2   Turn RIGHT at the Stop sign onto unmarked Caves Road.

10.5   At the Stop sign, continue STRAIGHT across Cedar Road.

On the southwest corner is an enclosed geodesic dome designed as a one-family dwelling.

Be prepared for a steep downhill to OH 322.

11.5   Turn RIGHT onto OH 322.

This was once the main intersection in the village of Scotland, named for Porter Scott who owned the area land. Once a lively town with a feed mill, ice house, school, interurban line depot, and general store, it faded with the passing of the C & E Electric Line. On the northwest corner is the Scotland schoolhouse, restored to its 1847 stature with a reconstructed woodshed and outhouse behind it. Also at the site is the 1842 Tanner House, the restored depot, and the 1850 Chester Town Hall. A tenth of a mile east along OH 322 is the old Scotland General Store. Visits to the Scotland buildings are by appointment, (216) 729–9031.

Commercial enterprises increase as you near the village of Chesterland, as does the traffic.

12.5   At the light, turn LEFT onto OH 306, Chillicothe Road.

Beautifully landscaped, with Gothic gazebo, ball fields, and tennis courts, the Chesterland town square is more a park than a village green. James A. Garfield attended the now defunct Geauga Seminary here and also met his future bride in this town.

One of the oldest thoroughfares in Ohio, Chillicothe road becomes relatively flat for a welcome few miles. On your right, the Market House has been converted into a small shopping complex.

13.9   Turn RIGHT onto Wilson Mills Road at the light.

On this east-west road, you'll encounter the rollercoaster dips and rises occurring regularly throughout Geauga County. Take special care when negotiating the winding and potentially difficult downhill about a mile along Wilson Mills Road.

18.9   At the four-way Stop sign, continue STRAIGHT on Wilson Mills Road, crossing Auburn Road.

21.4   Turn RIGHT at the light onto Chardon Road (OH 6).

A long, low hill takes you up to Chardon, the Geauga County seat. It's hard to imagine a better setting for the courthouse. Located within the town square, the courthouse was built of locally made bricks in 1869 at a cost of $88,862.00. With its ornate sandstone window moldings and the elaborate bracketed cornices, it remains one of the finest public examples of Italianate architecture.

The courthouse replaced a Greek Revival one built in 1826 that was destroyed by arson in 1865. The pride of the town, gallant efforts were made to save the building, but it was consumed by flames, as were most of the commercial buildings around the square. Residents donated enough money to rebuild the business district, resulting in some of the most distinctive blocks of commercial architecture in the Western Reserve.

Chardon hosts an annual Maple Sugar Festival each April, at which gallons of maple syrup flow liberally over mountains of pancakes. The three-day event includes antique shows and sugarbush tours. Those who prefer a more nourishing meal might choose to visit the Chardon Lakes Inn just south of town on OH 44. The tavern replicates a Western Reserve stagecoach stop, complete with fireplace.

21.9   Turn RIGHT onto South Street, which is OH 44.

22.2   Turn LEFT onto the diagonal road named *both* Claridon Road and Aquilla Road, one sign right below the other.

This road begins with a half-mile downhill. The land here is mostly wooded or uncultivated farmland and is serenely quiet. The little village of Aquilla, population 474, was not incorporated until the 1940s. It took the name of a nearby lake that was shaped like an eagle or, in Latin, *aquilla*. Now designated the Lake Aquilla Wildlife Area, the ninety-acre lake is known for its abundance of northern pike.

25.6   Turn LEFT at the Stop sign onto Mayfield Road, OH 322.
There are about two miles of busy traffic along this stretch.

27.5   Turn RIGHT onto Claridon-Troy Road.
The First Congregational Church on the east side of the town square was built in 1831 by volunteer labor under the direction of the town's two cabinetmakers. Noted for its unique twin entrances, it remains one of the most remarkable examples of Greek Revival architecture in the Reserve. The plans for the church are filed at the Library of Congress, and it is listed on the National Register of Historic Places.

29.7   At the Stop sign, continue STRAIGHT on Claridon-Troy Road as Taylor-Wells Road comes in on a diagonal from the right.

29.9   Turn RIGHT onto Butternut Road.
In a mile, be prepared for a long downhill into the valley of the West Branch of the Cuyahoga. The Grand, the Chagrin, and the Cuyahoga rivers all flow north to Lake Erie, and each has its source in the hills of Geauga County. After a respite along the valley floor comes the inevitable climb up to the next turn.

31.8   Turn LEFT onto Aquilla Road.
This wooded and shady road carries you back across the Cuyahoga's West Branch.

33.9   At the Stop sign, turn RIGHT onto unmarked OH 87.
You cross yet again the West Branch.

34.7   Go STRAIGHT on OH 87, crossing OH 44.
The Newbury Chapel to the left on OH 44 was built in 1856 by a group of irate Christians when the young James Garfield was refused the right to speak at the local church because he was a member of the Disciples of Christ church. Dedicated to freedom of speech, the church was used later by suffragettes such as Susan B. Anthony.

The downhill west of OH 44 is winding and potentially dangerous when traffic is heavy. As with all the freewheels you've enjoyed today, this one is followed by a long uphill climb.

36.1   Turn LEFT into the entrance of Punderson State Park.

The American Society for Minerals has its international headquarters in Geauga County beneath this towering aluminum frame geodesic dome.

Bicycle Repair Services

Spoke-N-Wheel Cycle Center, Inc., 100 Industrial Parkway, Chagrin Falls, Ohio 44022 (216) 247–7662.

Ski & Sport Haus, 22 West Orange Street, Chagrin Falls, Ohio 44022 (216) 247–4900.

Western Reserve Cycle Sport, 425 Water Street, Chardon, Ohio 44024 (216) 285–7433.

9
Amish Country

35 miles; moderate to strenuous cycling
Rolling to hilly terrain
County maps: Portage, Geauga

The followers of Menno Simons and Jacob Ammann were European Anabaptists or "rebaptizers," members of a major religious and social movement often considered the left wing of the Protestant Reformation. A diverse movement, many (but not all) Anabaptists believed in peace and nonresistance, adult baptism, and the separation of church and state. Such heretical notions made the established religious authorities of Europe very uncomfortable, and the Anabaptists were persecuted from the early sixteenth through the eighteenth centuries. An effective punishment for this deviance was an interdiction against their owning land, a severe penalty for these "plain living" people who saw farming as a godly vocation.

Quaker William Penn, whose faith also espoused the gospel of nonresistance, welcomed people of all religious persuasions to settle in the "peaceable kingdom" later known as Pennsylvania. The Mennonites were among the first to accept the invitation, settling in Germantown in 1683. By 1803, the first Mennonites arrived in Ohio. In 1809, the Amish followed suit. Today there are sixteen thousand Amish living in Ohio, giving it the world's largest Amish population. Forty-four of the 196 Amish districts in Ohio are in Geauga County, some spilling over into neighboring Trumbull and Ashtabula counties. With thirty-eight hundred members, Geauga has the fourth largest Amish population in Ohio.

This tour gives you the opportunity to see Amish farms, visit an Amish cheese factory, purchase Amish produce, and eat Amish-style meals. While traveling the hilly route, you might also hike in a unique state park, take a swim in an old quarry, visit a municipally owned sugar camp, dine in historic inns, and visit the beautiful campus of Hiram College where President James A. Garfield was both a student and college president.

The hills in northern Portage and southern Geauga counties account for much of the beauty of this trip. However, it is recommended that the rider be in reasonably good shape to handle the thirty-five rollercoaster miles and have a bike with gears in the lower ranges.

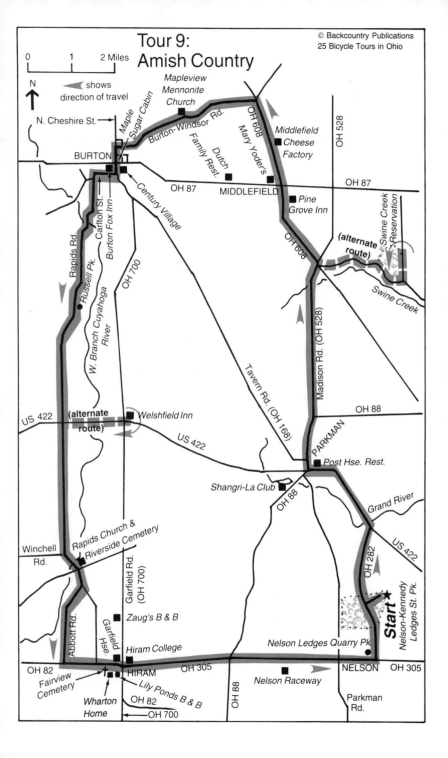

Tour 9:
Amish Country

© Backcountry Publications
25 Bicycle Tours in Ohio

0   1   2 Miles

N

shows
direction of travel

N. Cheshire St.

Mapleview
Mennonite
Church

Maple Sugar Cabin

Burton-Windsor Rd.

OH 608

Middlefield
Cheese
Factory

OH 528

BURTON

Dutch
Family Rest.

Mary Yoder's

OH 87

OH 87

MIDDLEFIELD

Century Village

Carlton St.
Russell Pk.
Burton Fox Inn

Pine
Grove Inn

(alternate
route)

Swine Creek
Reservation

OH 608

Swine Creek

Rapids Rd.

OH 700

W. Branch Cuyahoga River

Tavern Rd. (OH 168)

Madison Rd. (OH 528)

US 422

(alternate
route)

Welshfield Inn

OH 88

US 422

PARKMAN

Post Hse. Rest.

Shangri-La Club

OH 88

Grand River

US 422

OH 282

Winchell
Rd.

Rapids Church &
Riverside Cemetery

Garfield Rd.
(OH 700)

Nelson-Kennedy
Ledges St. Pk.

Start

Zaug's B & B

Abbott Rd.

Garfield
Hse.

Hiram College

Nelson Ledges Quarry Pk

OH 82

Fairview
Cemetery

HIRAM

OH 305

OH 88

NELSON

OH 305

Lily Ponds B & B

Wharton
Home

OH 82

OH 700

Nelson Raceway

Parkman
Rd.

The tour begins in the parking lot of Nelson-Kennedy Ledges State Park on OH 282, off US 422. US 422 can be reached from I-80 at exit 14 west of Warren (I-80 to OH 5 West, to OH 534 North) or from I-271 at exit 29 east of Cleveland.

0.0   Turn RIGHT out of the parking lot of Nelson-Kennedy Ledges State Park onto OH 282.

The startling formations of the Nelson-Kennedy ledges are carved from Sharon conglomerate, or "puddingstone," a coarse bedrock formed of quartz pebbles eroded from a former mountain range. In James Garfield's day, this spot was apparently used as a precursor of Camp David. Earlier still, the Cayuga Indians found the place ideal for hiding from enemies under the upturned ledges. Hiking the parks five major trails is a rewarding adventure, for they wind through narrow passageways like Dwarf's Pass and lead to natural marvels such as the fifty-foot Cascade Falls. Picnic tables and grills are provided, but there are no camping facilities.

Flea market fans should come on Sundays when the market just north of the parking area is in operation.

1.6   At the Stop sign, turn LEFT onto US 422.

This major route can be busy any time, but the two lanes provide ample space for bicyclists.

Just before reaching the village square in Parkman, you'll see the Post House Restaurant on your right. Formerly a Greyhound bus station, the restaurant features two murals in the former waiting room, one depicting the era of the stagecoach, and the other, the period when the Greyhound still passed through town. Today the Post House serves generous Amish-style meals and outstanding home-baked pies and cobblers.

The town received its name from Samuel Parkman, its Boston-based proprietor, and Robert Breck Parkman, his nephew and the town's first settler. Robert supervised the town's survey, and perhaps he deserves the credit for the attractive town square. The tiny brick post office on the west side of the green adds to the quaintness.

3.6   At the light, go RIGHT onto Madison Road, which is OH 528 and 88.

To watch champion waterskiers at practice, make a left at the light, then a quick right, following signs to OH 88. At the bridge you'll see a widening of this branch of the Grand River, used by the private Shangri La Club for waterskiing lessons and tournament training. To your left on the bridge is the picturesque gorge where Parkman's first mill operated until the beginning of this century.

As you head north, away from the village green, you'll face another hill to climb.

3.8 As Tavern Road (OH 168) goes off to your left, continue STRAIGHT on OH 88.

At this point, OH 88 is a wide and well-paved highway without much traffic.

4.9 As OH 88 goes off to the right, continue STRAIGHT on OH 528.

The road has a few dips, but you are generally climbing all the way to Middlefield. You'll begin to see the Amish buggy signs at this point and you'll note the prosperous and well-maintained farms on both sides of the road.

8.2 Follow OH 608 as it branches off to your LEFT.

A detour to the right at this intersection will take you to Swine Creek Reservation after about two and a half miles of dirt roads. The newest in the Geauga County park system, Swine Creek has nine marked trails, two of which go to a sugar bush — the site of maple sap collection and syrup production. Nature programs are offered at the lodge. A visit to the horse barn affords a closeup view of the Clydesdale horses that pull the naturalists' wagon through much of the park's 313 acres. For a schedule of interpretive wagon rides, call (216) 286–9504.

OH 608 continues the slow climb to Middlefield. Before reaching the town center, you may be surprised to see a number of small industries and manufacturing firms lining both sides of the road in this rural farming area. The increases in land prices and in the Amish population have led many of the "plain people" into nonagricultural trades. Some go into construction or small trades such as blacksmithing or harness making, and others work in these local factories, many of which manufacture plastic products. Although they are the major landholders in five Ohio counties including Geauga, half of the Amish are not full-time farmers.

On this side of town, at 15853 Grove Street, is the Pine Grove Inn where innkeeper Janice Schwendeman cooks, bakes, freezes, and cans everything that goes into her sumptuous breakfasts. Call (216) 632–0489 for reservations.

As you approach the next light, you'll see the fine home that now houses the Middlefield Historical Society on your right.

10.1 At the light in the center of Middlefield, go STRAIGHT on OH 608.

A left turn at this light onto West High Street (OH 87) brings you to downtown Middlefield. Mary Yoder's Amish Kitchen in the center of town is a highly recommended stop, as is the Dutch Family Restaurant a mile and a half further on. (Amish businesses are closed on Sundays).

You'll see the name Yoder frequently in these parts, a Swiss surname shared by seventeen percent of Ohio's Amish families. It is second only to Miller, used by twenty-seven percent of Ohio Amish residents. Troyer, Raber, Hershberger and Hostetler follow in frequency of occurrence. Indeed, the entire Amish population has only 126 surnames.

Middlefield got its name because it was midway between the thriving towns of Painesville to the northwest and Warren to the southeast. It was the first town in Geauga County to attract settlers, most of whom avoided the area because farming was difficult on the hilly and heavily forested terrain. This topography hindered the development of industry and cities, and many pioneers concentrated their efforts on dairy cattle. As a result, at one time there were sixty creameries in the county, and cheesemaking soon became one of Geauga's foremost enterprises.

About one mile out of town is the Middlefield Cheese Factory and Museum. Established as a cooperative in 1956, it produces more than twenty million pounds of cheese a year. The museum traces the history of cheesemaking, and a small theater shows a film detailing the cheesemaking process. The Cheese Chalet Shop offers, in addition to fine quality cheese, smoked meats, baked goods, portable drinks, and, of course, maple syrup. It is an excellent source of picnic supplies, and a table is provided outside the museum.

After the cheese factory, there is a rather steep downhill through astonishingly beautiful farm country.

12.0   Turn LEFT onto Burton-Windsor Road.

This road affords excellent opportunities for close views of several Amish farms and homes. It may amaze the tourist that such well-kept and prosperous farms can be maintained without the use of tractors, combines, and most other farm machinery. Their avoidance of modern machinery is based on religious beliefs that value community-based labor; however, the large families also allow labor-intensive farming to be more economical than investments in modern farm equipment.

Along this road, you'll see the Mapleview Mennonite Church, one of four in this area. The Amish do not build churches, instead holding their worship services in homes and barns on a rotating basis. Also, unlike their Amish neighbors, some Mennonites use cars and public utilities and may send their children to high school and college. Although many wear the plain clothes of their Amish neighbors, they are not required to do so.

15.1   At the four-way Stop sign, continue STRAIGHT on what is now called Goodwin Avenue, crossing Hickox Street.

15.4   Turn LEFT at the Stop sign onto North Cheshire Street.

You'll be greeted by the Burton water tower at this end of the village square. The area surrounding the square is called the Burton Village Historic District, and the homes here represent a fine collection of styles from the nineteenth century. The square has a homogeneity due to a hiatus in building after a 1903 bank failure. Here, even the Ford tractor shop blends in with its nineteenth-century neighbors.

Geauga County leads the state in maple sugar production. On the green itself is the only municipally owned sugar camp in the country, using sap from the maples growing there. The cabin is open every day during the sugaring season (late February through April) and sells maple products on weekends from May to December. The sugaring cabin was built in 1962, after a fire gutted the old one, which was a replica of Lincoln's birthplace erected in 1931.

15.5   At the Stop sign at the village square, follow the one-way sign around to the RIGHT onto North Park Street; then make an immediate LEFT onto West Park Street.

On the north side of the square you'll see the firehouse, which was formerly a theater. On the west side is the Burton Congregational Church and the library, followed by the popular Belle's Restaurant.

15.6   Continue around the square, going LEFT onto South Park; make an immediate RIGHT onto South Cheshire Street (OH 168 and 700).

After the turn onto South Cheshire, the Burton Fox Inn appears to your right. The original building was erected by Postmaster James Peffer in 1832, and north of the present fireplace was the door to the post office. Repeatedly enlarged, the property remained in the Peffer family until 1975. The present building uses portions of two old barns for a rear wing.

On your left, across from the Burton Fox Inn, is the renowned Century Village, a restored, nineteenth-century community maintained by the Geauga County Historical Society. The society's offices are in the Hickox Brick House, a Federal-style home on its original site on the southeast corner of the square. The fifteen other restored buildings were brought to the sixty-acre Century Village. They include other century homes, a blacksmith's shop, a B&O Railroad station and a twenty-ton caboose, a schoolhouse, a church, several shops, and the Crossroads General Store. Historical Society members conduct ninety-minute tours of the village May through November.

15.8   Halfway down the downhill as you leave town on South Cheshire Street, make a RIGHT onto Carlton Street.

16.3   At the Stop sign, turn LEFT onto Rapids Road.

Rapids Road is sometimes ill patched, but it is virtually empty and generally runs downhill to the tiny community of Hiram Rapids. A portion of the Buckeye Trail, a twelve hundred-mile state hiking route, goes along the entire length of Rapids Road.

In a little over three miles is the entrance to Russell Park on the left. Here are picnic tables, shelters, toilets, drinking water, nature trails, and a small arboretum with a nature program. Located along a quiet stretch of the West Branch of the Cuyahoga, the park is convenient for fishing and for canoeing up to Burton or down to Lake Rockwell near Kent.

The Chagrin Falls and Eastern Electric Interurban Railway line went through this park from 1902 to 1914. The concrete construction in the river near the parking area was the foundation of the former trolley bridge.

22.0   At the Stop sign, continue STRAIGHT on Rapids Road, crossing US 422.

A left turn onto US 422 will take you to Welshfield and its historic inn, which opened in 1842 as the Nash Hotel. As a stagecoach stop on the Pittsburgh to Cleveland route, its growing prosperity was reflected in its additions, including the impressive front portico. The East Room, which was part of the original 1842 structure, is still in use.

Rapids Road at this point supplies the bicyclist with refreshing descents matched by some challenging ascents. The road changes its name to Pope Road when you reenter Portage County.

25.0   At the Stop sign, turn LEFT onto Winchell Road.

In about a quarter mile, you'll cross over the Cuyahoga River, looking much less peaceful here than at Russell Park due to the "rapids."

25.1   At the Y-junction (so wide it almost looks like a T), take the far RIGHT arm, which is Allyn Road although it is not posted here.

A quick detour of a couple hundred yards on the left arm of this intersection will bring you to a picturesque corner with the historic Rapids Church and Riverside Cemetery.

25.2   At the Stop sign with the "No Outlet" sign ahead, turn LEFT onto Abbott Road.

25.3   At the Y-junction, follow Abbott Road to the RIGHT.

This road is relatively flat as it runs along the valley of the Cuyahoga to your right.

27.2 At the Stop sign, turn LEFT onto OH 82.

There will be more traffic on this highway than on most parts of the tour, although the berm is a little wider than usual here. As you climb towards the town water tower, you'll appreciate the fact that Hiram, at thirteen hundred feet, is the highest point in the Western Reserve. You will, however, be rewarded with a long downhill into the village of Hiram. On your right is the Fairview Cemetery, established in 1824, where two of President Garfield's children are buried. Immediately east of the cemetery is a fine Gothic Revival house, formerly known as the Wharton Home. Here the children of missionaries of the Disciples of Christ were sent while their parents went abroad spreading the gospel. The Disciples, or Campbellites as they were called after their founder, Alexander Campbell, were one of many new sects that evolved during the religious fervor that swept the frontier in the first half of the nineteenth century.

Near the intersection with OH 700 is the Lily Ponds Bed and Breakfast on the right, a cozy, secluded hideaway on twenty-two acres of fields and woods. Call Marilane Spencer for reservations at (216) 569–3222.

28.6 Go STRAIGHT at the light onto OH 305, as OH 700 and OH 82 go to the right.

At this corner you'll be at the southwest portion of the campus of Hiram College. With a strong following in the area around Hiram and Nelson, the Disciples of Christ chose Hiram hill for the site of its Western Reserve Eclectic Institute, which opened in 1850 with eighty-four students and three teachers. A progressive institution, the school was co-educational from its inception and became a college in 1867. Hiram's most famous alumnus is James A. Garfield, who attended the institute from 1851 to 1854 and served as its president from 1857 to 1863.

Garfield lived in the home at 6825 Hinsdale Street, next to "Bonney Castle," a former inn built in the Greek Revival style during the 1830s. The latter has been restored by the college as offices and classrooms for English faculty and students. Hinsdale Street is named for the school's third president, and OH 700, which you cross at this intersection, is known here as Garfield Road.

To the left here on OH 700, just north of town, is Esther Zaugg's Bed and Breakfast at 12689 Garfield Road. Call (216) 569–7541 for reservations. About two miles to the right on OH 700, Joseph Smith, the founder of the Mormon church, and a follower named Rigdon were tarred and feathered by outraged Hiramites, who considered Smith a fraud and a cheat.

You'll experience one of the most difficult portions of the tour at this point, with strenuous uphills and steep downhills and more traffic than one would care for on such terrain.

30.8   At the Stop sign, go STRAIGHT, crossing OH 88.

33.3   At the Stop sign at the village circle in Nelson, follow the circle around to the RIGHT; passing the first junction with Parkman Road, make a RIGHT at the next junction onto the continuation of OH 305.

Surprisingly, this quiet village with its typical Western Reserve style is best known for its speedway, where Paul Newman has been a race participant.

34.1   Very carefully due to the downhill, turn LEFT onto OH 282.

In a little over half a mile is Nelson Ledges Quarry Park on your left, a privately owned recreation area that offers swimming and scuba diving in a former sand and gravel quarry. With depths up to forty-five feet, divers can explore rusted cars and sunken boats in lieu of coral reefs and tropical fish. Admission to the park is $2.00 on Monday through Thursday, and $3.00 Friday through Sunday. Overnight camping is available for $3.00 per person.

35.4   A long downhill from the quarry takes you back to the parking area at Nelson Ledges State Park.

Bicycle Repair Services
Western Reserve Cycle Sport, 425 Water Street, Chardon, OH (216) 285–7433.
Star Cycle, 18324 Main Street, Parkman, OH 44080 (216) 548–8121.

10

Portage County Potpourri

42 miles; easy to moderate cycling
Level to rolling terrain, with a few gradual hills
County maps: Portage; small portion of northern Stark

In this forty-two mile loop there is something to please almost everyone, from the golfer, swimmer, angler, and wine sampler to the architecture buff, anthropologist, and naturalist. This tour takes in portions of five different lakes and passes through five Western Reserve townships, all named for Connecticut towns or Connecticut natives and each with the characteristic village green. You'll pass several golf courses and can tour one of the newest wineries in the state. The tour also dips for a few miles below the border of the Western Reserve, crossing the forty-first parallel to visit the fascinating Amish/Mennonite community of Hartville, with its famous restaurant and flea market. A six-mile detour to the village of Atwater features the Congregational Church, considered one of the jewels of Western Reserve architecture, second only to the First Congregational Church in Tallmadge. Several historical cemeteries can been visited, one of which is located in the beautiful Quail Hollow State Park. The combination of lush farmland and residential enclaves provides the visitor with a fine modern example of what the early "developers" may have envisioned when they first settled the Western Reserve.

The tour starts in the historic village of Brimfield on OH 43, immediately south of exit 33 on I-76 east of Akron. Parking is available in the town square parking lot.

0.0   Turn RIGHT out of the parking lot onto Tallmadge Road.
Amid tall maples and conifers, Brimfield's town square has a picturesque gazebo and covered picnic areas with running water. Very little has changed in Brimfield in the last two centuries except its name. First labeled Swampton due to the low-lying land, the locals soon switched the name to Greenbriar. Still unsatisfied, residents then named it Wylestown for one of the proprietors, then Thorndike for the other. When he failed to give land for a public square (no small matter to these Yankees), the settlers selected Brimfield, the Connecticut home of John Wyles, Jr.

Just behind the parking area is a shopping plaza with a restau-

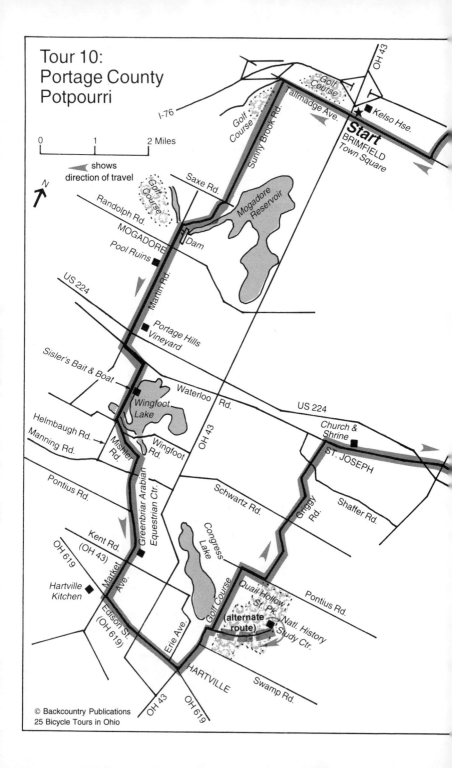

Tour 10:
Portage County
Potpourri

0   1   2 Miles

shows
direction of travel

N

I-76

OH 43

Golf Course

Tallmadge Ave.

Kelso Hse.

Start
BRIMFIELD
Town Square

Golf Course

Sunny Brook Rd.

Saxe Rd.

Mogadore Reservoir

Randolph Rd.

Golf Course

MOGADORE

Pool Ruins

Dam

Martin Rd.

US 224

Portage Hills Vineyard

Sisler's Bait & Boat

Waterloo Rd.

US 224

Wingfoot Lake

Church & Shrine

ST. JOSEPH

Helmbaugh Rd.

Manning Rd.

Mishler Rd.

Wingfoot Rd.

OH 43

Shaffer Rd.

Griggy Rd.

Pontius Rd.

Greenbriar Arabian Equestrian Ctr.

Schwartz Rd.

Kent Rd. (OH 43)

OH 619

Congress Lake

Market Ave.

Hartville Kitchen

Golf Course

Quail Hollow St. Pk.

Pontius Rd.

Edison St. (OH 619)

Erie Ave.

(alternate route)

Natl. History Study Ctr.

HARTVILLE

Swamp Rd.

OH 43

OH 619

© Backcountry Publications
25 Bicycle Tours in Ohio

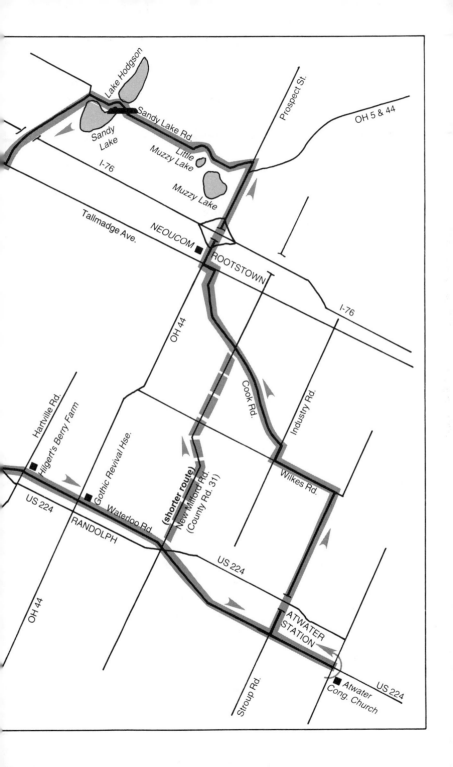

rant, and on the corner opposite the park is a take-out delicatessen.

0.1 At the stop light in the center of town, go STRAIGHT across OH 43 and continue on Tallmadge Road.

A quarter mile to the right at this intersection on OH 43 is Kelso House, built in 1833 as a stage stop and now used as a community center. In less than half a mile along Tallmadge Road you will see the Green Hills Golf Course on your right. The road here can have a lot of traffic and, like most of the roads on this tour, has no berm.

1.4 Shortly after crossing the Norfolk Western Railroad tracks, turn LEFT onto Sunny Brook Road.

Here you'll pass along the eastern boundary of the Sunny Brook Golf Course; Maplecrest Golf Course is a half mile further east along Tallmadge Road. There are over two hundred golf courses in Ohio, and, as the favored game of Columbus native, Jack Nicklaus, it is an extremely popular spectator sport here as well as a participatory one.

2.5 At the top of the hill, continue STRAIGHT at the Stop sign, crossing the unmarked Old Forge Road.

The area now becomes one of small farms, and the road, one of small pot holes.

3.6 At the Y-junction, bear LEFT onto Sunny Brook, not straight onto Saxe Road.

In about half a mile you'll see the western-most branch of the sprawling Mogadore Reservoir. After the lake appears, the road becomes narrow and shady. Watch out for turtle crossings! A half mile after your first view of the lake, you'll see the Mogadore dam. There are two hundred thousand acres of water in Ohio, excluding Lake Erie, but only sixty-seven hundred acres are comprised of natural lakes. Built for water supply, stream flow augmentation, flood control, or recreation, many reservoirs were created in the 1920s and 1930s by state conservancy districts or the Army Corps of Engineers. Mogadore's abundant water makes the name of this village and reservoir, taken from a town in Morocco, even more incongruous in this Anglo-Saxon Western Reserve.

4.5 Turn LEFT at the Stop sign onto Martin Road.

A pleasant downhill leads across the outflow from the dam. The imposing hill out of this valley is poorly paved and gives scant view of the Mogadore Country Club to your right, the third golf course passed in fewer than five miles. For the next two and a half miles you'll follow the route of the blue-blazed Buckeye Trail, a twelve hundred mile loop encircling the state. Information on the trail is available from the Buckeye Trail Association, Inc., P.O. Box 254, Worthington, Ohio 43085.

5.0   Go STRAIGHT at the Stop sign, crossing Randolph Road.
A half mile to your right at this intersection is the village of Mogadore, useful if you're in need of a Dairy Queen but not noted for having retained its Western Reserve heritage.

6.6   Go STRAIGHT at the Stop sign, crossing the intersection at US 224 with care.
If you're a wine fancier, ride the gravel road on the northeast corner of this intersection a quarter mile to the Portage Hills Vineyards Winery. In addition to tours, the Glaus family will supply samples of their wines and sell bread, cheese, salami, crackers, and soda. The cathedral ceiling and all-glass wall permits a fine view of the vineyards from comfortable pine tables. Restrooms are provided. The winery is open Monday through Thursday from noon to 6 PM, and Friday and Saturday from noon to 11 PM.

US 224 was the main east-west thoroughfare before I-76 was built. It parallels the southern boundary of the Western Reserve a few miles to the south.

6.9   At the Stop sign, make a LEFT onto Waterloo Road.

7.4   At the bottom of the hill, turn RIGHT onto Mishler Road.
You'll get your first view of Wingfoot Lake in about a half mile, with lake access at Sisler's Bait and Boat shortly thereafter. Sisler's provides picturesque, if primitive, pit toilets.

8.3   Follow Mishler Road as it bears LEFT at the Y-junction; do not go straight on Heimbaugh Road.

8.5   At this Y-junction, head STRAIGHT on Mishler Road, not left on Wingfoot Road (unmarked).

9.3   Ride STRAIGHT across the intersection with the unmarked and unpaved Manning Road.

9.8   Go STRAIGHT at the junction with Pontius Road on your right.
Signs indicate that you have just entered Lake Township and Stark County, at which point the name of the road changes to North Market Avenue and the road surface improves markedly. Pontius Road marks the southern boundary of "New Connecticut" or the Western Reserve, thus you are now at the same latitude as the southern border of the Constitution State. Ironically, this northeastern corner of the Buckeye State is larger than the entire state of Connecticut.

Soon after the short uphill, you'll pass through gently rolling and attractive farm country. About a mile into Stark County appear the lush pastures of the Greenbriar Arabian Equestrian Center.

11.1   Turn LEFT at the light at the intersection of Market Avenue and Edison Street (OH 619).

This is a busy intersection, and the left-hand turn should be made with care. A major cause for the traffic is the Hartville Kitchen on the southwest corner, and the Flea Market behind it. Famous for its Amish/Mennonite cooking, the Hartville Kitchen sells salad dressings, rolls, cookies, candies, and delectable pies, in addition to excellent country-style meals, all at exceptionally reasonable prices. The Hartville Kitchen is open Mondays, 10 AM to 6 PM; Tuesdays, 11 AM to 8 PM; Thursdays through Saturdays, 11 AM to 8 PM; closed Wednesdays and Sundays. At standard meal times, expect at least a half-hour wait in line. No reservations are taken. Those who prefer a picnic lunch will find an ample array of salamis, cheeses, and baked and home-canned goods if you arrive on Monday, which is flea market day.

Hartville is primarily a Mennonite town. Although less well known than the Amish, the Mennonite sect was the parent group from which the followers of Jacob Amman came. Less conservative than the Amish, most Mennonites drive motorized vehicles and wear modern attire, except for the white organdy caps worn by Mennonite women. The Mennonnites, unlike their Amish cousins, encourage higher education and approve of commercial enterprise.

11.9   Ride STRAIGHT at the light, crossing Kent Road (OH 43).

12.4   At this next light, where OH 43 South turns off to the right, turn LEFT on the unmarked street just before the railroad crossing. (There is a sign pointing to Erie Avenue, but that refers to the road to the left of the one for this route.) The unmarked road becomes Congress Lake Avenue.

In less than a mile, you'll pass the entrance to the private Congress Lake Country Club and ride alongside the beautifully groomed— you guessed it—golf course.

13.3   Turn RIGHT onto the gravel road into Quail Hollow State Park if you want to ride the mile to the Natural History Study Center. Otherwise, continue STRAIGHT along Congress Lake Avenue.

The study center, a Greek Revival/Federal home built in 1838, was formerly called the Minnie Taylor Farmhouse. It was erected on the Brumbaugh Estate, a vast acreage that Conrad Brumbaugh laid claim to after his arrival from Maryland in 1811. The Center is open

for visitors from 1 to 4 PM on weekends, where information on the ten
miles of interpretive nature trails can be obtained.

14.2   At the T-junction, turn RIGHT onto Pontius Road.
You now return to the official Western Reserve territory.

14.9   Turn LEFT onto Griggy Road (County Road 20).
After about one mile, at the intersection with Schwartz Road, Griggy
changes from a county to a town highway, and the paving deterio-
rates considerably. Cyclists should use caution on the short downhill
after Shaffer Road.

**17.4   Turn RIGHT at the Stop sign where Griggy forms a T-junction with
Waterloo Road, which still handles a lot of traffic for a rural road.**
In a little over a quarter mile, you'll enter the village of St. Joseph, a
cluster of homes dominated by the attractive Catholic church and
school. The first Catholic parish in Portage County and the sixth in
Ohio, the congregation originated with six families from the Alsace
region in 1831. By 1835 they had built a church and a school. The
present church, erected in 1904, is the third on this site. Behind the
school is Our Lady of Lourdes Shrine, a replica of the grotto at
Lourdes, France.

**19.2   Go STRAIGHT at the Stop sign through the unmarked intersection
with OH 224.**
In about a quarter mile, you'll cross the unmarked Hartville Road.
The Randolph Hillside Cemetery is to the left of this intersection, and
Hilgert's Berry Farm and Market is just beyond it. In addition to a
varied and abundant supply of fresh-picked and pick-your-own
fruits and vegetables, Hilgert's offers bottled drinks, candy, and
snack food.

**20.6   At the traffic light, continue STRAIGHT on Waterloo Road, cross-
ing OH 44.**
Randolph is known locally for hosting "the biggest little fair in Ohio"
in the next-to-last week of August. Bela Hubbard, a pioneer resident, was reportedly the originator of hubbard squash. Note the
striking Gothic Revival home on the east side of the village green.

**22.3   If you wish to continue on to Atwater, ride STRAIGHT at the
intersection with New Milford Road (County Road 31). Those wishing to shorten the ride by a little over six miles can make a left turn
here onto New Milford Road and pick up the rest of the tour at
mileage point 32.9.**

**22.4   Ride STRAIGHT at the Stop sign on Waterloo Road, crossing OH
224 (again).**

23.4 At the five-way Stop sign, go STRAIGHT on Waterloo Road.

24.6 Ride STRAIGHT through the intersection with Stroup Road.

The village of Atwater Station, considerably more populated than Atwater itself, grew up around the Penn Central Station. Beware: the tracks are quite uneven here.

25.9 At the four-way Stop sign, turn RIGHT to visit the Atwater Church; then RETRACE your route back (west) along Waterloo Road, through Atwater Station to Stroup Road (1.3 miles).

Waterloo Road ends here and turns into OH 224, making this quite a busy intersection. Just south of the intersection on OH 183 is the Atwater Congregational Church, completed in 1841. Long considered one of the finest churches in the Western Reserve, the Atwater Church attests to the mix of Greek and Gothic Revival styles prevalent at the time. The pointed Gothic windows and domed cupola are at variance with the predominantly Greek features, most notable of which are the paired outermost columns used by the Greeks to add stability to temple fronts.

27.3 Turn RIGHT onto Stroup Road.

29.8 At the T-junction and Stop sign, turn LEFT onto the unmarked Wilkes Road.

30.9 At the Stop sign, turn RIGHT onto the unmarked Industry Road.

31.1 Turn LEFT onto Cook Road.

32.9 At the Stop sign, go STRAIGHT on Cook Road, crossing New Milford Road. If you omitted the ride to Atwater, this is the point at which you pick up the tour again.

All these roads are straight, flat, and unbusy, making for fast cycling if the prevailing westerlies are not against you.

34.5 At the Stop sign at the Rootstown village square, make a LEFT onto Tallmadge Avenue, then a RIGHT onto OH 44.

This tiny community is home to the extensive Northeastern Ohio Universities College of Medicine (NEOUCOM), which is on your left as you head north on OH 44. The college is a medical consortium of the universities at Kent, Akron, and Youngstown. The town was named after a chief stockholder in the Connecticut Land Company, Ephraim Root.

35.7 As OH 5 and 44 go off to the right, continue STRAIGHT on unmarked Prospect Street.

36.1 Turn LEFT onto Sandy Lake Road.

Our Lady of Lourdes shrine, an exact model of the grotto in Lourdes, France, was built in a former gravel pit in 1926 in the tiny Suffield township village of St. Joseph.

In a little over half a mile, the road makes a jog to the right and back again to curve around Little Muzzy Lake on your left.

38.4   Be prepared to stop at the bottom of the long downhill at the five-way Stop sign, then continue STRAIGHT on Sandy Lake Road.
You'll pass over Lake Hodgson and by the northern tip of Sandy Lake.

39.1   At the Stop sign at the T-junction, follow Sandy Lake Road as it turns off to the LEFT.

40.9   At the Stop sign, turn RIGHT onto Tallmadge Road.

42.4   Turn RIGHT into the parking lot by the Brimfield town square, where the tour began.

Bicycle Repair Services
Great Outdoors, 820 North Main Street, Akron, OH (216) 762-4001.
Sypherd's Bike Shop, 652 Canton Road, Akron, OH (216) 784-6832.
Merriman Valley Cyclery, 1670 Merriman Road, Akron, OH (216) 864-1674.
Wheel & Wrench, 408 East Main Street, Kent, OH (216) 678-6110.
Eddy's West, 3989 Medina Road, Akron, OH (216) 666-2453.

11

A Tale of Two Townships

16.5 miles; easy bicycling
7 miles of bike trail; rural and urban streets with gently rolling terrain
County maps: Summit, Portage

The Summit County Metropolitan Park District's Bike and Hike Trail has been a model for similar bike paths across the country since its opening in 1972. Beginning less than a mile east of the Summit/Portage county line in the city of Kent, the Bike and Hike Trail continues for seventeen miles through the Summit County townships of Stow, Hudson, Boston, and Northfield. In Cuyahoga County, it links up with the Cleveland Metroparks All-Purpose Trail for another eighteen miles, winding through the Bedford and South Chagrin Reservation where it ends at Chagrin River Road. Another six miles of trail form a branch running through Hudson to northern Stow's Silver Springs Park.

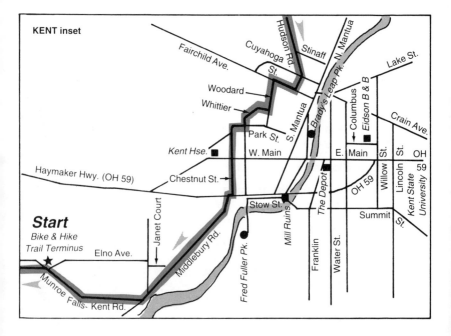

The trail was built with a crushed limestone compacted surface, but much of that has now been upgraded to asphalt. Marked with green and white bike route signs, the trail follows old railroad beds with no grades greater than three percent. Parking areas are located at most of the trail's road access points, and gates are constructed at these points to prevent the entrance of horses or motorized vehicles. The trail gates require

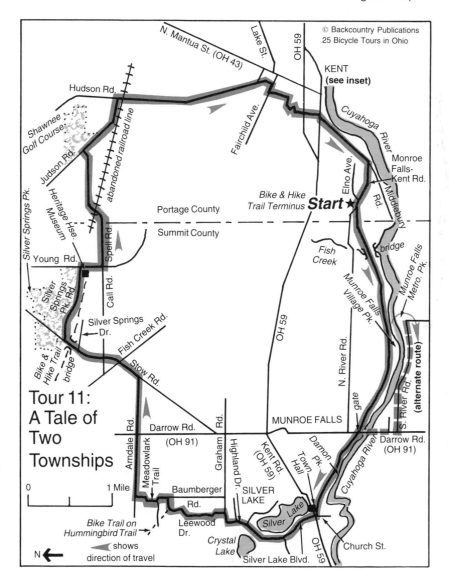

© Backcountry Publications
25 Bicycle Tours in Ohio

bicyclists to dismount in order to pass through them, thus encouraging riders to walk bikes across busy streets.

For four miles, this tour follows the former riverside railroad bed of the "Alphabet Railroad," so-called because it was the Akron, Bedford & Cleveland Railroad (the AB&C Interurban),before it merged with other Akron electric lines forming the Northern Ohio Traction and Light (NOT & L) Company. For another two and a half miles, the bike trail runs along suburban streets, affording intimate views of the relentless Cuyahoga River and tranquil Silver Lake. The route then leaves the established bike trail and heads northeast to Stow's Silver Springs Park. From the park, you'll reenter Portage County's Franklin Township along excellent rural roads, which give way to busier urban streets in the city of Kent.

Known locally in the early days of the Reserve as a flourishing milling and manufacturing center, Kent achieved national notoriety more recently as the site of the slaying of four Kent State University students and the wounding of nine more by the Ohio National Guard during a 1970 anti-war protest.

The tour begins at the entrance to the bike trail at Munroe Falls-Kent Road, .25 mile west of its junction with Elno Avenue. Munroe Falls-Kent Road can be reached by taking Middlebury Road south from OH 59. Middlebury is just west of the intersection of OH 59 and OH 43. OH 43 can be reached via I-80's exit 13 southeast of Cleveland, or via I-76's exit 33 east of Akron. Unfortunately, there is not yet a designated parking area at this terminus of the bike trail; however, there is room for a couple of cars off the roadway. There are no convenient sources of food until you return to Kent at the end of the tour.

0.0   Ride STRAIGHT (west) on the Metropolitan Park District Bike and Hike Trail.

Virtually all of the trail on this tour is well-maintained asphalt shaded by deciduous trees in surrounding woodlands.

In a quarter mile, you'll enter Stow Township in Summit County, where there are some gentle ups and downs until the long downhill to the bridge over Fish Creek near its junction with the Cuyahoga River. From this point you'll be riding along the north side of the river, along the former NOT&L Railroad bed. Near the one mile mark, note the thoroughbred horse farm on your right. A mile and a half past the farm, you'll have another gentle freewheel alongside the Munroe Falls Village Park, which occupies a narrow strip between the trail and the river. Directly across the river at this point is the 213-acre Munroe Falls Metropolitan Park, with a thirteen-acre swimming lake, a lawn beach, restrooms, changing rooms, and concession stand. You can reach the park by leaving the trail a half mile ahead and turning left onto Darrow Road, which will take you to the south side of the river. In another half mile, take the second left onto South River Road; you'll reach the park entrance in a little under a mile. Admission for swimming is two dollars for adults, and one dollar for children under thirteen.

After passing the Village Park, you'll have fine views of the Cuyahoga River as the bike trail hugs the river's north bank. Shortly before the next highway crossing is a short path to your left leading to a fine view of the falls that attracted the village's first entrepreneurs.

2.9 At the gateposts at Darrow Road (OH 91), dismount and walk STRAIGHT across busy Darrow Road.

There are covered picnic tables and grills by the riverside at this intersection. The highway is named for Joseph Darrow, the Connecticut surveyor who laid out the township for its owner, Joshua Stow. Darrow Road serves as Main Street for the village of Munroe Falls, named for the Munroe brothers, Edmund, William, and George, who came from Boston in the 1830s with a plan to make it a manufacturing center. They planted groves of mulberry trees and imported quantities of silkworms, expecting to use the abundant water power for silk production. The mulberry trees thrived in the northeastern Ohio climate, but the worms found it intolerable and promptly died. With true Yankee ingenuity, the Munroe syndicate switched to other types of milling and founded a bank, enjoying a brief period of prosperity until the Panic of 1837. Their bank failed, and without sufficient development of the surrounding countryside to support its enterprises, Munroe Falls reverted to a sleepy village until the encroachment of the Akron suburbs.

Shortly after crossing Darrow Road, you'll come to Damon Park, which also borders the river and has a small fishing pond.

4.2 At the recreation area behind the Silver Lake Town Hall, go STRAIGHT on the dirt path to the right of the tennis courts.

In the lovely "backyard" of the town hall, you'll find a water fountain amid the flowers in the island in the parking area. Restrooms are located next to the tennis courts. Up the paved hill, which allows access to the courts from Kent Road, is the small Ernest E. Fauser Arboretum, dedicated in 1989.

4.4 Turn RIGHT onto Church Street, following the bike trail sign uphill to the light.

Although you are still on the official bike trail, it now follows village streets for the next several miles. The bike route signs continue, indicating the safest and most easily traversed route through the village of Silver Lake.

4.5   At the light, go STRAIGHT, crossing Kent Road (OH 59), and continue on Silver Lake Boulevard.

Here you'll see the bike route sign on the signpost for Silver Lake Boulevard. The attractive concourse leads you downhill to the tree-shaded lakefront lined with large French, Mediterranean, Tudor, and Neo-colonial homes. This is Silver Lake Estates, occupying the prime real estate in what historian Harriet Taylor Upton called in 1900 "one of the most popular summer resorts in northern Ohio." Local residents have taken care of the crowding problem endemic to most resort towns: They have limited use of the lake to residents only.

5.4   At the intersection of Silver Lake Boulevard and Highland Drive, you'll see a bike route sign posted within a traffic triangle; bear LEFT onto Highland Drive.

5.6   At the traffic triangle (also with a bike route sign) at the Y-junction with Dover Road, bear LEFT onto Dover Road.

5.7   At the light, cross Graham Road and turn RIGHT onto the paved sidewalk on the left side of the street.

There's a bike sign on the northeast corner of this intersection, and the curb is leveled to allow one to ride easily from the street onto the sidewalk.

For this brief stretch, you are riding along the Mahoning Trail. An ancient Indian trail, it began at Fort Pitt (Pittsburgh) and followed the ridges and highlands to the famous Portage Path, or "carrying place," between the Cuyahoga and the Tuscarawas rivers in present-day Akron.

5.8   Turn LEFT onto Leewood Drive, following the bike route sign and returning to the right side of the street.

Although most of the tour thus far has been in Stow Township, it is not until this point that you enter the city of Stow itself. Joshua Stow was commissary of the surveying party headed by Moses Cleaveland, which was charged with laying out the five-mile square towns throughout the Western Reserve for the Connecticut Land Company. As such, it was Stow's job to secure the provisions for the entire party. A sort of warehouse for these supplies was erected in the Reserve's first settlement of Conneaut; it was the first building constructed in the Western Reserve and was named Stow's Castle in recognition of the young commissary.

During his forays for food, Stow selected for himself what he pronounced "one of the prettiest and romantic spots in the Western Reserve." He bought an entire township with the help of a partner for

$11,423. Stow made thirteen trips to the township he named for himself but never settled here.

6.5 **At this point, the Bike and Hike Trail goes to the left on Humming-bird Trail; on this tour, continue STRAIGHT on Leewood Drive.**

6.6 **Turn LEFT at the Stop sign onto Baumberger Road.**

6.8 **At the Stop sign at Meadowlark Trail is a very wide Y; bear RIGHT here, which puts you on the continuation of Meadowlark.**

7.0 **At the Stop sign, turn RIGHT onto Arndale Road.**

7.7 **Go STRAIGHT at the light, crossing Darrow Road (OH 91).**

8.4 **At the Stop sign, turn LEFT onto Stow Road.**

8.7 **At the light, continue STRAIGHT on Stow Road, crossing Fish-creek Road.**

As you cross the bridge after Silver Springs Drive, note the branch of the bike trail that runs under the bridge. It lies along the north side of the former railroad bed of the New York Central Railroad. This branch of the bike trail ends here at Silver Springs Park, although there are plans to continue the bike route further to the east.

9.5 **Turn RIGHT onto Silver Springs Park Road.**

Silver Springs Park, occupying 280 acres, is three times larger than all nine of the other Stow parks combined. It has excellent sheltered picnic areas with grills, and a swimming pavilion with a concession stand and water play equipment. Admission is charged to use the three-acre, spring-fed swimming lake. A unique feature of this town park is its campground—twenty-seven sites with electric outlets. Rent-a-Camp packages can be reserved by calling (216) 688–8238. On the east side of the park, at Young Road, is the Heritage Lake area with a fishing pond, an historical museum, and a pole barn where summer stock theater performances are held. The 1839 Heritage House Museum, formerly a tavern, is filled with objects known to have been used in 1804 when the first settlers arrived. It also has good examples of period furnishings and a handsome staircase with one spindle per step. The museum is open every Sunday from the first week in May to the second week in December from 1:30 to 4 PM. Admission is free.

10.5 **Turn RIGHT at the Stop sign onto unmarked Young Road.**

10.6 **At the four-way Stop sign, turn LEFT onto Call Road.**

As Call Road bears left, you can see the continuation of the abandoned railroad bed that you last saw at the west entrance of Silver Springs Park.

12.0   **Midway through the Shawnee golf course is a Stop sign and T-junction, with a sign indicating that Call Road becomes Spell Road here in Portage County; go RIGHT onto unmarked Judson Road.**

12.7   **At the Stop sign, turn RIGHT onto Hudson Road.**
You'll ride immediately under the railroad bridge, which is the continuation of the same abandoned line.

14.0   **At the three-way Stop sign, where Stinaff comes in from the left, go STRAIGHT on Hudson.**

14.2   **At the four-way Stop sign, go STRAIGHT on Hudson, crossing Cuyahoga Street.**

14.3   **At the Stop sign, go RIGHT onto Fairchild.**
A left turn onto Fairchild will lead you into a maze of busy, narrow, streets that access some of the most interesting reminders of Kent's colorful history. Although some may find it negotiable by bike, the sites are most easily visited on foot or by car. Brady's Leap Park, along the river, is where the most commemorated event in Kent's history reportedly took place some twenty-five years before the first white settlers arrived. A stone marker and two large spruces mark the spot where in 1780 Samuel Brady, captain in the Eighth Pennsylvania Unit during the American Revolution, supposedly jumped the twenty-one plus feet across the Cuyahoga River while being pursued by Indians. Without a pause to reflect upon this near superhuman feat, he ran, leaving a bloody trail, to the shores of a small lake three miles away where he seemingly disappeared. The Indians, assuming suicide, retreated after nightfall, allowing the ever-resourceful Brady to discard his hollow reed snorkel and emerge from the lake that now bears his name.

From Brady's Leap Park, one can walk the mile and a half Riveredge Park in the heart of downtown Kent to Fred Fuller Park and get a clearer picture of the Cuyahoga River's influence on Kent's development. In 1805, John Haymaker and his father, Jacob, who came from a family of German millers, became the first settlers, attracted by the river's potential for water power. Their gristmill became known as the best mill in Portage County, the foundation ruins of which can still be seen at the end of Stow Street. Settlers were attracted by the early industrial air of the town, which soon became known as Franklin Mills.

In 1832, the family of Zenas Kent, who moved here from nearby Ravenna, bought the Haymaker family mill and in 1836 built the Main Street dam to provide increased water power. By 1840, the ninety-three-mile Pennsylvania and Ohio Canal, more often called

The Summit County Metropolitan Park District leases miles of former railroad bed from the Ohio Edison Company for its Bike & Hike Trail.

the Cross-Cut Canal, was completed from Akron through Franklin Mills to Pittsburgh, and the first railroad arrived in 1851. In 1863, through the efforts of Zenas Kent's son, Marvin, the Atlantic and Great Western Railroad was routed through the town and, through his influence, was selected as the site for the railroad shops. In gratitude for all his development work, the residents of Franklin Mills petitioned for a name change, and in 1867, the Ohio legislature officially changed the name of the city to Kent. The township continues to be called Franklin.

The elegant Italianate railroad depot can be reached by crossing the river via the 1867 Main Street Bridge and turning right onto Franklin Street. Built in 1875, the tri-towered structure is one of only two Italianate depots in the country. Closed in 1970 when passenger service ended, it was rescued and restored by the Kent Historical Society and placed on the National Register in time for its one hundredth birthday. Upstairs it houses the offices of the Historical Society and the Chamber of Commerce, plus the Theodore Rowe Museum, open Wednesdays from 11 AM to 2 PM. Downstairs is the railroad memorabilia-bedecked Pufferbelly Restaurant, with a menu as imaginative as it is varied and a comfortable nineteenth-century ambience.

Behind the Pufferbelly, across the tracks, you can see vestiges of a P & O Canal lock and the flooded canal bed next to the dam. It was on this canal line that James A. Garfield worked as a "bower" during the summer of 1848 for fourteen dollars a month.

Northeast of the Pufferbelly, at 141 East Columbus Street, is the Eidson House Bed and Breakfast in a lovely 1910 Victorian home. Call (216) 673–5544 for reservations. The inn is found near Kent State University, thus in a convenient location for visiting the renowned Fashion Museum on the corner of Main and Lincoln streets, for attending a performance at the recently remodeled E. Turner Stump Theatre, or for visiting "blanket hill," that now-famous slope below Taylor Hall where a memorial to the four dead and nine wounded was finally dedicated on May 4, 1990, twenty years after that tragic, sunny spring day in 1970.

14.4   At the light, turn LEFT onto Woodard.

14.5   Turn RIGHT as Whittier comes in from the right.
After climbing this short hill, you'll see a School sign, at which Whittier makes a ninety-degree turn to the left and becomes level.

14.7   At the four-way Stop sign, turn RIGHT onto unmarked Park Street.

14.8   At this point, Park makes a ninety-degree turn to the left and

becomes Chestnut Street; after the turn, bear LEFT at the Y-junction, continuing on Chestnut.

14.9 At the Stop sign, go STRAIGHT on North Chestnut, crossing West Main Street.

A right turn onto West Main will bring you in a quarter mile to Marvin Kent's Victorian home at 408 West Main Street. Listed on the National Register, it is now the local Masonic Lodge.

15.1 At the light, go STRAIGHT, crossing Haymaker Highway (OH 59) onto Middlebury Road.

Fred Fuller Park is immediately to the left once you cross the four-lane highway. On its thirty acres, the park has picnic facilities, hiking trails, river fishing, and a ball park that is flooded for winter ice skating.

Beware of the broad stretch of railroad tracks in a quarter mile.

15.6 At the Stop sign, go STRAIGHT on Middlebury where Janet Court comes in from the right.

15.8 At the Y-junction, bear RIGHT onto Munroe Falls-Kent Road.

15.9 At the Stop sign where Ada comes in from the right, continue STRAIGHT on Munroe Falls-Kent Road.

16.3 At the Stop sign, as Elno comes in from the right, continue STRAIGHT on Munroe Falls-Kent Road.

16.5 You're now back at the eastern end of the Bike and Hike Trail where you began.

Bicycle Repair Services
Marty's Bike Shop, 3359 Kent Road, Stow, OH 44224 (216) 688-0814.
Eddy's Bike Shop, 3735 Darrow Road, Stow, OH 44224 (216) 688-5521.
Wheel & Wrench, 408 East Main Street, Kent, OH 44240 (216) 678-6110.

12

Portage Lakes

23 miles; moderate cycling
Rolling terrain
County map: Summit

The sprawling chain of waterways that make up the Portage Lakes begins in Coventry Township in the Reserve and continues through Franklin and Green, just outside the Western Reserve boundary. The Ohio-Erie Canal (for details on the canal see tours 15 and 16), which ran north-south through the county's center, accounted for the creation of many of the lakes in 1840 when dikes and dams were constructed to augment the water supply. As a result, the three original lakes that served the canal in these three townships grew to ten. After the canals were abandoned, the impounded water was used for urban water supply and, ultimately, recreation.

Today the Portage Lakes State Park contains 450 acres of land and 2,100 acres of water, with 37 miles of shoreline. In twenty-three largely tree-lined and shaded miles, the cyclist can circle all ten Portage Lakes and experience both the urban atmosphere of the northern portion and the rural ambience of the southern sector. There are ample opportunities for swimming, fishing, and duck-feeding. Those who prefer to travel only the rural portion of the ride are given directions for shortening the tour by two or five miles.

The tour starts from the parking area of Portage Lakes State Park on the west side of Turkeyfoot Lake. The entrance to the park is on OH 93, the Manchester Road exit off I-277 directly south of Akron. There are two parking areas in the park. The first is about a quarter of a mile down the entrance road; the second is another three-quarters of a mile further, adjacent to the beach and picnic area. The mileage is based on the beachside parking. Those wishing to camp can start the tour at the 8.0-mile mark, where there are abundant campsites at the Nimisila branch of the park.

0.0 Leave the parking lot by heading west along the park road.
This area is known as the park's Turkeyfoot Lake site, whose main attraction is a nine hundred-foot, sandy, swimming beach shaded by tall deciduous trees.

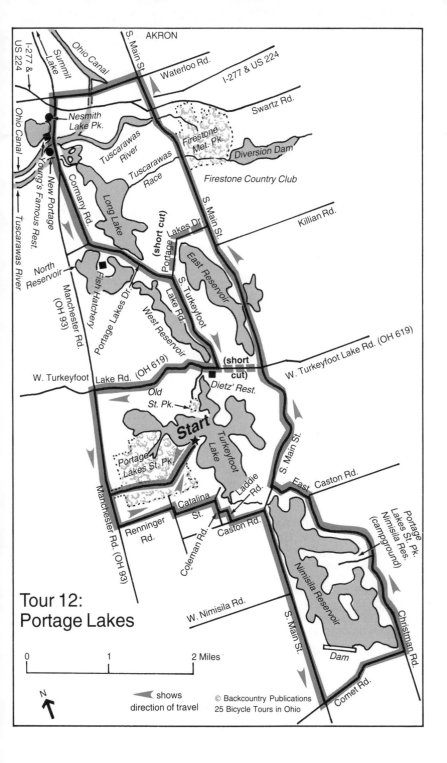

AKRON

I-277 & US 224

Summit Lake

Ohio Canal

S. Main St.

Waterloo Rd.

I-277 & US 224

Swartz Rd.

Nesmith Lake Pk.

Tuscarawas River

Firestone Met. Pk.

Diversion Dam

Ohio Canal

Young's Famous Rest.

New Portage

Tuscarawas Race

Firestone Country Club

Tuscarawas River

Cormany Rd.

Long Lake

S. Main St.

Killian Rd.

(short cut)

Portage Lakes Dr.

North Reservoir

Fish Hatchery

Portage Lakes Dr.

S. Turkeyfoot Lake Rd.

East Reservoir

West Reservoir

Manchester Rd. (OH 93)

W. Turkeyfoot Lake Rd. (OH 619)

W. Turkeyfoot Lake Rd. (OH 619)

W. Turkeyfoot Lake Rd. (OH 619)

(short cut)

Old St. Pk.

Dietz' Rest.

Start

Turkeyfoot Lake

Portage Lakes St. Pk.

S. Main St.

East Caston Rd.

Laddie Rd.

Catalina St.

Coleman Rd.

Caston Rd.

Portage Lakes St. Pk. Nimisila Res. (campground)

Renninger Rd.

Manchester Rd. (OH 93)

Nimisila Reservoir

Christman Rd.

Tour 12: Portage Lakes

W. Nimisila Rd.

S. Main St.

Dam

0   1   2 Miles

N

shows direction of travel

© Backcountry Publications
25 Bicycle Tours in Ohio

Comet Rd.

1.1 Turn LEFT at the Stop sign at the park exit onto unposted Manchester Road, which is busy OH 93 south.

Turkeyfoot Lake, one of the three natural lakes in this chain, is in Franklin Township, outside the Reserve.

1.4 Turn LEFT onto Renninger Road.

Here begins a gentle downhill toward the Turkeyfoot Lake basin.

2.1 At the Stop sign, follow Renninger Road around to the RIGHT. Make an immediate LEFT onto Catalina Street.

2.7 At the three-way Stop sign, turn RIGHT onto unmarked Coleman Road.

2.8 Turn LEFT onto Laddie Road; follow Laddie around as it makes a sharp right turn.

Turkeyfoot was a resort area long before the creation of the park in 1950, and many Akronites located second homes here.

3.0 At the Stop sign, ride LEFT onto unmarked Caston Road.

3.5 Turn at the Stop sign onto South Main Street.

This street is the southern extension of the road that runs through busy downtown Akron. The road is narrow, but there is a bit of a berm. South Main becomes increasingly steeper as you approach the traffic light.

The lake to your left, a favorite spot for anglers, is Nimisila Reservoir, stocked with large-mouth bass, northern pike, and walleye.

4.4 Go STRAIGHT at the light at the junction with West Nimisila Road.

You'll have some more hill climbing here, followed by some enjoyable downhills.

5.7 Turn LEFT onto Comet Road.

This southernmost portion of the lakes is a modest residential area, ranging from homes with large gardens to small farms. Comet Road curves downhill, then carries you up again.

6.8 Make a LEFT at the Stop sign onto Christman Road.

This intersection affords a fine view up the length of Nimisila Reservoir. Christman is flat but curves considerably as it passes right along the lake, providing access to fishing and boat launching sites. In a little over a mile, you'll see the entrance to Portages Lakes State Park Nimisila Reservoir. Here the park maintains 104 Class B campsites, with picnic tables, campfire rings, and latrines.

9.1 At the Stop sign, turn LEFT onto East Caston Road.

9.5   **Turn RIGHT at the traffic light onto South Main Street.**

At this intersection, you'll find sources for groceries or prepared foods. The ride at this point still remains largely wooded with farms and a mixture of old and new homes. In half a mile, you'll tackle a low, long uphill that extends for four-tenths of a mile.

11.1   **At the Stop sign, go STRAIGHT across West Turkeyfoot Road, OH 619. (To shorten this tour by about five miles, turn left onto 619 and return to the park.)**

At this point, South Main Street begins to show signs of its urban connections. The route becomes a mix of residential and commercial porperties as you ride along East Reservoir, which at one point is on both sides of the road.

12.6   **At the flashing yellow light at the junction with Killian Road, continue STRAIGHT.**

In a few hundred yards, you'll see the junction with Portage Lakes Drive on the left. Those who prefer to eliminate the most urban part of this tour can shorten the route by about two miles by turning left onto Portage Lakes Drive, picking up the tour again at mile 18.3. Those who continue up the long, low hill after the yellow signal will see areas of historical significance to the region.

The Firestone Metropolitan Park's 254 acres on your right provides walking and running courses, a children's stocked fishing pond, and excellent facilities for cross-country skiing, skating, and sledding. One hundred and eighty-nine acres were donated to the park district by the Firestone Tire and Rubber Company in 1949. It was largely farmland until park personnel and local Scout troops planted thousands of trees and shrubs. The Tuscarawas Race, which once channeled water from the Tuscarawas River to supply the canal, runs across the southwest corner of the park. Just to the east of the park, on the grounds of the Firestone Country Club, is the Tuscarawas River Diversion dam, completed in 1956. It created an elongated lake along the course of the Tucscarawas and caused certain areas of the park to turn into wetlands, providing a safe habitat for small mammals, birds, and amphibians. The Country Club hosts the American Golf Classic in August and the World Series of Golf in September.

South Main becomes two lanes at this point, and the automobile traffic increases considerably. There's another uphill just before the next light.

14.3   **At the light, go STRAIGHT at the junction with Schwartz Road.**

14.6   **Get into the left lane to make a LEFT turn at the light onto Waterloo Road, or walk your bike across the intersection.**

The beach at Portage Lakes State Park is a welcome sight for summer cyclists.

Although you are only halfway through Coventry Township, you are now within Akron city limits. The city occupies Portage Township and sprawls into all eight townships surrounding it. At this busy intersection, unlike most places visited in these tours, it is difficult to get a flavor of old Connecticut. Instead, due to the thousands who came to work here first on the canal and then in the factories, Akron represents the heterogeneity of the American melting pot.

15.7   At the light, get into the left lane and use the left arrow to turn LEFT onto Manchester Road, OH 93 (or make a pedestrian crossing).

15.8   At the light for the exits from routes I-277 and US 224, continue STRAIGHT on Manchester Road.

Soon you will see Nesmith Lake and its pleasant park on your right. The northernmost of the Portage Lakes, Nesmith is completely within Akron city limits. Young's Famous Restaurant overlooking Nesmith Lake was originally a Portage Lakes resort hotel. Built in 1850, it is the oldest restaurant in Summit County. Two miles north of Nesmith Lake is little Summit Lake, 395 feet above the canal port at Lake Erie. Located astride the continental divide, the lake was the highest point on the canal, hence the name. For Summit Lake to serve the canal, it needed to flow in both directions, north into the valley of the Cuyahoga and south into the Muskingum watershed. The lakes and reservoirs you have been circling provided the large quantity of water needed to facilitate this flow. For purposes of shipping and transport, Summit Lake was the reservoir that linked the Gulf of St. Lawrence with the Gulf of Mexico. Across Carnegie Street from Young's, you can see the still-watered canal with a wood baffle to control erosion. This view helps one appreciate the enormous amount of manpower it took to dig this ditch four-feet deep, twenty-six-feet wide at the bottom, and forty-feet wide at the top.

This corner was important, however, long before the arrival of the canal in 1827 or Young's in 1850. A few hundred feet beyond the canal on Manchester Road is a bridge crossing the Tuscarawas River. This spot marks the site of New Portage, the southern end of the Indian trail known as the Portage Path. Exactly eight miles, four chains, and fifty-three links to the north, according to the surveyors of the Connecticut Land Company, is Old Portage on the Cuyahoga (see tour 13). From Lake Erie, this strip is the only place where a portage was necessary to link the canoe traveler with the Ohio River and points south. Before the canal, the town of Coventry was considered to be the town of most promise in the Western Reserve, situated on this main north-south trade route. Manufacturing sites began to spring up at New Portage, and boats were constructed here to send northern produce down to New Orleans. Ironically, the construction of the canal along the route of the portage path caused trade and commerce to move north to Akron and the Great Lakes, and New Portage was eventually swallowed up by Akron.

16.5   At the blinking yellow light, turn LEFT onto Cormany Road; the road is posted but the sign may be obscured by trees.
Now off the busy highway and back onto country roads, you'll begin a gentle downhill towards the lake basin.

17.4   At the Stop sign, take the LEFT turn onto Portage Lakes Drive.
On the south side of Portage Lakes Drive is a parking lot for anglers. Beyond the lot is a causeway leading to an island in North Reservoir. Here is a state operated fish hatchery.

18.3   At the T-junction with South Turkeyfoot Lake Drive, turn RIGHT.
Be prepared for some climbing, for Turkeyfoot Lake Drive is hillier than most other parts of the route.

19.2   At the light, turn RIGHT onto Turkeyfoot Lake Road, OH 619.
The *Portage Princess*, an enclosed paddle-wheeler, leaves from Dietz' Restaurant for an hour-long narrated cruise. For information, contact John Roessner at 1–800–BOAT–OHIO.

Across the street from Dietz' Restaurant is State Park Road, leading to the Old State Park. Still used for boat launching, this lovely shaded picnic area is crowded with ducks and provides access to Turkeyfoot Lake at one of its most picturesque points.

21.7   At the light, turn LEFT onto Manchester Road, OH 93.
There's a bit more hill climbing before a welcome downhill to the state park entrance.

22.9   At the sign for Portage Lakes State Park, turn LEFT.
There is no light or Stop sign here, so take care not to roll right by the entrance.

Bicycle Repair Services
R-D Bike Shop, 899 Wooster Road West, Barberton, Ohio 44203 (216) 825–3821.
Barberton Bike & Train Depot, 356 4th Street NW, Barberton, Ohio 44203 (216) 753–5316.
Sypherd's Bike Shop, 654 Canton Road, Akron, Ohio 44312 (216) 784–6832.
Merriman Valley Cyclery, 1670 Merriman Road, Akron, Ohio 44313 (216) 864–1674.

13

Historic Akron

11 miles; moderate cycling
Rolling terrain with some flat areas
County map: Summit

The city of Akron is perched like a saddle atop the continental divide, which separates the waters of the Saint Lawrence River system from that of the Mississippi. While pioneer farmers were setting up homesteads and platting villages in other areas of the Western Reserve, the area within the present Akron city limits was neglected by almost all but trappers and traders until the canal was started in 1825.

Unlike the other towns in the Reserve, Akron was not named after a land proprietor, a family of settlers, or a village in New England. Akron comes from the Greek word *akros,* meaning "high point," and the lake at the apex of the canal route was named Summit Lake. Akron began to grow as it attracted canal laborers, then to flourish as businesses grew to serve the needs of canal travelers. The population grew so steadily that by 1840 residents were clambering to separate from Portage County. Akron was made the seat of the newly created Summit County, both named for the high point of the Ohio Canal.

True to its non-Yankee name, Akron didn't develop along the lines of a proper New England village. A rowdier, more ambitious crowd were attracted to this near-overnight boom town, and they were looking for big business. Ohio Columbus Barber (known as "O.C.") started a match company, moved it to a site further out in Summit County, and named the site Barberton. Ferdinand Schumacher started a milling complex that became Quaker Oats. And B. F. Goodrich, lured by a chamber of commerce brochure, built a plant in Akron in 1870 to manufacture rubber fire hoses and beer tubing. That was before the advent of the horseless carriage; from 1910 to 1920, Akron's population grew from 69,000 to 209,000 due to the demand for automobile tires. The rubber capital of the world built its last tire in the early 1980s, but most of the companies, some under new, foreign, or hyphenated names, maintain their corporate headquarters here.

Although this is an urban tour, several undulating miles go through Sand Run Metropolitan Park as well as through quiet residential streets.

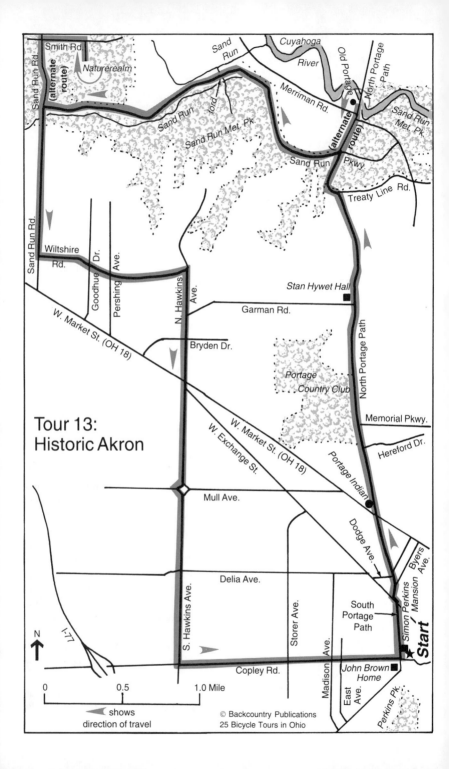

Tour 13:
Historic Akron

Smith Rd.

Naturerealm

Sand Run Rd. (alternate route)

Sand Run

Cuyahoga River

Sand Run

Old Portage

North Portage Path

Merriman Rd.

Sand Run ford

Sand Run Met. Pk.

(alternate route)

Sand Run Met. Pk.

Sand Run Pkwy.

Treaty Line Rd.

Sand Run Rd.

Wiltshire Rd.

Goodhue Dr.

Pershing Ave.

N. Hawkins Ave.

Stan Hywet Hall

Garman Rd.

W. Market St. (OH 18)

Bryden Dr.

Portage Country Club

North Portage Path

Memorial Pkwy.

Hereford Dr.

W. Market St. (OH 18)

W. Exchange St.

Portage Indian

Mull Ave.

Dodge Ave.

Byers Ave.

Delia Ave.

S. Hawkins Ave.

Storer Ave.

Madison Ave.

Simon Perkins Mansion

South Portage Path

East Ave.

Copley Rd.

John Brown Home

Perkins Pk.

★ Start

N

I-77

0   0.5   1.0 Mile

◄ shows
direction of travel

© Backcountry Publications
25 Bicycle Tours in Ohio

You'll have the opportunity to tour the homes of three famous Akronites: abolitionist John Brown, Akron founder Simon Perkins, and A. J. Seiberling, the Goodyear rubber baron. Riding along the ancient Portage Path, you'll travel the route trodden by millions of Indian moccasins, a path so vital to north-south river navigation that it was neutral territory for all Indian nations and for twenty years served as the western border of the United States. A pleasant route with a mix of business, residential, and park land, the town still it has the disadvantages of every major urban area. Watch carefully for traffic and don't ride the route alone.

The tour begins at the parking lot of the Simon Perkins Mansion on the corner of Copley Road and Portage Path, at the north end of Perkins Park. About a mile west of downtown Akron, the Perkins Mansion can be reached by taking the Copley Road exit off I-77.

0.0   Leave the Perkins Mansion parking lot and turn RIGHT onto South Portage Path.

In 1807, General Simon Perkins, land agent, surveyor, and founder of the Western Reserve Bank, bought a thousand acres straddling the continental divide for four dollars and change, the amount due for back taxes. Eighteen years later, as a commissioner of the Ohio Canal Fund, Perkins, along with partner Paul Williams, platted a town of three hundred lots and then set about convincing state officials that the best route for the canal would be through this near-empty town. By donating one hundred lots for canalbeds and lock basins, they gained the approval of the Canal Commission to make Akron the summit of the canal route.

Son of a Revolutionary War soldier, Simon Perkins, Sr., known as *General* Perkins, never resided in the town he founded. A surveyor, land agent, postmaster, general during the War of 1812, bank organizer, county auditor, and canal commissioner in turn, he raised his nine children in Warren, then the unofficial capital of the Reserve. His son, Simon Perkins, Jr., or *Colonel* Perkins, lived with his wife in Akron in what is now called the John Brown home. Their magnificent Greek Revival "Stone House" across the road, a gift from Perkins, Sr., reached completion in 1837. Both Warren and Akron are sprinkled with memorials to the two Simons in the form of Perkins Woods, Perkins parks, Perkins streets, and Perkins schools.

In 1844, the Colonel invited John Brown and his family to stay in the cottage he and his family had vacated in exchange for managing and expanding the Perkins' wool business. Dogged by ill luck and an unstable personality, Brown failed at sheepherding as he had failed at former occupations. By 1854 the partnership was dissolved amicably, and Brown joined four of his sons in Kansas, laboring with fanatic zeal to ensure that Kansas entered the Union as a free state. Captured by Robert E. Lee for attacking the government arsenal at Harper's Ferry, Brown refused to plead insanity despite the evidence of mental illness in his family and was hanged for treason in 1859. A monument to Brown stands in Perkins Park, adjacent to the home that now bears his name.

Tours of the mansion and John Brown home are given Tuesday through Sunday, 1 to 5 PM, and cost $2.00 for adults, $1.50 for children; admission is for both homes. The Perkins Mansion is also home of the Summit County Historical Society.

A few hundred feet after leaving the parking lot of the mansion, you'll see the first of twenty-two markers that indicate the route of the Portage Path. An eight-mile "carrying-place," as it was referred to in contemporary documents, and only one person wide, it enabled the Indians and, later, traders and settlers to travel by water from Lake Erie to the Ohio River and points south. In his 1911 volume on the portage, P. P. Cherry explained that "it was not only an Indian trail, but the center and keynote of all Indian communications in the entire northwest." Likewise, after the appearance of the white man, it was used as a boundary line in several treaties with the Indians and was seen as the obvious route for the canal, and then the railroad. As late as 1814, the trail was still on current maps of the United States, and its significance is still reflected in the frequent use of the word portage in the names of schools, lakes, streets, buildings, and for the township of Akron and the neighboring county.

0.3   At the light, make a LEFT onto West Exchange Street; at the next light, make a RIGHT onto South Portage Path. (Maps may indicate that South Portage Path is slightly to the right after West Exchange; in fact, there are two lights requiring the turns described above.)

0.4   At the Y-junction, continue STRAIGHT on South Portage Path, avoiding the right arm of the Y, which is Byers Avenue.

0.5   At the light, continue STRAIGHT on South Portage Path, crossing Dodge Avenue.

Note the large, striking profile of an Indian brave on the east end of the Portage Path Elementary School.

0.8   At the light, continue STRAIGHT onto North Portage Path, crossing West Market Street (OH 18).

On the southwest corner of this intersection is another plaque to remind you that you are pedaling along hallowed ground. After crossing the intersection, pause to visit the small park on the northeast corner. Here stands the Portage Indian, familiar even to Akronites who have never seen the statue because it is used so often as an emblem of the city.

1.3   At the light, go STRAIGHT on North Portage Path at the T-junction with Hereford Drive.

On your left is the Portage Country Club, also named for the re-nowned trail.

1.5   Go STRAIGHT at the light at the T-junction with Memorial Park-way.

2.2   At the T-junction with Garman Road, continue STRAIGHT on North Portage Path.

To your left is the entrance to Stan Hywet Hall and Gardens. Built by Goodyear founder, F. A. Seiberling, between 1912–1915, the sixty-five room mansion occupies the site of a stone quarry, or *stan hywet* in Anglo-Saxon. Not surprisingly, the basement of the mansion was cut from solid rock. Avid anglophiles, Mr. and Mrs. Seiberling made trips to England in anticipation of creating the largest private resi-dence ever built in Ohio and one faithfully designed after some of the most famous Tudor manor houses in the British Isles. The house contains a three-story great hall, a music room (described as one of the most beautiful rooms in America), an indoor swimming pool, fountain rooms, a billiard room, and individual bedroom suites for all family members and guests. Telephones are concealed behind wall coverings, and wood for the twenty-five working fireplaces is hauled from the basement by rope elevator. The garden landscape, also patterned on Tudor models by Warren Manning, is among the best examples of its kind in this country.

The estate stands as a testimony to the vast fortunes that were made during the heyday of the rubber industry. The motto over the door, *Non Nobis Solum* (not for us alone), is a generous sentiment but should not lead one to assume free admission. Paying visitors are welcome year-round, Tuesdays through Saturdays, 10 AM to 4 PM, and Sundays, 1 to 4 PM. The tour costs $5.00 for adults and $2.00 for children. The grounds charge of $2.50 is likely to be waived by the gatekeeper if you just want a closer peek at the exterior and gardens. Stan Hywet hosts many special events on the premises; for information, call (216) 836–5533.

2.9   Take the LEFT arm of the Y-junction at the sign for Sand Run Park, which is the continuation of North Portage Path (unposted).

The road going to the right is Treaty Line Road. The road and the historical marker commemorate the 1785 Treaty of Fort MacIntosh, limiting the white man's territory to lands east of the Portage Trail. Twenty years later, with the Treaty of Fort Industry, the Indians relinquished the rest of the Reserve west of the path for $18,000 and the usual rum, tobacco, and trinkets.

This is a steep descent as you enter the Cuyahoga Valley, with curves so tight that cars may come upon you suddenly.

3.2   Make a LEFT turn onto the unposted Sand Run Parkway.
If you continue straight on Portage Path for half a mile, crossing the railroad tracks and heading straight through the light at the intersection with Merriman Road, you will come to Old Portage, the point where the portage began.

The road through Sand Run Metropolitan Park is shaded and curves through a lovely wooded area, providing a pleasant relief from the traffic, Stop signs, and traffic lights. This park was the first metropolitan park in Summit County, with shelters and other structures built by the Civilian Conservation Corps in the 1930s. In about a mile and a quarter, the route requires that you ford Sand Run, a tributary of the Cuyahoga, named for the soil particles deposited here. Beware: This local landmark often prevents use of the parkway after heavy rains.

5.4   Turn LEFT at the Stop sign onto Sand Run Road.
A right turn here and another onto Smith Road brings you to the F. A. Seiberling Naturerealm in another one and a quarter miles. There is a convenient bike rack outside the visitors center, where naturalists begin guided walks as scheduled. There are nature exhibits and a one-way window facing a wildlife feeding station with a sound system that brings the bird songs indoors. The grounds are open until sundown during the summer and close at 4:30 during other seasons. The visitors center opens at 10 AM daily and noon on Sunday. Admission is free. For information, call (216) 867–5511.

The left turn on Sand Run Road carries you back out of the valley at a steep grade initially and continues to climb for a little over a mile.

6.4   Make a LEFT turn onto Wiltshire Road.

6.5   Go STRAIGHT through the next four Stop signs, crossing Winston Road, Goodhue Drive, Pershing Avenue, and Stoddard Avenue.

7.2   Make a RIGHT turn at the light onto North Hawkins Avenue.
The area continues to be residential, but Hawkins will have more traffic.

7.6   At the Stop sign, go STRAIGHT, crossing Bryden Drive.

7.8   Go STRAIGHT on North Hawkins through the major intersection with West Market and West Exchange streets.
This is a very busy intersection and must be crossed with care.

8.5   At the Stop sign, travel RIGHT around the traffic circle, passing

The Portage Indian has become an emblem for the city of Akron, guarding the historic Portage path which once marked the westernmost boundary of the United States.

the junction for Mull Avenue and continuing at the opposite side of the circle onto South Hawkins Avenue.

9.0   At the Stop sign and flashing red light, continue STRAIGHT, crossing Delia Avenue.

9.6   At the light, turn LEFT onto Copley Road. (Motorists have a green arrow to facilitate this left turn; walking pedestrian-style is the safest option.)

The area changes from residential to commercial on Copley Road, and the road climbs gently uphill.

10.3   At the next three lights, continue STRAIGHT, crossing Storer Avenue, Madison Avenue, and East Avenue.

11.1   At the light at the corner of Copley and Portage Path, turn LEFT, then RIGHT into the Perkins Mansion parking lot where the tour began.

For those who want to spend the night in this area, the 1917 Portage House offers attractive accommodations at a very reasonable price. The Pinnicks live in the former third floor ballroom of this Tudor mansion, which leaves five rooms for guests. The Portage House is just down the block from the Perkins and Brown homes at 601 Copley Road, Akron, Ohio 44320. Call (216) 535–1952 for reservations.

Bicycle Repair Services
Eddy's West, 3989 Medina Road, Akron, OH 44305 (216) 666–2453.
Great Outdoors, 820 North Main Street, Akron, OH 44310 (216) 762–4001.
Sypherd's Bike Shop, 652 Canton Road, Akron, OH 44313 (216) 784–6832.
Merriman Valley Cyclery, 1670 Merriman Road, Akron, OH 44313 (216) 864–1674.

14

Hudson Triangle

9 miles; easy to moderate cycling
Rolling terrain
County map: Summit

In 1798, Connecticut gentleman David Hudson joined five other Yankees to buy a township in the Western Reserve. Hudson was not simply an entrepreneur; as a pious Christian and direct descendant of explorer Henry Hudson, he had three life goals: to found a town on the western frontier, to "raise an altar to God in the wilderness," and to start a college.

The settlers had a rough start in the summer of 1799, when the swampy area bred so many insects they actually killed one of Hudson's oxen. Undaunted, Hudson returned the next year with his wife and six children to accomplish his mission. By 1826, he had founded the town, designed the green, built a Congregational church, and was instrumental in establishing Western Reserve College.

Never a commercial center, Hudson began and remained a focus of intellectual and educational activity. Nearly a century later, millionaire coal baron, James W. Ellsworth, worked to ensure that David Hudson's vision remained a reality. With the stipulation that the town remain "dry," Ellsworth had all the utility lines placed underground, had the clock tower on the green built in 1912, and endowed the Western Reserve Academy, which had become a prep school after the college was removed to Cleveland in 1882. Indeed, Hudson has remained so unspoiled that when filmmakers were looking for a New England setting for the film *The Gathering,* starring Ed Asner and Maureen Stapleton, they chose to film in Hudson (and nearby Chagrin Falls), because it had more New England ambience than any true New England town. Because the Hudson Heritage Association works to preserve the atmosphere of the early days, the tourist gets a feel for what it was like throughout the Western Reserve before progress took its toll.

The tour begins in the northeast corner of Hudson Township and follows a ragged, triangular route through the village and countryside. Park in the parking lot of the Stow-Middleton Park on the southwest corner of the intersection of Middleton and Stow roads. Middleton Road is east of OH 91, which can be reached from I-480 southeast of Cleveland or I-76 east of Akron.

0.0   Turn RIGHT out of the parking lot onto Stow Road.

One of eight parks in this twenty-five square mile town, Stow-Middleton Park has fields for baseball and soccer, a picnic pavilion, and grills. Water is not available here. Stow Road can have considerable traffic at busy times, so take the initial downhill ride with care.

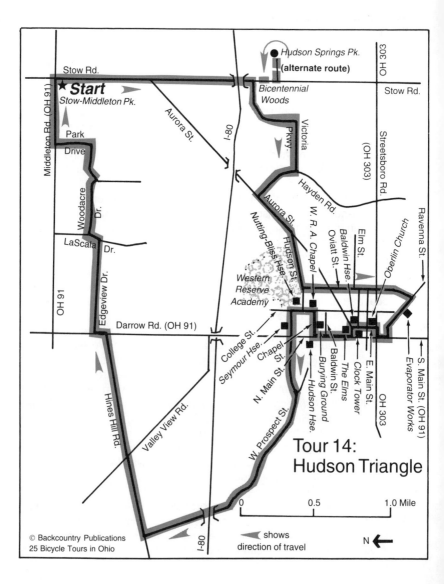

Tour 14:
Hudson Triangle

0   0.5   1.0 Mile

© Backcountry Publications
25 Bicycle Tours in Ohio

◄ shows direction of travel

N ◄

0.5   At the Stop sign, continue STRAIGHT on Stow Road.
Your long, freewheel downhill is now followed by a similarly sized uphill.

1.2   Take the first RIGHT after the overpass onto Victoria Parkway.
A few hundred yards ahead on the left is the 260-acre Hudson Springs Park. A half mile through this modern development, you'll see the entrance to Bicentennial Woods on your left. A gift from the citizens of Hudson in 1976, it is used frequently by area schools for nature and environmental study. The fine gravel path is closed to horses but not to bicyclists.

1.9   At the Stop sign, turn RIGHT onto Hayden Road (unposted).

2.2   Turn LEFT at the Stop sign onto Aurora Street.

2.5   At the Y-junction, bear RIGHT onto Hudson Street.

2.8   At the four-way Stop sign, turn LEFT onto Oviatt Street.
Along with the Hudsons, the Oviatt family was one of the first to settle in Hudson. You'll see some of the Western Reserve Academy buildings to your left. Note that you are now on an official bicycle route, indicated by the green bicycle signs.

2.9   At the Stop sign, continue STRAIGHT on Oviatt, crossing Aurora Street.

3.1   Continue STRAIGHT on Oviatt at the Stop signs at Elm Street, and Streetsboro Road, OH 303.

3.4   Turn RIGHT at the Stop sign onto Ravenna Street.
In 1877, the Oviatt Manufacturing Company made threshers and wagons on the site of the present Evaporator Works. When the company folded in the 1880s, the premises were bought by the G. H. Grimm Manufacturing Company, which produced evaporators for boiling down fruit or sap to make jams and maple syrup. Evaporators were made here until 1943, when the war-time shortage of tin brought production to an end. In 1978, the evaporator building was renovated and more buildings were added in a similar style to provide space for offices and shops.

3.7   At the Stop sign, turn RIGHT onto South Main Street.

3.8   At the light, turn RIGHT onto OH 303, Streetsboro Road; then make an immediate LEFT onto East Main Street.
On the southeast corner of this intersection is the Free Congregational Church, known as the "Oberlin" Church. Owen Brown, father of John Brown, established this church in 1843 as a protest against

the Congregational church, which had not taken a firm stand against slavery. Here the hot-headed abolitionist John Brown made his last speech to his fellow townspeople. Other notable buildings along this side of the green include the 1879 Town Hall, the 1841 Ellsworth General Store at 41 East Main, and the Hudson Library and Historical Society in the 1833 Baldwin House.

3.9   Turn LEFT onto Aurora Street, and make an immediate RIGHT at the light onto North Main Street.

At the corner are the 1930 Christ Episcopal Church and its annex to the right, a striking 1832 Greek Revival home. Further along on Aurora, the Elms, built in 1853, is the only stone Gothic mansion in the Western Reserve. It has been renovated into shops and offices. Inside, the Hudson Heritage Association can provide you with a brochure called "A Walk around the Green," which gives details on all the buildings here and along the lower part of North Main Street.

The bell tower on the northwest corner of the green was given to the village in 1912 by its benefactor, James W. Ellsworth. Locals tell of when John D. Rockefeller had his chauffeur drive him to Hudson so he could sit and listen to the tower chimes.

At the intersection of Main and Baldwin, note the stone marker commemorating the site of David Hudson's first log house and the birth of his daughter, Anner Marie, the first white child born in Summit County. In 1890, Anner Marie celebrated her ninetieth birthday in the Congregational Church her father had built.

4.1   Turn RIGHT onto Chapel Street through the entrance to Western Reserve Academy.

Western Reserve Academy was founded by David Hudson in 1826. Although it did not become the "Yale of the West" as he had envisioned, it did become the prestigious Western Reserve University when it was moved to Cleveland in 1882. The buildings were then taken over by the university's "preparatory department" until 1916, when it became the independently-operated Western Reserve Academy. From this portal is a splendid view of the school's 1836 Greek Revival Chapel, built of locally made brick, and based on classical models. Since many students would never view the antiquities of Greece and Rome, the college buildings served as instructional examples of classical theory and practice. In addition, given David Hudson's vision for the college and the Connecticut birthplace of the school's planners and builders, it is not surprising that many of the buildings are modeled after those at Yale University.

Halfway up the incline to College Street is the Old Hudson Burying Ground, with the gravestones of many of the original pioneers. Across from and a little north of the school's main entrance

Western Reserve tombstones often trace pioneers from their Connecticut home, through intervening states, to an Ohio settlement, as in this example in the Hudson Burying Ground.

on OH 91 (North Main Street) is the home of David Hudson. Built in 1807, it was occupied by his descendants until 1968. It is now used as a faculty residence and is owned by the academy.

4.3   At the Stop sign, turn LEFT onto unmarked College Street.
Buildings worth exploring on campus include the chapel, in particular the second floor of the building; the double-doored President's House to the left of the chapel, originally used as a residence for professors; the Athenaeum, now used as a dormitory; Hayden Hall, originally built as a cheese warehouse; and the Loomis Observatory, the second oldest observatory in the nation.

A short detour at the intersection of College and Hudson will take you to the Nutting-Bliss House at 79 Hudson Street. This 1831 Federal building was for many years the school's dining hall.

4.4   Turn LEFT onto Prospect Street.
Across from the tennis courts is the 1841 Greek Revival Seymour House, where you can pick up a guide to the academy.

4.6   Go STRAIGHT at the Stop sign, crossing North Main Street.
The shaded woodland of this route is in striking contrast to the Ohio turnpike you'll see as you traverse the overpass.

6.3   At the Stop sign, turn RIGHT onto Hines Hill Road.

6.8   Go STRAIGHT at the Stop sign across Valley View Road.

7.5   Turn LEFT at the Stop sign onto unposted Darrow Road (OH 91).

7.6   Turn RIGHT onto Edgeview Drive.

8.2   At the Stop sign, turn LEFT onto La Scala Drive, then make an immediate RIGHT onto Woodacre Drive.

8.5   At the T-junction, turn LEFT onto the unmarked Park Drive.

8.9   Turn RIGHT at the T-junction onto Middleton Road.
On your left is a sign pointing out a restored 1847 farm home.

9.3   Turn RIGHT onto Stow Road and turn into the parking lot where the tour began.

Bicycle Repair Services
Hudson Wheel & Wrench, 46 Ravenna Road, Hudson, OH 44236 (216) 650–4105.

15
CVNRA—South

14 miles; moderate cycling
Rolling terrain
County map: Summit

"Summit County," writes historian Harriet Taylor Upton, "bears out the general rule that the ultimate importance and destiny of any locality are largely the result of geological forces." The handiwork of those forces was particularly fortuitous when it came to carving out the Cuyahoga Valley. The last glacier left two large lakes in the county divided by a ridge now called the Portage Escarpment. This hogback, running east-west through the center of the county, formed the continental divide that separates the Ohio and Mississippi drainage basin from the Great Lakes drainage basin. The lake north of this divide became the Cuyahoga River, a twisting, confused tributary that formed a sharp U when it smacked up against the escarpment as it attempted to flow south. Though nearly a hundred miles long, the river, because it turns back to the north, empties into Lake Erie only thirty miles from its double-tongued source.

The Cuyahoga is smaller than many fishing streams at some points, yet it is a pivotal river in the history of the United States. It has been found correctly located on maps of the seventeenth century, before cartographers could accurately draw even the Great Lakes or the Gulf of Mexico. A crucial component in the only route to the south coast, the river was neutral territory for the Indians, and, until an 1805 treaty, it marked the westernmost boundary between the Indian nations and the new republic.

After the treaty gave the white man control of the Western Reserve, it wasn't long before the river bed of the gentle Cuyahoga was chosen as the ideal location for the Erie-Ohio Canal. This strip, from the "summit" of the escarpment at what became Akron to Lake Erie, proved the most difficult and the most expensive to build in the whole state. Forty-two locks in thirty-five miles were required to accommodate the four hundred-foot drop between Akron and Cleveland. This topography may sound ominous to the bicyclist; however, by sticking close to river and canal, you can take advantage of the level pathway the river cut through the undulating landscape left by the glacier.

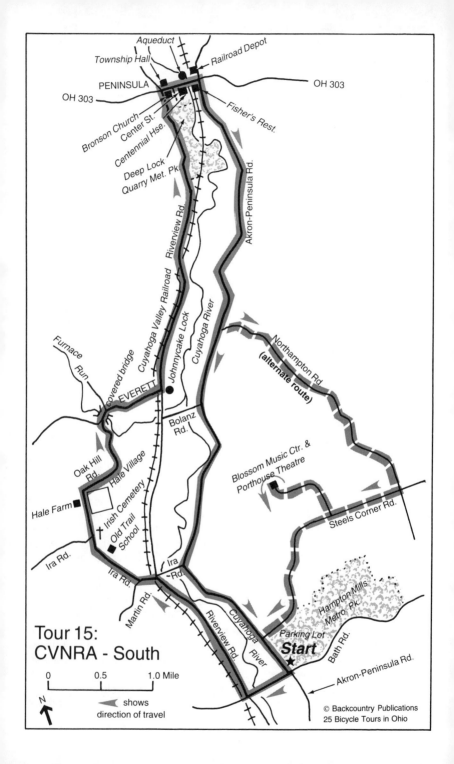

Aqueduct

Township Hall

Railroad Depot

PENINSULA

OH 303

OH 303

Fisher's Rest.

Bronson Church

Center St.

Centennial Hse.

Deep Lock
Quarry Met. Pk.

Riverview Rd.

Akron-Peninsula Rd.

Cuyahoga Valley Railroad

Johnnycake Lock

Cuyahoga River

Furnace Run

covered bridge

EVERETT

Northampton Rd

(alternate route)

Bolanz Rd.

Oak Hill Rd.

Hale Village

Blossom Music Ctr. &
Porthouse Theatre

Hale Farm

Irish Cemetery

Old Trail School

Steels Corner Rd.

Ira Rd.

Ira Rd.

Ira Rd.

Martin Rd.

Riverview Rd.

Cuyahoga River

Hampton Mills
Metro. Pk.

Parking Lot

Start

Bath Rd.

Tour 15:
CVNRA - South

0   0.5   1.0 Mile

N

◄ shows
direction of travel

Akron-Peninsula Rd.

© Backcountry Publications
25 Bicycle Tours in Ohio

The dramatic story of the extraordinary growth of the Western Reserve, made possible through these natural and man-made waterways, is preserved forever in the Cuyahoga Valley National Recreation Area (CVNRA). Created by Congress in 1974, the CVNRA is restoring the pioneer homes, old canal towns, locks and locktender dwellings, aqueducts, and towpaths. By incorporating six metropolitan parks belonging to Cleveland and Akron, the CVNRA has provided an urban recreation area offering a seventeen-mile bike trail, downhill and cross-country skiing, miles of nature trails, swimming, picnicking, and horseback riding. Also located within the CVNRA is the Blossom Music Center, summer home of the Cleveland Orchestra, and the adjacent Porthouse Theatre, Kent State University's open air summer stock playhouse.

This tour leaves from the parking lot of the Hampton Hills Metropolitan Park at the corner of Bath Road and Akron-Peninsula road. Akron-Peninsula road can be reached via the Steels Corners exit off OH 8. OH 8 is accessible from I-80 southeast of Cleveland at exit 12 and I-76 east of Akron. Stores and restaurants are available in Peninsula at the halfway point of this tour. Toilets are available at both metroparks.

0.0   Turn LEFT out of the parking lot onto unposted Akron-Peninsula Road.

0.2   Turn RIGHT onto Bath Road.
You'll see the river as it flows under the road just before you reach the Stop sign.

0.6   At the Stop sign, turn RIGHT onto Riverview Road.
You will have a fine view of the river about a mile after your turn.

2.0   Turn LEFT onto Ira Road and immediately cross the tracks.
The Cuyahoga Valley Line runs every Saturday and Sunday from mid-June until the end of October. The cars on this steam-powered train were all built between 1914 and 1930 and carry passengers from the south Cleveland suburbs and downtown Akron to the Hale Farm and Village, one mile ahead on your route. Reservations must be made in advance by calling the Cuyahoga Valley Line Railroad at 1–800–468–4070.

2.1   Follow Ira Road as it curves to the RIGHT, avoiding Martin Road.
In about one-quarter mile, you'll pass Old Trail School, an independent, non-sectarian "country day" school founded in 1920 for students in preschool through the eighth grade.

2.6   At the three-way Stop sign in front of the Irish Cemetery, go STRAIGHT on Oak Hill Road; do not follow Ira Road, which goes off to your left.

Only bicyclists and walkers may use the Everett covered bridge, the only such bridge in the Cuyahoga Valley National Recreation Area.

This cemetery contains the Hale family plot, not far from their homestead just up the road. Hales lived on this property from 1810 until the death in 1956 of Clara Belle Ritchie, great granddaughter of pioneer Jonathan Hale, who had willed it to the Western Reserve Historical Society. The twenty-six stones tell a tale similar to other early settlements in the Western Reserve: "Jonathan Hale, born in Glastenbury [sic] Connecticut, moved to this township July 12, 1810, died May 14, 1854, age 77 years"; his wife, Mercy, who predeceased him by nearly thirty years, worn out by the drudgery and hardship that was the lot of pioneer women; his second wife Sarah, who bore him two boys and a girl, in addition to raising her own three and Mercy's five; a hapless Hale christened Othello W.; and "Little Lizzie, born May 31, 1876—died June 29, 1876."

The farm portion of Hale Farm and Village centers around Old Brick, the house Jonathan and his sons built for Mercy in 1826. Built of bricks fired in his own kiln and composed of material found on his property, this was the first brick home in the Cuyahoga Valley south of Cleveland.

The village across the road is a recreation of an early Western Reserve town and is made up of structures from the entire region that were facing demolition. Rescued buildings are added as the need arises, so visitors have the opportunity to see restoration work in process. Gathered around the characteristic village green, these buildings are staffed with volunteers in early nineteenth-century attire who demonstrate traditional pioneer occupations with hands-on opportunities for youngsters.

The Hale Farm and Village is open May to October on Tuesday through Saturday, 10 AM to 5 PM, Sundays and holidays, noon to 5 PM. Admission is $6.00 for adults and $4.00 for children over six. A well-stocked snack bar provides a variety of edibles, and picnic tables are scattered throughout the spacious grounds of the Old Brick.

Just beyond the homestead, Oak Hill makes a right-angle turn and goes downhill into a small creek valley, then makes a steep uphill followed by another downhill. This undulating and wooded landscape is typical of this region beyond the valley floor.

3.9   At the Stop sign at the wooden bridge, turn RIGHT, crossing the Everett covered bridge over Furnace Run; after the bridge, continue STRAIGHT on the paved path, which changes to a dirt path leading to a parking lot.

The Everett bridge was washed out May 21, 1975, shortly after it had been listed on the National Register of Historic Places. A detailed story of the bridge is posted on the covered bulletin board in the parking lot. Restored in 1986, it is open only to nonvehicular traffic, saving the bicyclist five miles.

4.2   At the Stop sign within the parking lot, turn RIGHT onto the unmarked Everett Road.

The abandoned dwellings in the old canal town of Everett are being restored to serve as an artist-in-residence community.

4.6   At the Stop sign, turn LEFT onto Riverview Road.

A few paces northeast of the ranger station at this intersection is the notorious Lock 27, which filled with sand during a sudden flood in 1828. Because the stranded passengers had nothing to eat but cornbread, it became known as Johnnycake Lock.

Riding along Riverview Road, you'll notice the railroad to your left and the upper half of tall trees to your right. At this point, the canal is dry; the trees you see from such a peculiar perspective are growing in the bottom of the canal bed, some six or more feet below the level of the surrounding terrain.

After a mile on Riverview, the road crosses to the left of the tracks and in another mile leads to Deep Lock Quarry Metropolitan Park. A short walk along the Towpath Trail will take you to the remains of Lock 28, the deepest lock on the Ohio Canal between Akron and Cleveland. The Quarry Trail follows an old railroad bed scattered with millstones and hewn blocks, with interpretive signs explaining the connection between millstones, train, and quarry. The trail ends at the vast abandoned quarry, which was the source of millstones and building material throughout the area.

7.6   **Turn RIGHT at the light onto OH 303. OH 303 can be very busy, especially when major activities are going on in the national park. Be prepared for this traffic and for a steep downhill into the valley floor.**

On the northeast corner of this intersection is the Township Hall, a classic example of Victorian Stick architecture and one of many preserved structures in this village that was placed on the National Register of Historic Places in 1974. A little further downhill on OH 303 on your right is the Bronson Memorial Church, a Greco-Gothic building constructed in 1839 with the gift of one thousand dollars given by Herman Bronson. Bronson made his money through a sawmill that he astutely placed in the river valley just two years before the village became a booming canal town. By 1960, the church had been closed for ten years, and the Hale Homestead wanted to remove the church to the pioneer village. Local residents raised $18,500 to restore the church and provide for its maintenance in order to keep it in Peninsula. Also, don't miss Bootie's, a fine Gothic Revival general store on the north side of the street that sells cards and gifts and also serves as the Peninsula Post Office.

Just after crossing the Cuyahoga River, turn left, following the railroad tracks, to see the Peninsula Depot, a ticket office for the Cuyahoga Valley Line. Ironically, this depot with its picturesque red caboose represents the end of an era for the boom town of Peninsula, which was once larger than Cleveland. If you cross the tracks, you can see the stone abutments of the aqueduct that carried the canal from the west to the east side of the river. The meander in the river at this point almost doubled back on itself, forming the twenty-acre "peninsula" that gave the town its name. The meander was "removed" during the construction of the canal.

Just before your next turn is Fisher's Restaurant, known for its good food and outstanding homemade pies. For those interested in staying in Peninsula, Centennial House, at 5995 Center Street is a bed and breakfast establishment. Reservations can be made by calling (216) 657–2506.

8.0   At the light, turn RIGHT onto Akron-Peninsula Road. (Those who would like to visit the grounds of the Blossom Music Center can make a four-mile detour by turning LEFT onto Northampton, then RIGHT onto Steels Corner Road, rejoining Akron-Peninsula Road just above the Hampton Hills parking area.)

There is heavy traffic on this route during activities at Blossom Music Center. Since these can be almost nightly in the summer, it's best to do the tour before 5 PM.

The Blossom Music Center, completed in 1968, is a major source of revenue for the Cleveland Orchestra. Its enormous, fan-shaped shell is the largest shingled area in the country, with perfect acoustics both for the five thousand seated in the pavilion and the thirteen thousand patrons on the lawn. Sharing the eight hundred acres with the Music Center is Kent State University's Porthouse Theatre, an open-air facility with performances scheduled regularly during the summer. Tours of Blossom are available on Mondays from 11 AM to 4 PM during the season. Information on schedules and tours is available by calling (216) 920–1440.

After Bolanz Road, the Akron-Peninsula Road becomes flat, wooded, and shady, with some opportunity to ride right alongside the Cuyahoga.

13.7   Turn LEFT into Hampton Hills Metropolitan Park parking area.

Bicycle Repair Services

Big Wheels, 1601 West Mill Street, Peninsula, OH 44264 (216) 657–2212.

Merriman Valley Cyclery, 1670 Merriman Road, Akron, OH 44313 (216) 864–1674.

Falls Wheel & Wrench, 1730 Portage Trail, Cuyahoga Falls, OH 44221 (216) 928–0533.

16

CVNRA—North

19.5 miles; moderate to strenuous
Hilly terrain, with nine miles of bike trail
County maps: Cuyahoga, with a small portion of Summit

In 1974 President Ford signed a measure making the Cuyahoga Valley the nation's third National Recreation Area. Incorporating portions of the Cleveland metroparks' Emerald Necklace and several of the Akron metropolitan parks, the CVNRA today is a microcosm of the cultural and natural history of northeastern Ohio.

The major features of the park's cultural history are located along the twenty-mile segment of the Ohio and Erie Canal, which runs through the park. The towpath, mill, locktender's house, aqueducts, and lockworks tell of the hardships faced by Western Reserve pioneers and their dogged persistence in building a civilization in the wilderness.

The earliest settlers came to the Cuyahoga Valley just after the turn of the nineteenth century, tempted by cheap land and water power from the Cuyahoga River. Farmers and early entrepreneurs erected mills along the river, expecting to profit from the large grain harvests. But word soon trickled back east that transporting goods in a vast, roadless forest was virtually impossible. To avoid loss from spoilage, most millers chose to use their grain for distilling whisky. It soon became apparent, however, that without a dependable means of transport, settlers would cease to come, those already here would return, and the area would revert once again to wilderness.

In 1825, work began on a canal to run from Lake Erie 308 miles south to the Ohio River. The plan had its opponents, but, mindful of the success of New York's Erie Canal, its developers opened the thirty-eight mile portion from Cleveland to Akron in 1827. Just this portion required forty-two locks to lift the barges up the 395-foot climb between Lake Erie and the Portage escarpment. Within a year, wheat going to Cleveland for purchase by Buffalo merchants increased from 1,000 to 250,000 bushels per year. Akron and Cleveland became boom towns, exporting wheat, oats, corn, flour, cheese, and whisky; and importing nails, glass, cloth, salt, coffee, and tea.

Ironically, the first railroad was started in the east in 1825, the same year the canal was begun in Ohio. By 1852, Akron and Cleveland were

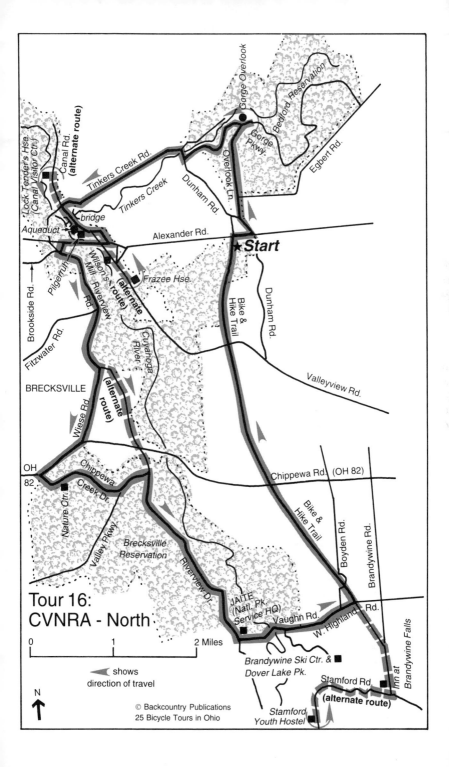

Tour 16:
CVNRA - North

★ Start

shows
direction of travel

N

0   1   2 Miles

© Backcountry Publications
25 Bicycle Tours in Ohio

Lock Tender's Hse.
(Canal Visitor Ctr.)

Canal Rd.
(alternate route)

Tinkers Creek Rd.

Tinkers Creek

bridge

Aqueduct

Brookside Rd.

Pilgeruh

Fitzwater Rd.

BRECKSVILLE

Wiese Rd.

OH
82

Nature Ctr.

Chippewa
Creek Dr.

Valley Pkwy.

Brecksville
Reservation

Riverview Dr.

Wilson's
Mill
Riverview Rd.

alternate
route

Frazee Hse.

Cuyahoga
River

(alternate
route)

Dunham Rd.

Alexander Rd.

Bike &
Hike Trail

Dunham Rd.

Valleyview Rd.

Chippewa Rd. (OH 82)

Bike &
Hike Trail

Boyden Rd.

Brandywine Rd.

Gorge Overlook

Gorge
Pkwy.

Overlook Ln.

Bedford Reservation

Egbert Rd.

JAITE
(Natl. Pk.
Service HQ)

Vaughn Rd.

W. Highland Rd.

Brandywine Falls

Inn at
Brandywine

Stamford Rd.

(alternate route)

Brandywine Ski Ctr. &
Dover Lake Pk.

Stamford
Youth Hostel

linked by rail, and the quarter-century supremacy of the canal came to an end. Still used occasionally for freight in the 1860s and 1870s, the canal was leased for a time to private companies. The state took it back in 1877, but it remained a poorly maintained pleasure route through the turn of the century. Finally, the water that gave life to the canal brought about its end when the flood of 1913 tore through its banks and washed out its towpaths. For an idea of what things were like before the canal's demise, tourists can visit the newly opened Canal Visitor Center.

By the time of the flood, a line of tracks had been laid (or sometimes blasted) through the often torturous landscape of the Cuyahoga Valley. Now, it too has been abandoned, and the park has turned the old roadbed of the Penn Central into a pleasant, gravel-bedded bike trail. Five miles of this tour is along the former railroad right-of-way, and another four miles follows all-purpose, nonvehicular trails through the Bedford and Brecksville reservations. The rest of the trip uses public roadways, many of which twist picturesquely and steeply in and out of narrow valleys. These roads can often have heavy traffic on weekends, so this route is recommended for the experienced and cautious cyclist; those looking for gentler park or bike trail rides should look at tours 11, 15, and 21.

The tour starts at the bike trail parking lot on Alexander Road just west of its intersection with Dunham Road. You can reach it by taking the Alexander Road exit off I-77.

0.0 **Leave the parking lot via the all-purpose trail at the east end of the lot. Follow the trail onto Alexander, immediately cross Alexander, and continue on the all-purpose trail paralleling Alexander on the left side of the road.**

0.2 **At the light, the trail crosses Dunham Road and travels along its right side; in other words, you are making a LEFT turn onto the Dunham Road portion of the trail.**

0.5 **The trail makes a RIGHT turn to continue along the right side of Egbert Road.**

0.8 **The trail crosses Egbert Road and continues STRAIGHT along the right side of Overlook Lane.**
     This is the entrance to Bedford Reservation, named for the surrounding town of Bedford.

1.7 **Follow the trail as it curves to the RIGHT at the T-junction of Overlook Lane and Gorge Parkway; the trail is on the right side of Gorge Parkway.**

1.9 **Take the bike path exit to the LEFT, heading to the gorge overlook across (on the left side of) Gorge Parkway. After viewing the**

gorge, return to the bike path and retrace your route for a quarter mile to the intersection of Gorge Parkway and Overlook Lane.

From here you'll have a spectacular view of Tinker's Creek gorge, designated a National Natural Landmark. The longest of the Cuyahoga's tributaries, Tinker's Creek got its name from Joseph Tinker, the chief boatman for Moses Cleaveland's surveying party that first mapped out the Reserve in 1796. The layers of rock in the gorge include Berea sandstone on the bottom, Bedford shale, Bedford sandstone, Cleveland shale, and Chagrin shale at the top, 190 feet above the ground.

2.1   Leave the bike path and cross the road to the RIGHT side of Gorge Parkway, heading west and down the hill.

This part of Gorge Parkway should be taken with extreme care. In addition to the steepness, the curves often limit sighting distance for drivers. It is not recommended for child riders.

In half a mile the road flattens out, bringing you to the Hemlock Creek picnic area where water and restrooms are available. You can walk from the road to wade in Tinker's Creek.

3.1   At the Stop sign, turn RIGHT onto Dunham Road.

Across the street is an attractive snackery called Park Place. If you want more fashionable dining, the Astorhurst Country Club and Restaurant is behind Park Place.

3.2   Just after crossing the bridge over Tinker's Creek, turn LEFT onto Tinker's Creek Road.

This level road, which runs to the right of Tinker's Creek, has little traffic and provides a pleasant respite after the ride through the gorge.

3.8   At the light and T-junction, turn LEFT onto Canal Road.

A half-mile ride to the right at this junction will bring you to the newly rehabilitated Locktender's House, which opened as the Canal Visitor Center in December 1989. Like most lockside buildings, this one had an eclectic background; it was used as a saloon, hotel, dance hall, grocery store, and blacksmith shop. There are no records to indicate that it ever actually housed a locktender. "Because of unspecified entertainment upstairs," says canal historian Jack Geick, "[the house] was also known among canalers as Hell's Half Acre." Transformed into the new visitor's center, the building's upper floor is now as respectable as the first, featuring a narrated slide show and fascinating dioramas and media displays of the history of the canal. It also serves as a starting point for tours led by park rangers. Restrooms and drinking fountains are provided, and there is a small book shop.

The house is adjacent to twelve-mile lock, so named because it was twelve miles from the canal's starting point on Lake Erie. Here much of the stonework, iron work, and even some of the woodwork of the old lock is still intact.

As you ride south on Canal Road from the junction with Tinker's Creek Road, you'll cross a bridge over the creek. Immediately after the bridge, pause to read the two historical markers on your right. One is for the aqueduct, which runs alongside the bridge on the right. The aqueduct actually carried the canal across intervening waterways, thus avoiding the damage that swift-flowing creeks and rivers could cause to the wall of the canal. It also produced the odd phenomenon of having water flow across water.

The second marker commemorates the site of Pilgerruh, a Moravian mission that was established here over ten years before any other white settlers arrived in the valley. The Moravians were a German sect, said to be the first Protestant denomination in the world. They founded Ohio's first white settlement as early as 1772 with the object of converting the Indians to Christianity while maintaining the Indian culture. Disliked by the non-Christian Indians and erroneously suspected of pro-British leanings by many whites, their settlements were objects of attack from both groups. Escaping from hostile groups at their mission south along the Tuscarawas River, they established this mission at the site of an old Ottawa Indian town at the confluence of the Cuyahoga and Tinker's Creek.

Canal Road can be busy with traffic, but the view of the canal and towpath along its west side is excellent here.

4.6   At the Y, bear LEFT on the slight uphill to go to Pleasant Valley Road; at the next Y, bear RIGHT and ride on the bridge across the canal.

Going straight here along Canal Road for about a quarter mile will take you to Wilson's Mill. Called Alexander's Mill when it was first built in 1853, it is now the last operating mill along the canal. Powered today by electricity, it originally had an interior horizontal turbine instead of the more common and picturesque overshot wheel. The mill is located next to fourteen-mile lock, the ruins of which can be seen behind the millworks. Mills were often located on the spillway just above a lock to take advantage of the additional water power, and the leasing of such locations was a good source of state revenue. This use often led to a widening of the channel above or below the locks to provide a boat basin. As a result, locks often became a social gathering place, making the siting of a mill there even more advantageous.

Another quarter of a mile on the left is the Simon Frazee House.

Built in 1820, it is one of the earliest buildings in the valley and is under restoration by the park service.

While crossing this bridge and the one immediately following, you'll get a splendid view of the history of transportation; you'll ride over the canal, the towpath, the Cuyahoga River, and the railroad.

5.2   Turn LEFT at the sign for Bike Route "N" onto Brookside Road.
Bike Route "N" follows the path of the Iowa to Maine Bike Route mapped by Bikecentennial. It is part of a 25,000-mile network of bike trails begun in 1976. Maps of this network and other statewide bike routes can be obtained by contacting the Columbus Council of the American Youth Hostels Association.

5.3   At the Stop sign, turn LEFT onto Riverview Road.
There is a steep uphill here for about a quarter mile.

6.2   At the Stop sign, continue STRAIGHT on Riverview Road, crossing Fitzwater Road.

7.1   Turn RIGHT onto Wiese Road at the T-junction.
(If you continue straight on Riverview at this point you can shorten the trip by about 2 miles and eliminate some hill-climbing; you will also eliminate a visit to the Brecksville Reservation.)

The road makes a steep climb for about a quarter mile, then levels out in a residential area.

8.0   At the blinking red light and Stop sign where Wiese Road forms a T-junction with Chippewa Road (SH 82), turn RIGHT onto Chippewa Road.
OH 82 usually has a considerable amount of traffic, but you'll be on it for only three-quarters of a mile.

8.7   Turn LEFT onto Chippewa Creek Drive at the sign for "Metroparks Brecksville Reservation: Chippewa Road Entrance," and take the all-purpose trail on the left.
In three-quarters of a mile, there is a trail to the right leading to the Brecksville Nature Center. Called the Brecksville Trailside Museum, it has been operating since 1939. Inside are excellent displays, some recalling the days of the Civilian Conservation Corps, which built this and many other features in the park. It is open daily from 9.30 AM to 5 PM.

Across from the nature center entrance is the Harriet Keeler Memorial Woods, with an asphalt paved hiking trail to be used by the visually impaired and those in wheelchairs.

In a little under three miles after entering the Brecksville Reservation you'll reach the junction of Valley Parkway and Chippewa

Creek Drive. There is a ford to cross after this point, and the road is closed, but the all-purpose trail continues via a convenient bridge that crosses the ford.

10.7   At the Stop sign, turn RIGHT onto Riverview Road.
This section of Riverview is hilly and twisting with no berm and lots of traffic. In a little under two miles, you'll come to a very steep, curving downhill that lasts for a quarter mile.

13.1   At the Stop sign, turn LEFT across the bridge onto Vaughn Road (leading to West Highland Road).
At this intersection is the abandoned town of Jaite, built in 1906 as the company town for a papermill. The two-and-a-half-story building on the corner of Vaughn and Riverview was a company store, with a post office and an upstairs dorm for mill hands. The four gambrel-roofed bungalows east of the store were houses for workers, as were the two duplexes south of the store on Riverview. The structures were bought by the park service in 1980 and renovated for use as park administration buildings. The entire town is on the National Register of Historic Places.

Across the river, on the north side of the road, is Lock 34. (Unlike the mileage *names* given to the locks, which are calculated from Lake Erie, the *numbers* assigned to the locks begin at the summit in Akron.) Also referred to as Red Lock, it is built of substantial sandstone blocks.

After crossing the bridge and the railroad tracks, there's a steep uphill on West Highland Road that goes on for a mile and a half, with the steepest part at the beginning. While climbing this hill, you won't be surprised to pass the entrance to Brandywine Ski Area just past the bridge on the right. In the summer, the area becomes Dover Lake Park, with camping, swimming, and other water sports.

14.7   In one-and-a-half miles past Jaite, pick up the bike trail just after the junction with Boyden Road on the left. You'll see a Bike and Hike Trail sign on your right, where you will turn LEFT onto the bike trail.
This five-mile section of the Bike and Hike Trail was completed by the park service in 1977. The gravel surface, which provides a good base on the flat sections of the trail, can be loose and slippery at the points where the trail climbs or descends at road crossings.

A right onto the bike trail at this point will take you in a half mile to Brandywine Road. Here the bike route follows Brandywine Road for another half mile to sixty-three-foot Brandywine Falls and the Inn at Brandywine Falls, a deluxe bed and breakfast accommodation.

A view of the falls, superb gourmet food, and a barnyard full of

The locktender's house, under restoration in this photo, is now the new Canal Visitors Center for the Cuyahoga Valley National Recreation Area.

animals (including an assiduous "watch-rooster") only begin to list the delights of a stay at the inn. For reservations, call (216) 467–1812.

For those on a more modest budget, a right turn onto un-marked Stanford Road, just beyond the falls, will take you along a steep and unpaved road for about one mile to the Stanford Youth Hostel. The cost here is $7.00 per night, plus a $1.50 bedding charge. The standard hostel arriving time (between 5 PM and 9 PM) and leaving time (9 AM) apply here, but there is no AYH membership requirement. For more information, call (216) 467–8711.

19.7   The Bike and Hike Trail ends at the Alexander Road parking lot where you began.

Bicycle Repair Services
Royal Cycle, 451 Broadway, Bedford, OH 44146 (216) 439–6170.

17

Emerald Necklace East—Chagrin Valley

30 miles; moderate to difficult cycling
Hill-and-dale terrain, occasional steep hills
County maps: Cuyahoga; small portions of Lake and Geauga

Looking at a map of Cuyahoga County, with a vivid imagination it is possible to see the city of Cleveland as a woman's neck and throat, and the line of the lakeshore as her shoulders. If you can manage this feat, then you can picture the irregular line of green looping from the lowered right shoulder to the uplifted left as a lengthy, if somewhat lopsided, necklace. Dubbed the "Emerald Necklace" by the Cleveland Metroparks System, this area contains nearly nineteen thousand unspoiled acres within its twelve parks and Zoo, most within fifteen miles of downtown Cleveland. These parks abound with activities for all ages and all interests. A call to the Cleveland Metroparks System at (216) 351–6300 will get you a free subscription to the *Emerald Necklace,* a newsletter detailing the parks' programs for each month. The nearly fifty miles of paved bike trail in the metropark system is known officially as the All-Purpose Trail and is open to hikers, bikers, and cross-country skiers.

This route up and down the Chagrin River Valley includes visits to two of the twelve Cleveland metroparks. The North Chagrin Reservation ride takes you from the Sunset Wildlife Preserve, with its beautiful Sanctuary Marsh Nature Center, by the Buttermilk Falls Overlook, to the ghostly Squire's Castle. At South Chagrin Reservation, you can visit the Cleveland Natural Science Club's Look About Lodge, see the carvings on Squaw Rock, walk through the Arboretum, and stop at the Sulphur Springs. In between, you'll see the metropark's Polo Club, plus the numerous attractive equestrian farms and lush pastures that make up the Chagrin Valley horse country. Visits to the riverside suburban villages of Gates Mills and Chagrin Falls will add fascinating social history to the natural history of the parks. The Chagrin River, quiescent or spirited, depending on the terrain, will keep you company through most of the ride.

Two miles of the route are along North Chagrin's All-Purpose Trail, as is the detour into South Chagrin. Most of the remainder is along narrow country roads. Today, although bypassed by many large highways, these roads are often heavily traveled on weekends and during rush hours. This fact, combined with swift descents on twisting parkways, requires cautious bike handling by a mature rider.

The tour begins at the parking lot of the Sanctuary Marsh Nature Center on Buttermilk Falls Parkway. You can reach the parkway by entering the Chagrin Falls North Reservation via the Sunset Lane entrance, which is on SOM Center Road (OH 91) northeast of downtown Cleveland. OH 91 is easily reached from US 6, I-90, or I-271.

0.0   Leave the Sanctuary Marsh Nature Center via the All-Purpose Trail on the left side of the auto entrance. The trail turns LEFT to travel along the left side of Buttermilk Falls Parkway.

The expansive Sunset Wildlife Preserve is a waterfowl and wildlife management area that includes the Nature Center, the Nature Education Building, Sanctuary Marsh, and Sunset Pond. The striking Nature Center, overlooking Sunset Pond, is designed to operate on solar power. There are touchable exhibits inside, and outside, numerous waterfowl come greedily out of the pond searching for handouts. The Nature Center is open daily from 9.30 AM to 5 PM, with extended hours in the summer months. There are restrooms and a pay phone.

Across the parkway from the Wildlife Preserve is the A. B. Williams Memorial Woods—sixty-five acres of beech-maple forest where Williams, the park system's first naturalist, did much of his research.

In one-tenth mile, you'll reach the Buttermilk Falls Scenic Overlook.

0.5   Continue STRAIGHT as the trail crosses Sunset Lane, which comes in from the left.

Here the paved trail veers away from the road and winds through the trees and grasslands of the wildlife management area.

1.1   Continue STRAIGHT on the trail as it crosses from the left to the right side of Buttermilk Parkway; this switch occurs just before the junction of the parkway with Strawberry Lane on the left.

Just before the park exit, the trail joins the parkway, which leads to the Stop sign.

2.1   Turn RIGHT onto Chardon Road (US 6).

This heavily traveled road has a narrow berm and heads generally downhill.

2.7   At the light, turn RIGHT onto Chagrin River Road (OH 174).

Be prepared immediately to begin a difficult curving downhill toward the Squire's Castle Picnic Area, which is on the left in a half mile. The

Castle itself is about one-tenth mile away from the road. Built at the turn of the century, it is actually neither a castle nor was it ever owned by a squire. The structure was built as a gatehouse by Feargus B. Squire, a past president of Standard Oil, who intended it as the entrance to his large country estate. The Metropolitan Park Board bought the place in 1925, and people now use it as a somewhat regal picnic shelter. Restrooms and water are available at the picnic area.

About 5 miles into your ride, you'll leave the park, at which point the road begins to decline more precipitously with sharper twists and turns.

5.4   At the flashing red light and Stop sign, go STRAIGHT at the junction of Wilson Mills Road on the right, crossing the bridge over the Chagrin River.

5.6   Continue STRAIGHT at the flashing red light and Stop sign, where Brigham Road comes in from the left.

Soon you'll see the sign for the village of Gates Mills, although you may wonder just where the village is. A very chic, residential hamlet, most of Gates Mills is made up of the sort of beautiful, old, well-maintained homes on nearly estate-sized tracts of land that you see now along River Road.

6.9   At the light, continue STRAIGHT across Mayfield Road (US 322).

A large nursery stretches down the valley to the west of the road

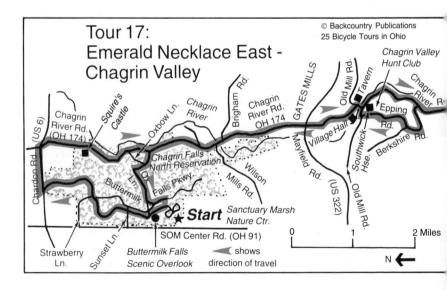

Tour 17:
Emerald Necklace East -
Chagrin Valley

© Backcountry Publications
25 Bicycle Tours in Ohio

Start
Sanctuary Marsh Nature Ctr.

SOM Center Rd. (OH 91)

0   1   2 Miles

Strawberry Ln.

Buttermilk Falls
Scenic Overlook

◄ shows direction of travel

N ◄

here. Soon you'll reach the village hall, post office, and Cahill's grocery. A little further on, to the right, is the Old Livery Tavern, which was once a stage stop and now houses private offices.

7.8   Turn RIGHT at the Stop sign onto Old Mill Road and cross the bridge over the Chagrin River; at the Y-junction, bear LEFT to stay on Chagrin River Road, as Old Mill Road goes off to the right.
At this point, you'll have your first extended stretch of riverside

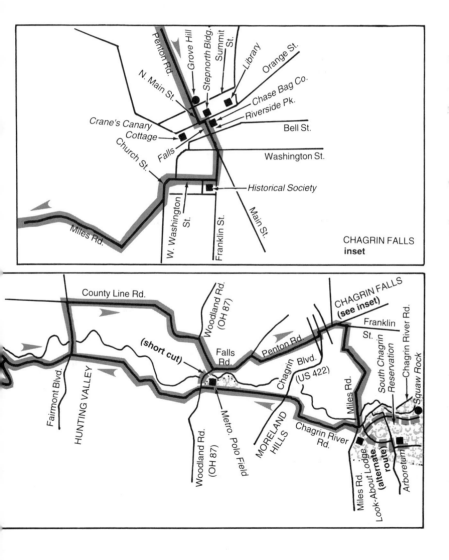

riding. The river is narrow and shallow here, with natural and man-made mini-rapids. The road curves in and out with the river, but, because you stay in the valley, your route is level, with a canopy of trees overhead. In about a mile and a half, you'll see a calligraphic sign for the village of Hunting Valley, and soon afterwards, the road pulls away from the river and begins an uphill climb.

9.9   At the light, turn LEFT onto Fairmont Boulevard.

Soon you'll cross the Chagrin River and begin to climb out of the valley.

10.8   Turn RIGHT onto County Line Road, which appears suddenly, with no Stop sign.

County Line Road, as its name implies, takes a quite straight course for a couple of miles, with some exercising, but not exhausting, roller coaster hills. Towards the end of this road, however, you'll encounter significant curves and a serious downhill that ends, rather abruptly, at a Stop sign.

13.3   At the Stop sign, turn RIGHT onto Woodland Road (OH 87).

13.8   At the Stop sign, turn LEFT onto Falls Road. (Because of traffic on OH 87, this left can be difficult to make; watch for traffic making a left onto your part of OH 87. Those wishing to shorten the tour by 6 miles and avoid Chagrin Falls can turn right here onto the continuation of OH 87 and pick up the tour at mileage point 20.1.)

Falls Road is brick and, although quaint and attractive, is difficult for bicycling, especially as it begins to climb.

14.5   Turn RIGHT at the sign pointing to "Chagrin Falls Village"; the sign says North Main Street, but on the map it is called Penton Road, leading to North Main. This road is not brick, but it does continue uphill most of the way, with a mile of climbing in all.

15.5   At the Stop sign, continue STRAIGHT, crossing Summit Street.

You'll find yourself perched at the top of an awe-inspiring drop of one-tenth mile down into Chagrin Falls. This high point is called Grove Hill, and you may be more comfortable dismounting and walking down the hill at a more reasonable speed than you'll be experiencing if you ride down it.

15.6   Continue STRAIGHT at the light on North Main Street and East Orange Street.

Chagrin Falls, says columnist Martha Coardes Towns, is "the little town everyone grew up in or wishes he had." Indeed, when filming *The Gathering*, a movie about the poignant Christmas reunion of a

New England family, starring Ed Asner and Maureen Stapleton, filmmakers chose Chagrin Falls and nearby Hudson as ideal models of New England villages. Locals work hard to keep it that way. Here at the northeast corner of this intersection is the Stepnorth Building, with offices, stores, a restaurant, and a wonderful Bavarian bakery. Formerly a car dealership, the building was considered a step north of the "real" town, hence the name. To the left on East Orange Street is the Stoneman-Nokes House at number eighteen, a fine Victorian home built about 1873 and made of local brick. At the far end of this block is the excellent Chagrin Falls Public Library, poised above the river with a brick trail down to a riverside walkway that leads to Main Street.

Looking the opposite way, towards the west at this intersection, you'll see a yellow building that looks something like a sprawling bungalow. This used to be Crane's Canary Cottage, a well-known restaurant patronized by guests such as John D. Rockefeller and Charles Lindberg. It was run by C. A. Crane, inventor of Life Saver candy, who built the "cottage" in 1927. C. A. was the father of Hart Crane, famous poet and troubled alcoholic who ended his life by jumping into the paddlewheels of the steamer he was taking back from Mexico. On the lawn of the Canary Cottage each year, members of the Hart Crane Society recite his poetry.

The central portion of the cottage was recently renovated as a fifteen-room inn and opened in December 1990. This portion was the section the elder Crane built, including the dining room area of the restaurant. Reservations for The Inn of Chagrin Falls can be made by calling (216) 247–1200.

As you come to the center of town, you'll see Riverside Park on your left and the stairway to the major falls on your right. A walk through the park and a trip to the falls, where the viewing deck is close enough for you to reach out and touch the powerful cataract, explain the attraction of this little town. It is on this deck that the arresting opening scenes of The Gathering take place.

This location, with such ideal water power, was attractive to early settlers for reasons quite different from its scenic virtues. Historian Harriet Taylor Upton wrote in 1910 that Chagrin Falls was "a thriving industrial village about eighteen miles southeast of Cleveland, its prosperity being founded upon a considerable water power . . . caused by the fall of the river of about 150 feet. Several iron foundries, paper mills, wooden-ware factories and other plants are in operation."

Today, the Chase Bag Company, formerly Adams Bag, is the only factory within the village limits. It is located along the river adjacent to the park. The man-made falls in the river was built for the use of this paper mill. Across from the park and next to the stairway is the Popcorn Shop, selling exquisite homemade ice cream.

15.8 At the light, continue STRAIGHT as Bell Street comes in from the left. At the Y-junction, as Main Street goes straight, bear RIGHT onto unmarked South Franklin Street, riding on the right side of the village "triangle."

15.9 At the light, turn RIGHT onto West Washington.

In one-tenth mile is Walnut Street on your left. A few houses down on the left is the Shute Building, which houses the Chagrin Falls Historical Society, open 2 PM to 4 PM on Thursdays or by appointment.

16.0 At the Stop sign, continue STRAIGHT. You'll see a very narrow Y-junction ahead; follow the LEFT arm, which becomes Church Street as it makes a ninety-degree turn to the left.

16.1 At the Stop sign at the junction with Center Street, continue STRAIGHT on Church Street.

At 48 and 54 Church Street, you'll see some good examples of the woodworking skills of Joe O'Malley on these Carpenter Gothic buildings. O'Malley had a lumberyard and woodworking shop in town and was a masterful operator of the power-driven jigsaw developed after the Civil War. Samples of his work can be seen throughout the town.

16.2 At the light, turn RIGHT onto Miles Road.

Here you'll cross back over the river, entering the village of Moreland Hills. In about half a mile, the road curves to the right and begins a slow ascent. The river valley is below to your left, with woodland providing plenty of shade on your right.

17.4 Turn RIGHT onto Chagrin River Road.

A left turn here will take you into South Chagrin Reservation. An All-Purpose Trail leads to Squaw Rock, a sandstone boulder carved with a rattlesnake and other images that make it look vaguely "Indian." It was, in fact, carved in 1885 by local sculptor and eccentric Henry Church, Jr. On the south side of the park is the arboretum. The Sulphur Springs flow from the massive, fine-grained Berea sandstone formations that underlie the park. Evidence of quarrying for this valuable stone can be seen at the Quarry Rock picnic area.

Continuing straight at this intersection for another quarter mile will take you to Look About Lodge, which offers displays and programs by the Cleveland Natural Science Club (open 2 PM to 5 PM on summer Sundays).

The "River Road," as this stretch of the route is referred to

locally, is narrow, and the curves make it difficult for passing motorists to see bicyclists.

**18.8 At the Stop sign, continue STRAIGHT on Chagrin River Road,
crossing unmarked Chagrin Boulevard (US 422).**

In just under a mile, you'll see the Metroparks Polo Field, which
continues for a quarter mile to the intersection of OH 87. The
Cleveland Polo Club plays here on summer Sundays at 2 PM.

**20.1 At the Stop sign, continue STRAIGHT on Chagrin River Road,
crossing Woodland Road (OH 87).**

Soon you'll re-enter Hunting Valley, which is dotted with horse farms,
some half hidden in wooded ravines. Given the obvious expense of
maintaining acres of wooded stableland this close to the city, it does
not come as a surprise to learn that Hunting Valley is the most
wealthy community in Ohio, with an average per capita income of
$63,000.

**22.3 At the light, cross Fairmont Boulevard, continuing STRAIGHT on
Chagrin River Road.**

For the next mile, you'll retrace the route you took coming south.

23.4 Turn LEFT onto Berkshire Road.

Berkshire begins with a steep uphill, which levels out after about half
a mile.

24.0 At the Y-junction, bear RIGHT onto Epping Road.

In a little over half a mile, after passing some of the most impressive
and expensive homes in the Cleveland area, you'll come to the
grounds of the Chagrin Valley Hunt Club, which adjoins the old polo
fields on your right.

**24.8 Turn RIGHT onto Old Mill Road; just to the right of the church of
St. Christopher's-by-the-River, turn LEFT onto a pathway and pedestrian bridge over the Chagrin River behind the church.**

On the southeast corner of Epping and Old Mill is the 1834 South-
wick House, which now houses the Gates Mills Historical Society
and the smallest library in the Cuyahoga County system. Behind the
house is an old mill race, today looking somewhat like an attractively
landscaped irrigation ditch.

Old Mill Road runs through the heart of Gates Mills, a village
that, writes Ohio historian Harlan Hatcher, "embodies twentieth century man's dream of early nineteenth century Connecticut gracious-
ness and peace." The inception of the village occurred in 1826,
when Holsey Gates bought 130 acres and built a sawmill/gristmill on
the Chagrin River. Much of its New England ambience is due to the
church and the Chagrin Valley Hunt Club across the street. The

The privileged waterfowl who live at the Sanctuary Marsh Nature Center receive only Center-approved goodies from their numerous visitors.

1853 Greek Revival church is by far the most photographed church in the Western Reserve, standing in pristine beauty at the edge of the Chagrin River. Each year, the Blessing of the Hunt takes place in front of the church. The Hunt Club was organized in 1906 when members bought the Maple Leaf Inn for its headquarters. It was formerly the home of Holsey Gates, although little but the door remains of the original French style edifice, which was destroyed by fire in 1935.

After crossing the bridge, you'll see an arboretum to your left with steps leading down to the river. On your right is the Old Livery Tavern, which you passed on the way down.

25.0   Turn LEFT off the pathway onto Chagrin River Road (now OH 174).
Again, you're retracing the route you took earlier through "center village" Gates Mills, with the town hall, post office, and Cahill's grocery.

25.9   At the light, continue STRAIGHT on Chagrin River Road, crossing Mayfield Road (US 322).

27.2 **At the Stop sign and blinking red light, continue STRAIGHT as Brigham Road comes in from the right.**

27.3 **Continue STRAIGHT at the Stop sign and blinking red light, as Wilson Mills Road comes in from the left.**

27.5 **At the Y-junction, bear LEFT to continue on Chagrin River Road.**
Here's your chance to ride again on that curving downhill you took some twenty miles ago—but now in the opposite direction.

28.3 **Turn LEFT onto Oxbow Lane.**

28.6 **At the Y-junction, bear LEFT onto unmarked Ox Lane, avoiding the right arm, which is the continuation of Oxbow Lane.**
Ox Lane climbs for about one-quarter mile.

29.3 **At the Y-junction, bear LEFT; at the Stop sign, continue left onto Buttermilk Falls Parkway.**

29.4 **Turn RIGHT into the parking lot of the Sanctuary Marsh Nature Center.**

Bicycle Repair Services
Solon Bicycle & Fitness, 6291 SOM Center Road, Solon, OH 44139 (216) 349–5225.
Bike One, 1891 Coventry Road, South Euclid, OH 44118 (216) 932–4830.
Shaker Cycle, 16730 Chagrin Boulevard, Shaker Heights, OH 44120 (216) 283–2422.
Mayfield Cycles, 5651 Mayfield Road, Cleveland OH 44124 (216) 461–7725.
B & K Bicycle, 4298 Mayfield Road, South Euclid, OH 44121 (216) 382–9966.
Lyndhurst Cycle and Fitness, 5416 Mayfield Road, Cleveland, OH 44124 (216) 461–1616.
Spoke-N-Wheel Cycle Center, Inc., 100 Industrial Parkway, Chagrin Falls, OH 44022 (216) 247–7662.
Ski & Sport Haus, 22 West Orange Street, Chagrin Falls, OH 44022 (216) 247–4900.
Bicycles & Exercisers, 29145 Euclid Avenue, Wickliffe, OH 44092 (216) 585–3839.

18

Emerald Necklace West — Rocky River

34 miles; easy to moderate cycling
Gently rolling terrain; 13 miles of paved bike trail
County map: Cuyahoga

This tour takes in three of the parks in the Cleveland Metroparks System: Rocky River, Huntington Beach, and Bradley Woods. Each park has its own unique feature: Rocky River is the largest, with the longest stretch of paved bike trail; Bradley Woods is the newest and least developed; and Huntington Beach, one of the oldest parks in the system, is the only one located on the lake.

Of all the Great Lakes, Erie is the shallowest, the busiest, the oldest, and the dirtiest of them all, requiring diligent effort and stringent regulation to effect a change for the better. Although not yet given a clean bill of health, Lake Erie is well on the road to recovery, and swimmers once again dot the Cleveland area beaches. On this tour, in addition to Huntington Beach, you'll see a long stretch of shoreline with majestic homes and charming parks that reflects present-day Cleveland's pride in its "North Coast." The Rocky River serves as a companion for much of this trip, as you visit the historic and cultural suburbs of Berea, Westlake, North Olmsted, and Bay Village.

The Rocky River Reservation is just south of Lake Erie on the west side of Cleveland. The tour begins at the Scenic Park Picnic Area on Valley Parkway at the north end of the Rocky River Reservation. Valley Parkway is reachable from Detroit Road (OH 254). There is a Detroit Road exit off I-90. Because the parking area at Scenic Park is so large, the mileage count begins at the Stop sign where the parking area exits onto Valley Parkway.

0.0 **At the Stop sign at the parking lot, turn RIGHT onto Valley Parkway. Follow the All-Purpose Trail, which begins immediately on the right side of the parkway.**

The Emerald Necklace Marina is at the far end of Scenic Park. Here private boats can be launched and boat rentals are available. Near the boat docks is a well-stocked bait and tackle store that also sells snack food. The entire length of Rocky River within the park is open to fishing, and the river is stocked with trout and salmon. The park also rents bicycles from this picnic site. Fee and regulation information is available by calling (216) 226–5646. The picnic area has restrooms, a public telephone, and a refreshment stand.

As you leave the picnic area, you'll immediately cross a bridge that permits spectacular views of the Rocky River Gorge.

0.1   Just past the Lakewood Water Treatment Plant, the trail crosses the road to the left side; here is a Stop sign and a sign reading "Walk Bike." At this point, the trail becomes a paved path separate from the roadway.

After three-quarters mile, you'll pass under the magnificent, slim, towering arches of the I-90 bridge that carries the traffic over the entire span of the Rocky River Valley.

In one and a quarter miles, the trail crosses a parking area and travels to the right side of Valley Parkway, as the parkway crosses to the east side of the river. Here the trail hugs the river on the west side of Memorial Field, while the parkway stays on the east side of the field.

Just before the 2-mile mark, you'll see Hogsback Lane to your right, leading up to the Stinchcomb-Groth Memorial and Scenic Overlook. To visit this obelisk-shaped monument, you'll need to leave the trail and climb a steep quarter mile.

After Hogsback Lane, the trail continues to parallel the river for another mile until the trail and parkway join to cross the river.

3.8   At Old Lorain Road by the Little Met Golf Course, the trail crosses Valley Parkway for the fourth time in 4 miles and is now on the left side of the road.

In less than a mile, you'll pass the Big Met Golf Course, one of three in the Rocky River Reservation. Both the Big Met and the Little Met golf courses have restrooms, telephones, and refreshment stands. The ranger station is near Big Met.

5.6   At the Stop sign, continue STRAIGHT across Puritas Road, making a pedestrian crossing.

Metroparks Rocky River Stables and the Mastick Woods Golf Course are to the left. In addition to its seventeen miles of All-Purpose Trail, Rocky River, in combination with Mill Stream Run, maintains fifteen miles of bridle trails.

The area of the park from Puritas Road to Shephard's Lane is considered the finest example of a floodplain forest in northern Ohio. A floodplain forest is characterized by an abundance of willow, sycamore, and cottonwood—trees common to bottomlands and streambanks that intermittently lie under water.

As you cross under the bridges for I-480 and Brookpark Road,

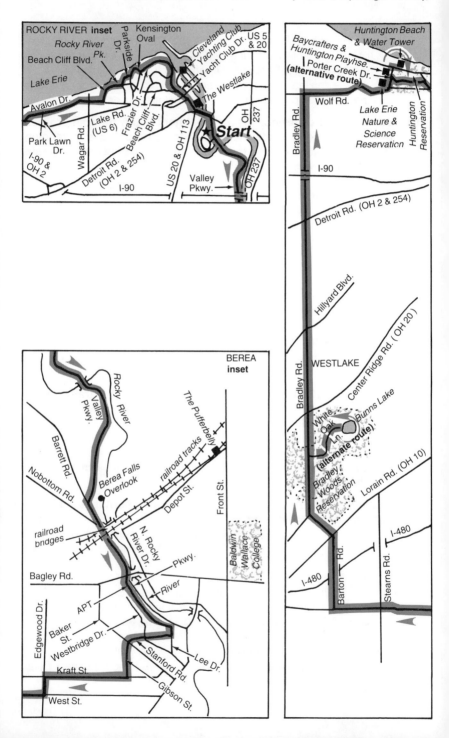

ROCKY RIVER inset

Rocky River Pk.
Parkside Dr.
Kensington Oval
Cleveland Yachting Club
Yacht Club Dr.
US 5 & 20
Beach Cliff Blvd.
Lake Erie
The Westlake
Avalon Dr.
Lake Rd. (US 6)
Frazier Dr.
Beach Cliff Blvd.
OH 237
★ **Start**
Park Lawn Dr.
Wagar Rd.
Detroit Rd. (OH 2 & 254)
US 20 & OH 113
I-90 & OH 2
I-90
Valley Pkwy.
OH 237

Huntington Beach & Water Tower
Baycrafters & Huntington Playhse.
Porter Creek Dr. **(alternative route)**
Wolf Rd.
Bradley Rd.
Lake Erie Nature & Science Reservation
Huntington Reservation
I-90
Detroit Rd. (OH 2 & 254)
Hillyard Blvd.
Bradley Rd.
Center Ridge Rd. (OH 20)
WESTLAKE
White Oak Ln.
Bunns Lake
Bradley Woods Reservation
(alternate route)
Lorain Rd. (OH 10)
I-480
Barton Rd.
Stearns Rd.
I-480

BEREA inset

Rocky River
Valley Pkwy.
The Pufferbelly
railroad tracks
Barrett Rd.
Nobottom Rd.
Berea Falls Overlook
Depot St.
Front St.
Baldwin Wallace College
railroad bridges
N. Rocky River Dr.
Pkwy.
Bagley Rd.
River
Edgewood Dr.
APT
Baker St.
Westbridge Dr.
Stanford Rd.
Lee Dr.
Kraft St.
Gibson St.
West St.

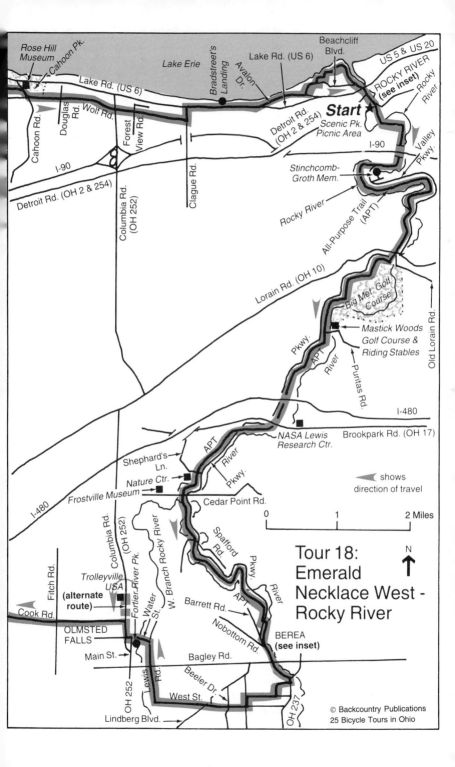

Rose Hill
Museum

Cahoon Pk.

Lake Erie

Bradstreet's
Landing

Lake Rd. (US 6)

Avalon
Dr.

Beachcliff
Blvd.

US 5 & US 20

Lake Rd. (US 6)

ROCKY RIVER
(see inset)

Rocky
River

Cahoon Rd.

Douglas
Rd.

Wolf Rd.

Forest
View Rd.

Detroit Rd.
(OH 2 & 254)

Start

Scenic Pk.
Picnic Area

I-90

Valley
Pkwy.

I-90

Detroit Rd. (OH 2 & 254)

Columbia Rd.
(OH 252)

Clague Rd.

Stinchcomb-
Groth Mem.

Rocky River

All-Purpose Trail
(APT)

Lorain Rd. (OH 10)

Big Met. Golf
Course

Mastick Woods
*Golf Course &
Riding Stables*

Old Lorain Rd.

Pkwy.

APT

River

Puritas Rd.

I-480

Brookpark Rd. (OH 17)

NASA Lewis
Research Ctr.

APT

River

Shephard's
Ln.

Nature Ctr.

Pkwy.

I-480

Frostville Museum

Cedar Point Rd.

shows
direction
of travel

0   1   2 Miles

Columbia Rd.
(OH 252)

W. Branch Rocky River

Spafford
Rd.

Pkwy.

Tour 18:
Emerald
Necklace West -
Rocky River

N

Fitch Rd.

*Trolleyville
USA*

**(alternate
route)**

Fortier-River Pk.

Water
St.

APT

River

Cook Rd.

Barrett Rd.

OLMSTED
FALLS

Nobottom Rd.

BEREA
(see inset)

Main St.

OH 252

Lewis
Rd.

Bagley Rd.

Beeler Dr.

OH 237

West St.

Lindberg Blvd.

© Backcountry Publications
25 Bicycle Tours in Ohio

the Cleveland Hopkins International Airport and the NASA Lewis Research Center are to the left. The Lewis Visitor Information Center is open to the public Monday through Friday from 9 AM to 4 PM, Saturday from 10 AM to 3 PM, and Sunday afternoons from 1 to 5 PM. Several exhibit areas display the history of space exploration and the practical applications of space research.

8.2   The bike path crosses the Valley Parkway again and continues along the right side of the road.
In half a mile on the right is the Rocky River Nature Center. The center is exceptionally beautiful, with an immense, glass-walled observation area overlooking the area's geologic exposures. Impressive wildlife displays line the walls and are suspended from the ceiling. Behind the center is the West Channel Pond, dammed in 1974 to become a management area for waterfowl, and the Ron Hauser Wildflower Garden. The center is open daily from 9:30 AM to 5 PM.

9.0   Continue STRAIGHT on the trail after making a pedestrian crossing at the trail's intersection with Cedar Point Road.
To the right along Cedar Point Road is the Frostville Museum, open Sundays 2 to 5 PM from Memorial Day to the end of October. This re-creation of a farm household in the early settlement days of the Rocky River Valley includes a Victorian farmhouse with post–Civil War memorabilia, a barn with an agricultural display, and a general store. There is no admission charge.

Across the road, a small bridge carries the All-Purpose Trail across the river. Parkway traffic must ford the river.

9.7   At the Stop sign and "Walk Your Bike" sign, walk your bike across Spafford Road.
Two more trail bridges lie at river fords along this stretch.

In two miles, you'll reach the Berea Falls Scenic Overlook, where the trail crosses to the left side of the parkway once again to carry you to the overlook. The tumultuous tumble of water over jagged rock and shale cliff is an apt illustration of the Indians' name for *Sinquene Thipe,* or Stony Creek.

12.0   The trail joins the parkway at this point, leading to the Stop sign at the junction with Barrett Road, where you turn LEFT.

12.1   Continue STRAIGHT on Barrett Road at the Stop sign at the intersection with Nobottom Road. Immediately after this junction is another Stop sign with a blinking red light; continue STRAIGHT under the railroad bridges.

12.3   Go STRAIGHT at the light, crossing Bagley Road, and re-enter the Rocky River Reservation via Valley Parkway; pick up the All-Purpose Trail on the left side of the parkway.

At this point is the main intersection of Berea, a town first settled by Jared Hickox who cleared a site here on Bagley Road in 1809. Hickox froze to death in a winter storm a year and a half later, leaving Connecticut native John Baldwin to become the town's founding father. Baldwin arrived in 1827 with two colleagues, hoping to set up a social colony called the "Community of United Christians," a religious enclave dedicated to the pursuit of agriculture, industry, and science. The group failed to prosper, but Baldwin did not. While digging the foundation for his home in 1837, he discovered a fine-grained sandstone that formed the bedrock of the entire area. Baldwin soon was in the quarry, grindstone, and building stone business, and quarry workers populated the town he laid out. His workers soon began dying of "grindstone consumption," a lung disease caused by breathing in the flour-like dust produced when the stone was cut. Having developed his own lathe for stone-cutting, Baldwin next invented a blower that forced the dust away from the workers.

Remaining true to his original ideals, Baldwin used his fortune to build the Baldwin Institute in 1845, which later merged with the German-Wallace College in 1913. A left turn on Bagley will thus bring you in a half mile to Baldwin-Wallace College, a pleasing mixture of historic buildings and newer ones in a Georgian Colonial design. The college is most famous for its Conservatory of Music and holds an annual Bach Festival the third week in May. Its renowned Bach Library has over twenty-five hundred pieces related to the great baroque master. Just north of the college, at 30 Depot Street, a fine old 1876 railroad depot built of Berea sandstone now houses the Pufferbelly Restaurant. On a still-active railroad line, the depot with its eighteen-foot ceilings, slate roof, and forty-five-foot tower was placed on the National Register of Historic Places in 1980.

As for Baldwin's quarrying business, its Berea sandstone became famous the world over, used in the Palmer House in Chicago, the Parliament Building in Ottawa, and the Garfield Monument in Cleveland. The industry flourished until the end of World War II, when carborundum wheels superseded grindstones and Portland cement replaced building stone. When the industry ended, the quarries became parks and lakes. The Bradley Reservation, visited later in this tour, and parts of Rocky River Park were quarry lands. Baldwin and Wallace lakes, just south of Bagley Road, were once quarry pits.

12.7   Turn RIGHT onto Lee Drive, which takes you out of the park.

12.8   Turn RIGHT onto Stanford Road.

12.9   At the Stop sign, continue STRAIGHT, crossing Westbridge Drive.

13.0   Continue STRAIGHT at the Stop sign, crossing Baker Street, where the road changes to Gibson Street.

13.1   At the Stop sign, turn RIGHT onto Kraft Street.

13.5   Turn LEFT at the Stop sign onto Edgewood Drive.

13.6   Turn RIGHT at the Stop sign onto West Street.

13.8   At the Stop sign, continue STRAIGHT on West, crossing Beeler Drive.

14.0   Continue STRAIGHT at the four-way Stop sign, crossing Lindberg Boulevard.

14.9   The road makes a right-angle turn to the right and becomes Lewis Road.

15.3   At the light, continue STRAIGHT on Lewis Road, crossing Bagley Road.

15.7   **At the Stop sign, turn LEFT onto Water Street.**

Just after making this turn, you'll cross a bridge over the west branch of the Rocky River. Immediately to the left is the David Fortier River Park, with picnic tables, shelters, fishing, and scenic trails. This town park of Olmsted Falls has been carved out along the river in this densely populated residential area.

The township got its name from Aaron Olmstead, a Revolutionary War soldier and one of the first to invest in the Western Reserve. First named Kingston, then Lennox, the town acquired its present name when Charles Olmstead offered his five hundred-book library to the town if they would name it after his father. The books were brought here from Connecticut in an ox cart, and some are still displayed in the North Olmsted library.

15.9   At the Stop sign right after the bridge, continue STRAIGHT on Water Street, crossing Main Street.

16.0   At the light, turn RIGHT onto Columbia Road (OH 252).

16.3   At the light, which has a green arrow for those turning left, turn LEFT onto Cook Road.

If you continue straight on Columbia Road for another quarter mile, you'll come to Trolleyville U.S.A., a museum of streetcars and interurbans. A thirty-minute trolley ride includes a visit to the car barn, while guides give an historic commentary on the cars and the role they played in the history of public transportation. The museum is open Sundays and holidays during the summer. For information, call (216) 235–4725.

17.2   At the four-way Stop sign, continue STRAIGHT on Cook, crossing Fitch Road.

18.3   Continue STRAIGHT on Cook at the four-way Stop sign, crossing Sterns Road.

19.0   Turn RIGHT onto Barton Road.

20.0   At the light, continue STRAIGHT, crossing Lorain Road (OH 10).

20.4   Turn RIGHT at the Stop sign onto Bradley Road.

In a quarter mile is the Bradley Woods Reservation. Acquired in 1960, this park is the only one in the system classified as a swamp forest—with flat terrain and poor drainage. The reservation is underlain by an extensive formation of Berea sandstone, which can be seen in the old quarry pits dotting the area. Over fifty years ago, this area was an industrial site rather than a quiet woodland, turning out hundreds of millstones and grindstones. Rock suitable for these stones was a rare commodity, and the demand throughout the country made the work of dressing and shipping the stone well worth the effort.

Halfway along this road through the park, you'll see White Oak Lane to the right. Three-quarters of a mile down this lane is Bunns Lake, a waterfowl and wildlife habitat developed in 1986. The lake is a quiet retreat for anglers and nature lovers. The area features picnic facilities, restrooms, and a telephone.

21.7   At the light, continue STRAIGHT on Bradley, crossing Center Ridge Road (OH 20).

As you leave the park, you'll enter the town of Westlake. In 1900, this area was the second largest grape-growing center in the country. Today, Dover Vineyards and Limpert Winery on Detroit Road are the only hints of the previous industry here.

Bradley Road is straight and flat, but, with no berm, it can be an uncomfortable route at busy times.

22.8   At the next two lights, continue STRAIGHT on Bradley, crossing Hillyard Road and Detroit Road (OH 254).

26.0   At the light, turn RIGHT onto Wolf Road.

26.2   At the next three lights, continue STRAIGHT on Wolf Road.

27.1   Turn LEFT onto the bike trail at the sign indicating Porter Creek Drive and the entrance to Huntington Reservation.

The Lake Erie Nature and Science Center, located at the entrance to the park, has been in operation since 1959. It features live animals that can be petted and held, a deer run, a waterfowl sanctuary, and a marine tank. There are also classrooms and a reference library. The center is open daily, except Wednesdays, from 1 PM to 5 PM. Next door is the Shuele Planetarium, with educational astronomy programs for scheduled school groups.

27.3   At the Stop sign, turn RIGHT to follow the sign indicating the Wolf Road Picnic Area.

You'll note a roadblock for cars a few hundred feet in. The bike trail goes around the barrier and continues onto the Bay Village City bike trail.

By continuing straight at the Stop sign for another quarter mile on Porter Creek Drive, you'll come to Baycrafters and the Huntington Playhouse on the grounds of the former Huntington estate. The park is one of the oldest reservations in the metropark system, acquired from the heirs of Mrs. John Huntington in 1927.

John Huntington had been an active industrialist, involved in oil, lake shipping, and the Cleveland Stone Company, which he founded. He just as energetically pursued his avocational interests, bringing back uncommon plant specimens from Europe and experimenting in viticulture. The reservation still has many samples of his botanical interests, and the water tower along the lakeshore was used to irrigate his grapes.

Until 1970, the Huntington Playhouse was housed in a former Huntington estate barn. Next to the new playhouse is Baycrafters, a nonprofit arts organization. The Station Shop, open 1 to 5 PM Tuesday through Sunday, sells members' works, while the Gallery Shop, open 10 AM to 5 PM weekdays and 1 to 5 PM on weekends, provides gallery space for local artists. The Queen Anne house between the two serves as the park office.

Across Lake Road is Huntington Beach, right next to Huntington's water tower that is now on the National Register of Historic Places. Often mistaken for a lighthouse, the tower was enclosed with siding to protect the interior beams from weathering. A concession stand is now attached to the tower.

28.0   From the bike trail, you can see a Yield sign on the road before you, where you turn RIGHT onto Cahoon Road.

At this point, you are in Cahoon Park, given to the community by Ida Marie Cahoon along with the ancestral home, now known as Rose Hill Museum, just to the north and facing onto Lake Road. The house was built in 1818 by Joseph Cahoon, who came to what is now Bay Village in 1810 with his wife and eight children. He built the Western Reserve's first gristmill west of the Cuyahoga at this location in 1813 and went on to construct the house with hand-hewn timber. Unable to secure nails, Cahoon pegged the house with wooden tree nails. Ironically, Cahoon developed the first nail-making machine in the country but was defrauded of his patent by a dishonest patent clerk. The home is now a museum of early pioneer living, with a gristmill, sawmill, fish house, and other outbuildings. It is open on Sundays from 2 to 4:30 PM, with expanded hours in the summer.

28.1   At the Stop sign and light at Wolf Road, turn LEFT onto Wolf Road.

28.3   Continue STRAIGHT at the next three lights, crossing Dover Center Road, Douglas Road, and Columbia Road.

29.6   Continue STRAIGHT at the flashing yellow light, crossing Forest View Road.

30.4   Turn LEFT onto Clague Road at the Stop sign and light.

30.6   Turn RIGHT onto Lake Road (US 6).

In three-quarters mile, you'll reach Bradstreet Landing Fishing Pier, next to the Harbor View Motel. Open to the public, the pier area also attracts numerous windsurfers. The park commemorates the unpropitious landing site of Colonel Bradstreet and his sixty-boat expeditionary force returning from Fort Detroit in October 1764. Erie, because of its shallowness, is always a capricious and treacherous lake, growing more so in the fall of the year. Ignoring safe harbor in the mouth of Rocky River some three miles to the east, Bradstreet ordered his men to land on the exposed shore. For three days and nights a storm battered the whaleboats, destroying boats, supplies, and ammunition, including six cannon. Forced to return to Fort Niagara through the wilderness without supplies, many did not live to finish the trip.

31.7   Turn LEFT at the light onto Avalon Drive.

Now off US 6, the traffic in this wealthy residential area will lighten up, and you'll have ample opportunity to marvel at the architecture and landscaping of these lakefront homes.

31.8   Continue STRAIGHT at the next two four-way Stop signs, crossing Parklawn Drive and Wagar Road.

32.4   Turn LEFT onto Beachcliff Boulevard, following one of the Bike Route signs that will guide you throughout the rest of this tour.

32.7   At the four-way Stop sign, turn LEFT onto Parkside Drive.

At this corner is the entrance to Rocky River Park, a pleasant neighborhood lakefront hideaway with restrooms, playground equipment, and benches perched along the cliffs overlooking the lake.

32.8   At the Stop sign, turn LEFT onto Kensington Oval.

32.9   Turn LEFT at the Stop sign onto Frazier Drive.

As Frazier bears to the right to follow the riverfront, you can catch glimpses of the Cleveland Yacht Club far below on the island at the mouth of Rocky River. The island was formerly used by the Indians to store their canoes.

33.4   At the Y-junction, stay to the RIGHT and make an immediate LEFT onto unmarked Beachcliff Boulevard; Beachcliff soon merges with Yacht Club Drive.

As you near the light at the next turn, you'll see the pink Westlake Hotel hovering on your left. Formerly the site of Wright's Tavern, a wayside station built in 1816, the Westlake was built in 1920. It is on the National Register of Historic Places.

33.7   Turn LEFT at the light onto Detroit Avenue and cross over the Detroit Avenue Bridge.

33.8   Turn RIGHT onto Valley Parkway, entering Rocky River Reservation.

34.1   Turn RIGHT into the parking lot of the Scenic Park Picnic Area.

Bicycle Repair Services

Fairview Cycle, 22230 Lorain Road, Fairview Park, OH 44126 (216) 734-2266.

Tim's Cycles, 27093 Bagley Road, Olmsted Township, OH 44138 (216) 235-2455.

Roger and Wray's Bikes, 27313 Wolf Road, Bay Village, OH 44140 (216) 871-2772.

Great Northern Schwinn, 25140 Lorain Road, North Olmsted, OH 44067 (216) 779-1096.

North Coast Cyclery, 26745 Brookpark Extension, North Olmsted, OH 44070 (216) 734-8141.

Marty's Cycle and Hobby Center, 32087 Electric Boulevard, Avon Lake, OH 44012 (216) 933-4204.

Berea Bicycles, 815 North Rocky River Drive, Cleveland, OH 44017 (216) 243-3332.

Lorain Triskett Schwinn, 15718 Lorain Road, Cleveland, OH 44111 (216) 252-3333.

Schneider's Bike Shop, 10001 Lorain Road, Cleveland, OH 44111 (216) 631-7187.

The Rocky River Nature Center is beautifully designed with attractive displays inside and striking geologic formations outside.

Raleigh Bicycles of Rocky River, 19353 Detroit Road, Cleveland, OH 44116 (216) 333-9155.

Westgate Cycle, 20180 Center Ridge Road, Cleveland, OH 44116 (216) 333-7121.

Lakewood Cycles, 14515 Madison Road, Lakewood, OH 44107 (216) 228-7865.

19

Medina Meander

43 miles; moderate to difficult cycling
Frequent hills with some steep inclines
County maps: Medina, Summit

On display at Cleveland's Western Reserve Historical Society is a 1798 manuscript map drawn by Seth Pease, a surveyor and astronomer who was third in command of the surveying party that mapped out the Western Reserve. The right half of the map shows a carefully surveyed area, neatly divided into five-mile-square townships. Superimposed on the left half of the map, however, over an area showing nothing but the carefully drawn courses of the Rocky River and the Black River, are the words "unsurveyed land and subject to Indian claims." Earlier treaties with the Indians had cleared the title to all land east of the Cuyahoga, and the treaties had been confirmed by Congress. It was thus a felony to settle west of the Cuyahoga.

By 1805, at the Treaty of Fort Industry, representatives of Congress and the Connecticut Land Company induced certain Indians to part with the Western Reserve lands west of the Cuyahoga for $18,916.67. According to surveyor Abraham Tappan, "It is said by those who attended this treaty, that the Indians, in parting with and making sale of the above lands to the whites, did so with much reluctance, and after the treaty was signed, many of them wept."

In the spring of 1806, Seth Pease again set to work, extending the southern boundary line of the Reserve, and Abraham Tappan ran the township lines. By 1807, the land was made available to purchasers, but settlement lagged. Heavily forested and still inhabited by Indians who did not feel bound by the Treaty of Fort Industry, Medina County was so named because it was seen by some as the end of the trail for the restless Yankee migration to the west. Of the few settlers who braved the hills, swamps, and forests of this western outpost, most retreated eastward when the War of 1812 brought raids from the Indians who fought on the side of the British.

After the war, white settlement began to pick up in Medina County, and it soon became one of the major wheat and corn producers of the Reserve. Today, farming is still the largest industry in terms of dollar value. As is often true in hilly rural areas, dairying has become one of the major agricultural industries.

The good roads in this county encourage bicycling, and the Medina County Bicycle Club is one of the most active in the Reserve. Given the challenging terrain of much of the county, you'll find on this forty-three-mile tour, that when you aren't riding down a hill, you're climbing up one, a fact that explains the frequent signs warning of "Limited Sight Distance." On a windy day, the combination of wind resistance gathering force over open farmland and roller coaster topography can provide a real workout. You'll be richly rewarded, however, with some of the finest rural scenery the Western Reserve has to offer.

The tour starts at the Buzzard's Roost parking area of the Hinckley Reservation on State Road, in the northeast corner of the county. The Hinckley Reservation is directly south of greater Cleveland and just north of I-271. State Road can be reached from I-271 via OH 3 and OH 303.

0.0 From the Buzzard's Roost parking lot, turn RIGHT onto State Road.

The Hinckley Reservation is the southernmost of the Cleveland Metropark System's "Emerald Necklace," a semicircle of park land surrounding the greater Cleveland area. The reservation's 2,288 acres are dominated by the ninety-acre Hinckley Lake, created in 1927 by damming the east branch of the Rocky River. The most outstanding natural feature of the park are its ledges, uplifted layers of sandstone conglomerate that rise some 350 feet above the lake. By far the most celebrated feature of these ledges is their attraction for the Hinckley buzzards. These turkey vultures, like the Capistrano swallows, return each year on March 15, reclaiming their homes in the ledges, cliffs, trees, and fields of the Hinckley Reservation.

Each year since 1957, thousands of people arrive on "Buzzard Sunday," the first Sunday following the fifteenth of March, to greet the returning migrants. At that time, naturalists are on duty from 8 AM to 6 PM with their Naturemobile, ready to dispense buzzard lore and hot chocolate. A massive Buzzard Activity Chart is erected near the pen of a lonely turkey vulture whose job it is to give the human welcoming committee a better view of his species' distinctly homely countenance than can be obtained through field glasses and spotting telescopes.

Although the turkey vulture is low on the scale of bird beauty, naturalists consider him, with his six-foot wingspan, the "epitome of avian perfection," soaring effortlessly on rising thermals as he scours the countryside for decomposing delicacies. The question most frequently asked on March 15 is, "Why Hinckley?" Scientific answers include references to the excellent nesting accommodations and the open field patterns. Since the turkey vulture can't be bothered with nest-making, she needs sequestered cliff ledges, hollow trees,

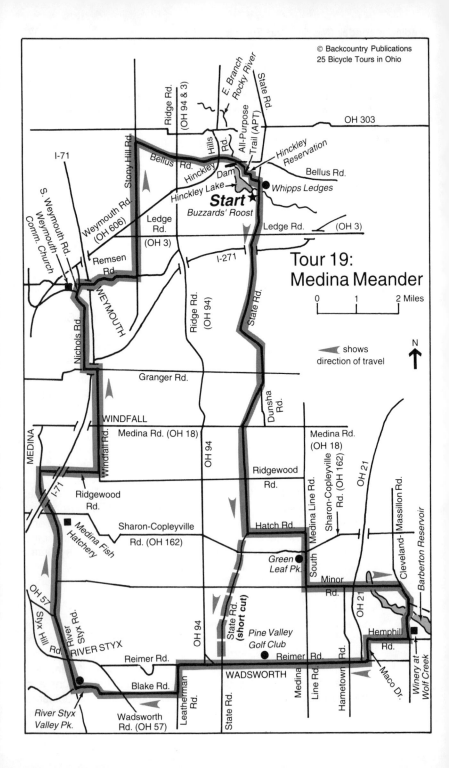

© Backcountry Publications
25 Bicycle Tours in Ohio

Ridge Rd. (OH 94 & 3)

E. Branch Rocky River

State Rd.

OH 303

I-71

Stony Hill Rd.

Bellus Rd.

Hinckley Hills Rd.

All-Purpose Trail (APT)

Hinckley Reservation

Bellus Rd.

Hinckley Dam

Hinckley Lake

Start ★
Buzzards' Roost

Whipps Ledges

S. Weymouth Rd.

Weymouth Comm. Church

Weymouth Rd. (OH 606)

Ledge Rd. (OH 3)

Ledge Rd.

(OH 3)

**Tour 19:
Medina Meander**

Remsen Rd.

I-271

State Rd.

0   1   2 Miles

Nichols Rd.

WEYMOUTH

Ridge Rd. (OH 94)

N

Granger Rd.

shows direction of travel

Dunsha Rd.

WINDFALL

Windfall Rd.

Medina Rd. (OH 18)

OH 94

Medina Rd. (OH 18)

MEDINA

I-71

Ridgewood Rd.

Ridgewood Rd.

Sharon-Copleyville Rd. (OH 162)

OH 21

Medina Fish Hatchery

Sharon-Copleyville Rd. (OH 162)

Hatch Rd.

South Medina Line Rd.

Cleveland-Massillon Rd.

Barberton Reservoir

Green Leaf Pk.

Minor Rd.

OH 21

OH 57

Styx Hill Rd.

River Styx Rd.

RIVER STYX

State Rd. (short cut)

Pine Valley Golf Club

Hemphill Rd.

Winery at Wolf Creek

Reimer Rd.

OH 94

Reimer Rd.

Medina Line Rd.

Hametown Rd.

Maco Dr.

Blake Rd.

Leatherman Rd.

State Rd.

WADSWORTH

River Styx Valley Pk.

Wadsworth Rd. (OH 57)

and cavern floors on which to lay her pair of eggs. The same open countryside that allows headwinds to challenge struggling bicyclists provides turkey vultures with rising thermals and unobstructed hunting grounds.

0.9   Continue STRAIGHT at the four-way Stop sign, crossing Ledge Road.

Once out of the park, State Road runs through some beautiful farmland with well-maintained farmhouses, lots of trees, and lots of hills. You are now in the town of Granger, named for Gideon Granger, President Jefferson's postmaster general and a major stockholder in the Connecticut Land Company, although he never settled in the Reserve himself.

4.6   At the Y-junction, bear RIGHT to continue on State Road, avoiding Dunsha Road on the left.

5.7   At the Stop sign, continue STRAIGHT on State Road, crossing Medina Road (OH 18).

The busy OH 18 is a bit of a shock after the pastoral peacefulness of State Road. Medina Road is a divided highway with no traffic signal and should be crossed with care.

7.0   At the Stop sign, continue STRAIGHT on State Road, crossing Ridgewood Road.

8.2   At the Stop sign, turn LEFT onto Hatch Road.

Hatch Road sports even more hills than you've encountered thus far, most of them uphill when approached from this direction. To avoid this climb and cut down the mileage by about 8.5 miles, continue straight on State Road, picking up the tour at mileage point 19.8 on Reimer Road. This shortcut will eliminate a visit to the Winery at Wolf Creek.

9.7   Turn RIGHT onto South Medina Line Road.

A steep downhill leads to the next Stop sign in just under half a mile.

10.1   At the Stop sign, continue STRAIGHT, crossing Sharon-Copley Road (OH 162).

At the southwest corner of this intersection is Green Leaf Park, a thirty-three-acre county park that was once a gravel pit. Here you can see the pioneer residence of the Hard family. At twenty-one-by-twenty-seven-feet, the building qualifies as a log *house,* larger than the sixteen-by-sixteen-foot dimensions of the standard log *cabin.*

10.9   Turn LEFT onto Minor Road.

Here you begin a seven-mile sojourn into Summit County.

12.1 At the Stop sign, continue STRAIGHT, crossing OH 21.

OH 21 is another major divided highway with fast-moving traffic and no traffic signal. It is advisable to walk your bike. After the highway, you'll cross the northern tip of Barberton Reservoir, an enlarged portion of Wolf Creek.

13.1 At the Stop sign, turn RIGHT onto Cleveland-Massillon Road.

Cleveland-Massillon Road has more traffic than most of the other roads on this tour. In a little over half a mile, you'll cross the Barberton Reservoir again and begin a steep uphill between ledges similar to those in the Hinckley area. At the crest of the hill, less than half a mile from the reservoir crossing, is the entrance on your left to the Winery at Wolf Creek. Open Tuesday through Thursday from noon to 8 PM and Fridays and Saturdays until midnight, the Winery at Wolf Creek has an indoor tasting room and a large deck with picnic tables overlooking Wolf Creek far below. Wines are available by the glass, bottle, or case, and soda and juices are obtainable. Snack baskets with fruit, cheese, bread, and crackers are sold, or you can bring your own picnic with you.

14.6 Turn RIGHT onto Hemphill Road.

15.8 Follow Hemphill Road as it makes a ninety-degree turn to the LEFT and becomes Maco Drive.

Enjoy Maco Drive for a few tenths of a mile; it is virtually the only flat stretch in this entire tour.

16.3 At the Stop sign, turn RIGHT onto Reimer Road.

16.6 At the four-way Stop sign, continue STRAIGHT on Reimer Road, crossing the unmarked Hametown Road.

17.7 At the Stop sign, continue STRAIGHT on Reimer Road, crossing Medina Line Road.

In about half a mile, you begin a quite steep uphill that peaks in about a quarter mile at the Pine Valley Golf Club.

19.8 At the Stop sign, bear LEFT onto State Road, coming immediately to another Stop sign where you turn to the RIGHT. Making these turns keeps you on Reimer Road, which for a short distance here is OH 94.

20.1 As OH 94 bears off to the right, continue STRAIGHT on Reimer Road.

20.8 Turn LEFT onto Leatherman Road.

21.5 Turn RIGHT onto Blake Road.

22.8 At the Stop sign, continue STRAIGHT on Blake Road, crossing Wadsworth Road (OH 57).

Blake is a side road that has no traffic and goes through some lovely farmland with large fields. In half a mile, you'll enter Guilford township, so named for towns in Connecticut and upstate New York where many of its settlers hailed from.

23.9 At the Stop sign, turn RIGHT onto River Styx Road.

On the northwest corner of this intersection is eighty-three acres that the county plans to develop into the River Styx Valley Park. In half a mile, you'll pass the River Styx Cemetery on your right and the River Styx Cider Mill on your left.

24.6 At the Stop sign, continue STRAIGHT on River Styx Road, where Styx Hill Road comes in from the left; at this point, River Styx Road becomes OH 57 for a short time.

The River Styx Market at the northwest corner of this intersection marks the center of the community of River Styx. Early surveyors found the swampy town of Guilford so like "the infernal regions" that they memorialized their misery by naming the area after the mythological stream in Hades.

Soon you'll cross into Montville township, named after towns in Connecticut and Vermont. It is aptly named, for through this township cuts the continental divide separating the waters running to the south toward the Ohio River and the waters flowing north to the Great Lakes.

25.6 At the Y-junction, bear RIGHT on River Styx Road, avoiding Wadsworth Road (OH 57), which bears left.

28.0 At the Stop sign, continue STRAIGHT on River Styx Road, crossing Sharon-Copley Road (OH 162).

A right turn here onto the moderately busy highway will bring you to the Medina Fish Hatchery in less than half a mile. Here the elongated hatchery troughs are stocked with trout, catfish, walleye, bluegill, and white bass. There is a clubhouse on the premises, and fishing is open to the public in the summer from 7 AM to 6.30 PM and in winter from 8 AM to 5 PM. The charge is $7.50 for adults, $6.50 for seniors, and $3.50 for children.

As you continue north on River Styx Road you'll make your first of several passes over or under I-71, which travels from Cleveland to Cincinnati and on to Louisville, Kentucky.

29.1 Turn RIGHT onto Ridgewood Road.

A hilly road, Ridgewood takes you under I-71 again in half a mile.

30.6 At the three-way Stop sign, turn LEFT onto Windfall Road.

31.5   At the light, continue STRAIGHT on Windfall Road, crossing Medina Road (OH 18).

This intersection is the community of Windfall, today a suburb. To the left on OH 18 is the city of Medina, laid out in 1818 as the county seat. Medina grew steadily into a city of small business and industry. Its best-known enterprise is the A. I. Root Company, begun in 1869 when retired jeweler Amos Root paid a dollar for a swarm of bees. The company is now a major manufacturer of beeswax candles and beekeeping supplies. This and Medina's other entrepreneurial endeavors left a legacy of historic Victorian homes and storefronts, many of which cluster around the Public Square originally donated by the town's proprietor, Elijah Boardman.

The Oakwood B&B, an antique-furnished Victorian home at 226 North Broadway, is located just north of the public square on the walking tour of the Victorian village. The modest price includes complimentary wine and a generous continental breakfast. Bicycles are available for guest use. Proprietors Lonore and David Charbonneau can be reached at (216) 723–1162.

32.9   Turn LEFT at the T-junction onto Granger Road.

33.0   At the three-way Stop sign and blinking red light, just after you pass over the highway (I-71), turn RIGHT onto Nichols Road.

In about one-and-a-half miles, you'll begin heading down into the village of Weymouth, in the valley of the north branch of the Rocky River.

35.0   At the Stop sign, turn RIGHT onto South Weymouth Road.

A quarter mile to the left is the Weymouth Community Church, originally built by sixteen families as a Congregational church. Built in the Greek Revival style in 1835, its portico and belfry were added in 1855. The original pews remain. The village, named for an early settler's hometown in Massachusetts, is seated picturesquely above the river far below to the south.

35.1   Turn RIGHT onto Remsen Road at the blinking yellow light.

In less than a quarter mile, you'll encounter I-71 again, running north and south beneath Remsen Road.

36.7   Turn LEFT onto Stony Hill Road.

37.5   At the Stop sign, continue STRAIGHT, crossing Ledge Road (OH 3).

37.9   At the Stop sign, continue STRAIGHT on Stony Hill Road, crossing Weymouth Road (OH 606).

39.7   Turn RIGHT onto Bellus Road.

The Buzzard Scoreboard keeps record of each turkey vulture sighted by the thousands who gather to welcome them back to Hinckley each March.

After nearly forty miles of vigorous pedaling, you'll be gratified to know that the hills are in your favor, almost through the end of the tour. Take care when freewheeling down this hill, for a Stop sign comes up in a little over a mile.

40.8   At the Stop sign, continue STRAIGHT on Bellus Road, crossing Ridge Road (OH 3 and 94).

Be prepared for another Stop sign in a mile.

41.8 **At the Stop sign at the bottom of hill, continue STRAIGHT on Bellus Road, crossing Hinckley Hills Road.**

42.0 **Pass the West Drive entrance to the park and pull over to the bike path as it crosses the bridge over the spillway area; bear to the RIGHT, getting onto the All-Purpose Trail that leads into the bathhouse parking lot.**

In addition to the bathhouse, the spillway pool area has a concession stand during the summer season. The picnic area here is a delightful place for a long or short rest, with the water pouring over the dam making an attractive backdrop. The guarded pool below the dam is open for swimming from 9 AM to 10:30 PM from Memorial Day to Labor Day.

42.2 **Turn LEFT into the parking lot, exiting the lot at the Stop sign; cross East Drive to continue on the All-Purpose Trail on the left side of East Drive.**

Here you'll begin a half-mile uphill, where you'll get a good view of Hinckley Lake below on your right. The lake is stocked with pike, largemouth bass, channel catfish, crappies, and bullheads. Rowboats, canoes, and pedalboats can be rented from the boathouse located on the opposite side of the lake off West Drive. It is open from March 15 to October 31.

43.1 **At the sign "Stop Walk Bike," turn RIGHT and walk your bike across East Drive, continuing on the All-Purpose Trail as it goes along the right side of State Road.**

The trail goes downhill, past the Whipps Ledges picnic area on the left, which offers water, pit toilets, tables, and a shelter house. There are marked trails to the ledges themselves, lush with vegetation due to the water-holding qualities of the sandstone ledges.

After the trail carries you across the Hinckley Lake inlet via a trail bridge, it begins to climb out of the valley.

43.5 **Turn RIGHT into West Drive and Buzzard's Roost parking area.**

Bicycle Repair Services

Brunswick Schwinn Cyclery, 15029 Pearl Road, Brunswick, OH 44136 (216) 572–2920.

Brunswick Bicycle and Repair, 3335 Center Road, Brunswick, OH 44121 (216) 225–6167.

Medina Bicycle Shop, 322 East Smith Road, Medina, OH 44256 (216) 723–4027.

Murray's Bicycle Shop, 141 West Smith Road, Medina, OH 44256 (216) 725–5902.

Wadsworth Bike & Stuff, 141 Main Street, Wadsworth, OH 44281 (216) 334–6361.

20

Three-Day College Loop

108 miles; easy to moderate cycling
level to hilly terrain; about 6 miles unpaved
County Maps: Lorain, Ashland, Wayne, Medina

Western Reserve pioneers brought with them a peculiar combination of conservative respect for their traditional New England roots and a passionate individualism that often led to the support of radical causes. Both notions found their greatest expression through the institutes of higher learning that the settlers established almost as soon as they arrived. Indeed, the site of Oberlin was total wilderness in 1833 when the spot was selected by two fervent ministers, Philo Stewart and John J. Shipherd, to train Christian teachers and leaders for the West dedicated to "the plainest living and the highest thinking." The College of Wooster was founded in 1866 by Presbyterians, and Ashland College, in 1878 by the United Brethren. Filled with ardent prohibitionists and abolitionists, and coeducational from their inception, these institutions reflected a pioneer combination of austere discipline and radical politics that seems almost paradoxical to us in the late twentieth century. Yet, by taking advantage of a Western Reserve society that was in a state of cultural and intellectual flux, the founders of these "western" educational institutions were able to attempt experiments that would have been doomed from the start in the tradition-bound East.

This three-day tour permits visits to each of the college towns mentioned above, connected by pleasant and often effortless miles through a countryside almost as rural and sparsely populated as when the schools were founded. The route actually extends beyond the southern boundary of the Western Reserve for nearly half of its 108 miles, but the themes of hard work, religious fervor, and free thinking united Wooster and Ashland to their northern neighbor in Oberlin. This tour omits much of the historical and cultural detail found in other tour descriptions because of its length; however, the Chambers of Commerce in Lorain, Ashland, Medina, and Wooster can supply additional information.

Although three days is suggested, the route can be split into two days, or it can occupy an entire week, depending on your stamina and the amount of time spent sight-seeing. Campers as well as those who prefer indoor lodging can be accommodated. Possible lodging sites

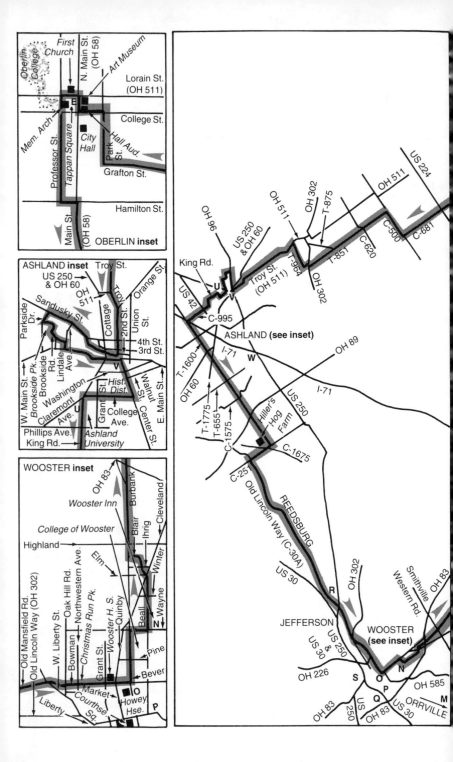

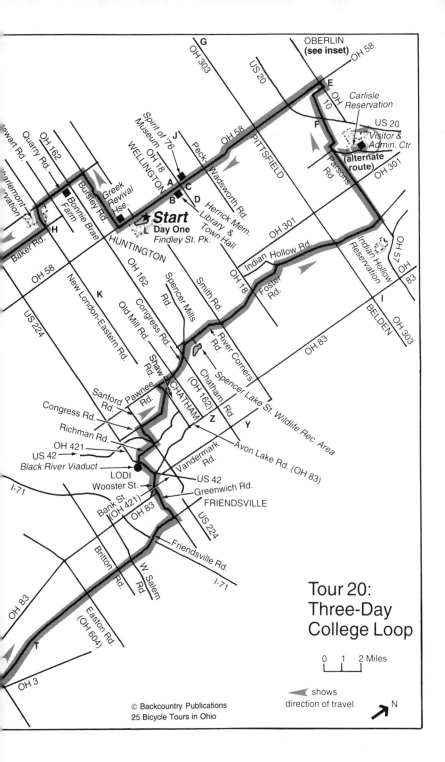

OBERLIN
(see inset)
OH 58

OH 303
G
US 20
E
OH 10

Spirit of '76
Museum
WELLINGTON
OH 18
Peck Wadsworth Rd.
J
OH 58
PITTSFIELD
Carlisle
Reservation
F
Parsons
Rd.
US 20
Visitor &
Admin. Ctr.
**(alternate
route)**
OH 301

Quarry Rd.
OH 162
Bursley Rd.
Greek
Revival
Hse.
A
C
B
D
Herrick Mem.
Library &
Town Hall
OH 301

Stewart Rd.
Charlemont
Reservation
Bonnie Brae
Farm
H
**Start
Day One**
L
Findley St. Pk.
HUNTINGTON
Indian Hollow Rd.
Foster
Rd.
Indian Hollow
Reservation
OH 57
OH 83

Baker Rd.
OH 58
OH 162
New London-Eastern Rd.
Spencer Mills
Rd.
Smith Rd.
OH 18
I
BELDEN
OH 303

US 224
K
Congress Rd.
Old Mill Rd.
Shaw
Rd.
River Corners
Rd.
Spencer Lake St. Wildlife Rec. Area
Chatham Rd
OH 83

Sanford
Rd.
Pawnee
Rd.
CHATHAM
(OH 162)
Z
Y

Congress Rd.
Richman Rd.
OH 421
US 42
Black River Viaduct
LODI
Wooster St.
Bank St.
(OH 421)
Vandermark
Rd.
Avon Lake Rd. (OH 83)
US 42
Greenwich Rd.
FRIENDSVILLE
US 224

I-71
OH 83
Britton
Rd.
W. Salem
Rd.
Friendsville Rd.
I-71

OH 83
T
Easton Rd.
(OH 604)
OH 3

**Tour 20:
Three-Day
College Loop**

0   1   2 Miles

shows
direction of travel

N

© Backcountry Publications
25 Bicycle Tours in Ohio

have been included in the tour description, and additional campsites and overnight accommodations for each county are listed at the end. It is recommended that you contact the Chambers of Commerce in each area for updated listings.

The route begins at the beach parking lot of Findley State Park, which is to the left of the park entrance. The park is on OH 58, 11 miles south of Oberlin, which is about 35 miles southwest of downtown Cleveland. You can reach Oberlin and OH 58 by taking OH 10 southwest from Exit 9 of the Ohio Turnpike, then taking the OH 511 exit to Oberlin. (Although many maps still show OH 10 leading to Oberlin, it has now been changed to OH 511.)

0.0 Turn LEFT out of the parking lot onto the park road.

0.1 Take the RIGHT arm of the Y-junction, which leads out of the park.

0.2 At the Stop sign, where the park entrance makes a T-junction with OH 58, turn LEFT (south) on OH 58.

OH 58 is flat and straight with no berm but relatively little traffic for a state highway. It passes through wooded areas with intermittent dwellings. One of these, 1.5 miles into the tour is an interesting pilastered Greek Revival house built about 1840.

1.6 Turn RIGHT onto Bursley Road.

Bursley is relatively flat, straight, and narrow with cultivated farmland on both sides. The lack of traffic makes it ideal for bicycling.

4.6 Turn LEFT onto Quarry Road (no Stop sign).

Quarry Road is so narrow that it is more like a paved bike path or a lane, with gentle dips and rises much like Bursley.

5.5 At the Stop sign, continue STRAIGHT on Quarry Road, crossing OH 162.

In three-quarters mile is Bonnie Brae Farm, a standardbred horse farm established just after the turn of the century. The marble headstone near the road is for the outstanding sire, "The Widower."

6.6 At the Stop sign, continue STRAIGHT on Quarry Road, crossing Stewart Road; immediately afterwards is another Stop sign in front of the Akron, Canton & Youngstown Railroad crossing.

In a quarter mile, Quarry Road becomes unpaved for a little over half a mile.

7.5 At the Stop sign, turn LEFT onto New London-Eastern Road.

The road goes through the Charlemont Reservation of the Lorain County Metropark System, which encompasses 540 acres of undeveloped land where pheasant and rabbit hunting is permitted in season.

8.6 Turn RIGHT onto Baker Road.

For nearly half a mile, Baker is poorly paved and only one-lane wide. After crossing into Ashland County, the road becomes County Road 681, and it widens into two lanes where the paving improves considerably.

11.4 At the Stop sign, continue STRAIGHT on County Road 681, crossing US 224.

The roads in Ashland County are numbered but unnamed.

13.8 At the T-junction, turn RIGHT onto County Road 500.

In neighboring Richland county to the west where roads do have names, this route is called Base Line Road, the southern boundary of the Western Reserve. This section goes through beautiful farmland grazed by dairy cattle.

15.4 Turn LEFT onto Township Road 851.

This road is generally unpaved, although paving usually appears in front of homes or former home sites.

16.9 At the Stop sign, continue STRAIGHT on Township Road 851, crossing County Road 620.

Because the road continues generally unpaved and begins to get hilly, it becomes more difficult to negotiate.

18.6 At the Y-junction, continue STRAIGHT on Township Road 851 as Township Road 875 goes to the right.

Township Road 851 now becomes paved. Within a mile, you'll find yourself in steeper hill country.

20.0 At the Stop sign, continue STRAIGHT on Township Road 851, crossing OH 302; the road now becomes Township Road 964 and becomes unpaved.

Township Road 964 makes three, right-angle turns through very rural countryside. The pavement picks up in a little over a mile.

21.5 At the Stop sign, turn LEFT onto OH 511, which becomes Troy Street.

In a little under 3 miles, you'll reach the outskirts of the city of Ashland. This state highway will be rather busy with traffic.

24.6 Continue STRAIGHT on Troy Street as OH 511 goes off to the right.

25.1 At the Stop sign, continue STRAIGHT on Troy Street, crossing Fourth Street.

25.2 At the traffic light, continue STRAIGHT on Troy Street, crossing Third Street; at the next Stop sign, turn RIGHT onto one-way

Second Street (a "Do Not Enter" sign prevents cars from continuing straight).

25.3 **At the Stop sign, continue STRAIGHT onto OH 96 (Sandusky Street), crossing Cottage Street, which is also US 250/OH 60/OH 511.**

This is a difficult intersection because there is no light here.

Originally called Uniontown, Ashland was named for the Kentucky home of Henry Clay. At this intersection is the Ashland County Courthouse, built in 1928 in the late Neo-classical or art deco style popular at the time. Inside is a plaque dedicated to native son Senator Edmund Ross, whose vote saved President Johnson from impeachment in 1868.

25.5 **At the blinking yellow light, continue STRAIGHT on OH 96 (Sandusky Street).**

26.0 **At the traffic light, turn LEFT onto Parkside Drive (following the sign for Brookside Park).**

Once inside the park, you'll cross a one-lane bridge and ride around to the left, then to the right, where you'll see the Johnny Appleseed Monument. The memorial was erected in 1915 by local schoolchildren for folk hero John Chapman, who lived for a time in the area of Ashland College. Following the "Keep Right" sign in the small traffic island, you'll continue around to the left, taking the one-way road to the left, called Brookside Road. The park has picnic shelters, restrooms, tennis courts, and a swimming pool.

26.4 **Turn RIGHT onto Lindale Avenue.**

26.5 **At the three-way Stop sign, turn LEFT onto West Main Street.**

26.9 **At the traffic light, continue STRAIGHT on West Main Street, crossing Claremont Avenue.**

27.1 **At the traffic light, turn RIGHT onto Center Street (OH 511 and 60).**

27.2 **At the traffic light, continue STRAIGHT on Center Street, crossing Washington Street.**

This area is the Ashland Historic District, which is on the National Register of Historic Places. At 302 Center Street is the Conrad Bockley Bed and Breakfast (see list at end of tour). The Ashland County Historical Society at 414 Center Street is in an 1859 Georgian Revival house and carriage house. Walking tour maps of the district are available within.

27.4 **At the traffic light, continue STRAIGHT on Center Street, crossing Walnut Street.**

27.5   Turn RIGHT onto College Avenue.

27.9   At the traffic light, continue STRAIGHT on College Avenue, crossing Grant Street.

Here you'll begin to see the buildings of Ashland University. Begun as Ashland College in 1878 by the Brethren Church, it is one of the few colleges in Ohio that still retains its religious affiliation. Many of the impressive buildings, such as the Hugo Young Theatre at this intersection, are modern.

28.0   Turn LEFT onto King Road.

28.4   At the four-way Stop sign, continue STRAIGHT on King Road, crossing Phillips Avenue.

28.6   At the four-way Stop sign, continue STRAIGHT on King Road, crossing Katherine Avenue.

The route soon becomes very rural, with more barns seen than auto traffic. In a bit under half a mile, you'll begin a downhill, with the Countryside Horse Farm at the bottom of the hill on the left.

29.3   At the Stop sign, continue STRAIGHT on what is now called County Road 995, crossing US 42.

In a little over a mile, you'll cross over I-71.

30.5   Just after the overpass, turn LEFT onto Township Road 1600.

31.7   At the next two Stop signs, continue STRAIGHT on Township Road 1600, crossing OH 511 and OH 60.

33.2   At the Stop sign, continue STRAIGHT on Township Road 1600, crossing Township Road 1775.

Township Road 1600 continues perfectly straight, with gentle downhills, exquisite farmland, and splendid vistas of sheep and white and red barns amid clusters of trees.

34.1   At the Stop sign, continue STRAIGHT on Township Road 1600, crossing Township Road 655.

At the northeast corner of the intersection is an old schoolhouse, one of many you'll see throughout this tour. The road has a downhill grade with several gentle inclines.

35.1   At the Stop sign, continue STRAIGHT on Township Road 1600, crossing County Road 1575.

36.2   At the Stop sign, continue STRAIGHT on Township Road 1600, crossing OH 89.

In about 1.5 miles, you'll pass Hiller's Hog Farm on the right, an engaging sight with large swine grazing like corpulent, fleeceless sheep.

38.0 **At the Stop sign and T-junction, turn RIGHT onto County Road 251.**

38.2 **At the Stop sign, continue STRAIGHT on County Road 251, crossing County Road 1675.**

County Road 251 becomes a less-than-ideal limestone surface for half a mile, with some significant hills.

39.2 **At the T-junction, turn LEFT onto County Road 30-A.**

30-A, called Old Lincoln Way, is a well-paved, undulating ribbon of highway carrying you into Wayne County. The road affords fine views of distant spaces because most of the area is open farmland with patches of woodland. In two miles you'll have a pleasant and long, but not steep, downhill where you'll see "Hine's Belgians," a Belgian horse farm with a century-old Italianate farmhouse.

This route takes you through the small Wayne County communities of Reedsburg and Jefferson. Wayne County, one of the most fertile counties in the nation, is the home of the Ohio Agricultural Research and Development Center, operated by the Ohio State University. Not surprisingly, the county, along with neighboring Holmes, Stark, and Tuscarawas counties, also boasts one of the world's highest Amish populations. More information on the Amish of Ohio is found in tour 9.

47.9 **At the Stop sign and blinking red light, continue STRAIGHT on Old Lincoln Way, crossing the divided US 250.**

49.3 **Make a sudden LEFT turn onto Old Mansfield Road, shortly after the City of Wooster Water Treatment Plant (Old Lincoln Way continues straight to merge with OH 302).**

In half a mile, you'll enter the Wooster city limits, with cornfields slowly giving way to small industry.

50.6 **At the traffic light, continue STRAIGHT as the road's name changes to Bowman Street, crossing West Liberty Street.**

You'll have a quarter-mile uphill at this point.

50.9 **At the Stop sign surmounted by a blinking red light, continue STRAIGHT on Bowman, crossing Oak Hill Road.**

51.0 **At the Stop sign, continue STRAIGHT on Bowman Street, crossing Northwestern Avenue.**

The road becomes smooth brick for one block, after which you will see the attractive City of Wooster Christmas Run Park on the left.

51.4   At the four-way Stop sign, continue STRAIGHT on Bowman, crossing Grant Street.

51.5   At the traffic light, continue STRAIGHT on Bowman, crossing Quinby/Market Street.

A right turn here onto Market Street takes you to the center of downtown Wooster and the courthouse square area. The interesting castellated building on the northeast corner of this intersection is Wooster High School.

51.7   At the traffic light, turn LEFT onto Bever Street.

A quarter mile to the right on Bever is Howey House, a bed and breakfast lodging in an 1849 Gothic Revival home replete with antiques (see list at end of tour).

Going north on Bever, you'll face a steady uphill. By the time you reach Pine Street, you'll begin seeing the light stone buildings of the College of Wooster, most of which are in the Gothic Revival style, complete with battlements.

52.3   Turn RIGHT onto West Wayne Street

You'll see the sign for the College of Wooster, founded 1866. Presbyterian minister James Reed chose this city as the site of his college; it opened its doors to thirty men and four women in 1870.

52.4   At the light, turn LEFT onto Beall (pronounced "bell") Street.

The street commemorates Revolutionary War General Reasin Beall, whose fine 1815 Georgian style brick home is open to the public a few blocks south of here at 546 East Bowman Street. The town of Wooster was named for another hero from that same war, General David Wooster, and the county itself is named for a third Continental Army general, Mad Anthony Wayne.

Continuing straight on West Wayne here would bring you to the Wooster Inn in a quarter mile. This colonial style bed and breakfast has seventeen sleeping rooms and a gourmet dining room (see list at end of tour).

52.8   At the traffic light, continue STRAIGHT on Beall Street, crossing Winter Street.

53.0   At the traffic light, turn LEFT onto Elm Drive; this left can be a little tricky since most traffic will continue straight on Beall, which becomes Cleveland Road.

53.1   At the Y-junction, take the RIGHT arm, which is Blair Boulevard.

53.3   At the blinking yellow light, continue STRAIGHT on Blair, crossing Ihrig Avenue. Blair then curves around to the left.

53.4 **At the Stop sign, turn RIGHT onto Burbank Road (OH 302).**

53.5 **At the traffic light, continue STRAIGHT on Burbank, crossing Highland Avenue.**

54.2 **At the Y-junction, take the RIGHT arm, which is Friendsville Road.**

54.4 **At the traffic light, continue STRAIGHT on Friendsville Road, crossing OH 83.**

55.5 **At the Stop sign and blinking red light, continue STRAIGHT on Friendsville Road, crossing Smithville Western Road.**
Friendsville Road passes through acres and acres of cropland and has little traffic and only a few, easy hills. In three miles, you'll pass Beck's Family Campground (see list at end of tour).

61.5 **At the Stop sign, continue STRAIGHT on Friendsville Road, crossing Easton Road (OH 604).**
In 1.5 miles is an attractive Holstein farm. Beef and dairy cattle are the focus of Wayne County agriculture.

63.5 **At the Stop sign, continue STRAIGHT on Friendsville Road, crossing Britton.**

64.2 **At the Stop sign, continue STRAIGHT on Friendsville Road, crossing West Salem Street.**
As the road crosses the Medina County line, it becomes Medina County Road 35. You are now back in the Western Reserve, where the hills become steeper and more challenging.

67.2 **At the Stop sign and blinking red light, turn LEFT onto Greenwich Road (County Road 97).**
This intersection is Friendsville, named for the Quakers who settled here. In 1.5 miles as the road enters Lodi, it curves around to the right and joins with OH 83 from which point it is called Wooster Street.

69.5 **At the traffic light, continue STRAIGHT on Wooster, crossing Church Street.**
Lodi, Medina County's oldest community, has an attractive small village square complete with gazebo. To the right of the square is a typical Victorian shopping block.

69.6 **At the traffic light, go STRAIGHT onto Bank Street (OH 421).**
Bank Street climbs as you leave town, leveling out in about half a mile.

70.6 **Just before the road curves under Black River Viaduct, make a sharp RIGHT onto West Street, which becomes Richman Road.**

The Black River Viaduct, built by the Baltimore and Ohio Railroad between 1892 and 1907, is considered an architectural masterpiece and is on the National Register of Historic Places.

71.7 **At the Stop sign, continue STRAIGHT on Richman Road (County Road 69), crossing US 224/OH 42.**

71.8 **Turn LEFT onto unpaved Sanford Road.**
The road becomes paved in half a mile.

72.9 **At the Stop sign, turn RIGHT onto Congress Road (County Road 29).**

75.3 **At the Stop sign, turn LEFT onto Shaw Road (County Road 99).**

75.7 **At the Stop sign, turn RIGHT onto Pawnee Road (County Road 28).**

The combination of architectural styles in the Wellington Town Hall make it one of the most photographed administrative buildings in the Reserve.

76.4 **At the five-way Stop sign, continue STRAIGHT onto Congress Road (still County Road 29), crossing Old Mill Road (Pawnee Road ends).**

77.5 **At the Stop sign, continue STRAIGHT on Congress Road, crossing Chatham Road (OH 162); Congress now becomes Spencer Mills Road (County Road 77).**

78.2 **At the Stop sign, turn RIGHT onto River Corners Road.**
In half a mile, Spencer Lake Road on the right leads into Spencer Lake State Wildlife Recreation Area, a wildlife and sport fish restoration area.

80.2 **At the Stop sign, continue STRAIGHT on River Corners Road as it becomes Foster Road, crossing Smith Road.**
You are now back in Lorain County.

82.4 **At the Stop sign, continue STRAIGHT on Foster Road, crossing OH 18.**

84.1 **Foster Road ends at this point, and Indian Hollow Road comes in from the left; by continuing STRAIGHT, you will remain on Indian Hollow Road.**

87.2 **At the Stop sign, continue STRAIGHT on Indian Hollow Road, crossing OH 303.**

89.8 **Turn LEFT onto Parsons Road.**
A right turn at this point takes you to Indian Hollow Reservation, a 291-acre facility with a nature trail, picnic shelters, well water, and toilets.

91.7 **At the Stop sign, continue STRAIGHT on Parsons Road, crossing OH 301.**
In two miles, a right turn onto Nickel Plate-Diagonal Road leads, in another two miles, to the Visitor and Administrative Center of the Lorain County Metropolitan Park District in the Carlisle Reservation. Covering 1,721 acres near the geographic center of the county, the reservation includes stocked ponds, hiking trails, shelters, baseball fields, a golf course, and an equestrian center. The Visitor Center is vast, with a nationally recognized Wildlife Observation Center, gift shop, restrooms, and drinking water.
Three miles past the reservation turn-off, Parsons Road enters the Oberlin residential area and becomes Grafton Street.

96.8 **Turn RIGHT onto South Park Street as Grafton Street ends.**

97.3 At the traffic light, turn LEFT onto East College Street.

97.5 At the traffic light, turn RIGHT onto South Main Street.

A turn to the left here will take you through "downtown" Oberlin.

Tappan Square is on your left, named for Arthur Tappan who promised financial backing to the new college if it would admit Negroes, which it did in 1835. Four women, admitted in 1837, were the first women in the country to receive A.B. degrees. At the southeast corner of the square is Oberlin Inn and gardens (see list at end of tour). Hall Auditorium on the square's east side was built by alumnus Charles Martin Hall, who discovered the electrolytic process for making aluminum and founded ALCOA. The 1953 building was called by the Cleveland *Plain Dealer* "the most controversial building in Ohio." The Allen Memorial Art Museum, on the northeast corner, opened in 1917 and houses the country's finest college art collection.

97.7 At the traffic light, turn LEFT onto Lorain Street (OH 511).

The First Church in Oberlin is on the right, founded in 1833, the same year this college community was hacked out of the wilderness. The Greek Revival building dates from 1842 and probably had the largest seating capacity in the Reserve at the time.

97.8 At the traffic light, turn LEFT onto Professor Street.

The Memorial Arch on the square was erected in 1903 to commemorate the Oberlin missionaries killed in the Boxer Rebellion in China. The thirteen-acre square once held five college buildings, the last of which was razed in 1927. A plaque on the arch notes that all of Oberlin College is on the National Register of Historic Places.

98.0 At the traffic light, continue STRAIGHT on Professor Street, crossing West College Street.

98.7 At the Stop sign and T-junction, turn LEFT onto West Hamilton Street.

98.9 At the Stop sign, turn RIGHT onto South Main Street, which becomes Ashland-Oberlin Road (OH 58).

99.8 At the traffic light, continue STRAIGHT on OH 58, crossing US 20.

In 2 miles, at the intersection with OH 303, is the community of Pittsfield, which was nearly wiped off the map by a tornado in 1965.

106.3 At the traffic light, after crossing several sets of railroad tracks, continue STRAIGHT on OH 58 (now Main Street), crossing OH 18.

Wellington is a comfortable Western Reserve village with about two hundred buildings listed on the National Register of Historic Places.

One of the nation's cheese capitals at the end of the last century, Wellington once had fifty-eight cheese factories within ten miles of the village.

Just past OH 18, on the left, is the Herrick Memorial Library, which houses a collection of paintings by Archibald Willard, painter of the famous *Spirit of '76*. The Spirit of '76 Museum at 201 North Main Street is a local history museum with walking tour maps of the village. Next to the library, facing the Willard Memorial Square, is the town hall, one of the most photographed in the Reserve. A pleasing amalgam of Byzantine, Greek, Gothic and Moorish architecture, it was built in 1885.

The American House Hotel occupied the site of the present library and was the focus of the Oberlin-Wellington Rescue court case. To protest the Fugitive Slave Law, a group of Oberlin and Wellington abolitionists rescued runaway slave John Price from the American House. He was being held there by slavecatchers after having been forcibly taken from Oberlin, a recognized haven for runaways. Twenty-four Oberlin residents and thirteen people from Wellington were indicted; however, popular sympathy was such that all were released from the Cuyahoga County jail after almost three months, being received in their hometowns with much fanfare.

108.7 Turn LEFT into Findley State Park.

Chambers of Commerce
Lorain County Visitor's Bureau, Inc., P.O. Box 567, Lorain, (216) 245–5282.
Ashland Area Chamber of Commerce, 508 Claremont Avenue, Ashland, (419) 281–4584.
Wayne County Visitor and Convention Bureau, P.O. Box 77, Wooster, (216) 264–1800.
Medina Area Chamber of Commerce, P.O. Box 160, Medina, (216) 723–8773.

Lodgings and Accommodations

Lorain County Lodgings
* A. The Deacon Edward West Home, bed and breakfast, 1872 Italianate home, downtown Wellington, (216) 674–5703.
* B. The Robinson-Hoyt Cottage, bed and breakfast, 1899 Queen Anne home, 238 South Main Street, Wellington, (216) 647–6219.
* C. The Wellington Inn, small inn plus restaurant, 214 Main Street, Wellington, (216) 647–3459.
  D. The Hillcrest Motel, 43885 OH 18 East, Wellington, (216) 647–2769.
* E. Oberlin College Inn, luxury inn, Main Street, Oberlin, (216) 775–1111.
  F. Sunset Motel-Oberlin, 44077 US 20, Oberlin, (216) 774–1629.

Lorain County Campgrounds
  G. Schaun Acres, 51468 OH 303, Oberlin, (216) 775–7122.

H. Clare-Mar Lakes, New London-Eastern Road, Wellington, (216) 647–3318.
I. The Maples, 17273 OH 83, Belden, (216) 926–3700.
J. Panther Trails Campground, 48081 Peck-Wadsworth Road, Wellington, (216) 647–5453.
K. Rustic Lake Campgrounds, 44901 New London-Eastern Road, Huntington, (216) 647–3804.
* L. Findley State Park, 25381 OH 58, Wellington, (216) 647–4490.

Wayne County Lodgings and Campground

M. Grandma's House Bed and Breakfast, 5598 Chippewa Road, Orrville, (216) 682–5112.
* N. The Wooster Inn, 801 East Wayne Avenue, Wooster, (216) 264–2341.
* O. Howey House Bed and Breakfast, 240 North Bever Street, Wooster, (216) 264–8321.
P. Best Western Gateway Inn, 243 East Liberty Street, Wooster, (216) 264–7750.
Q. EconoLodge, 2137 East Lincoln Way, Wooster, (216) 264–8883.
* R. Town and County Motel and Dining Room, Old Lincoln Way, Jefferson, (216) 264–5353.
S. LK Motel, 969 Timken Road, Wooster, (216) 264–9222.
* T. Beck's Family Campground, 8375 Friendsville Road, Wooster, (216) 345–9284.

Ashland County Lodging and Campground

* U. The Surrey Inn, 1065 Claremont, Ashland, (419) 289–7700.
* V. Conrad Bockley House Bed and Breakfast, 302 Center Street, Ashland, (419) 281–1898.
W. LK Motel, US 250 and I-71 Interchange, Ashland, (419) 281–0567.
X. Sloan's Hickory Lake Campground, 26 Perry Township Road, Rowsburg, (419) 869–7587.

Medina County Campgrounds

Y. Pier Lon Park, 5960 Vandermark Road, Lodi, (216) 667–2311.
Z. Sherwood Forest, Inc., 7454 Avon Lake Road, (216) 667–2156.

* Indicates lodgings found along the actual route.

Bicycle Repair Services

Ashland Schwinn Cyclery, 22 East Second Street, Ashland, OH 44805 (419) 289–1556.
Home Hardware, 140 Center Street, Ashland, OH 44805 (419) 281–4663.
John's Bicycle Shop, 15682 Avon-Belden Road, Grafton, OH 44044.
Bicycle Emporium, 16 South Main Street, Oberlin, OH 44074 (216) 775–2076.
Dale's Bicycle Specialties, 43239 US 20 East, Oberlin, OH 44074 (216) 774–8507.
Orrville Schwinn, 9658 West High Street, Orrville, OH 44667 (216) 682–1911.
Haidel's Schwinn, 4973 Cleveland Road, Wooster, OH 44691 (216) 345–7008.

21

Vermilion and the North Coast

26 miles; easy bicycling
Level terrain with some low hills
County maps: Lorain, Erie

In North America the phrase "from coast to coast" has traditionally meant from Atlantic to Pacific. However, officials of the Cleveland Convention Bureau, inspired by a bumper sticker marketed by the Western Specialty Company that read "The North Coast," recognized the image potential for northeastern Ohio in the idea of a coastline defined by Lake Erie. In 1980, "Cleveland on America's North Coast" and its accompanying sailboat-studded logo was registered as a trademark of the Cleveland Convention Bureau, and within ten years of its conception, the north coast notion took hold. Today, the north coast trademark has become for the greater Cleveland area what the "Big Apple" emblem is for New York City.

The north coast concept received official sanction when the Department of Commerce's Office of Coastal and Resource Management approved the creation of Old Woman Creek National Estuarine Sanctuary. Located some forty miles west of Cleveland, this research reserve, which houses the offices of the Ohio Center for Coastal Wetland Studies, is the first fresh water estuary to be recognized and preserved in the country.

Eight miles east of Old Woman Creek, the little lakeside city of Vermilion has borrowed the coastal concept for its travel and tourism promotions, calling itself "the heart of the North Coast." Although the developers of the idea justly assert that Cleveland is the central core of the country's newly recognized "north coast," historically and geologically the smaller city has some justification for its claim. For several decades after the opening of the Western Reserve, it remained highly uncertain which Lake Erie settlement would win the status of chief Ohio port. It at first looked like Sandusky, Huron, Lorain, or Vermilion would far surpass Cleveland, with its harbor of sandbars and its unhealthy malarial swampland at the Cuyahoga's mouth. Although the construction of the canal through Cleveland turned the tide in that city's favor, the numerous ship captains' homes that line the Vermilion streets attest to the strong competition it once gave its larger rival. The decision to place the Great Lakes Museum in Vermilion is another testament to its prominent and prosperous history, and today it has the distinction of being the largest small boat harbor on the Great Lakes. But perhaps Vermilion most merits its claim as the north coast's heart because of its red shale bluffs along the Vermilion River, the warm, red tones of which inspired French explorers to give the area its name.

In addition to visits to Vermilion, Old Woman Creek, and the Vermilion River Valley, this tour provides miles of excellent bicycling along the north coast. It begins about four miles south of Vermilion, which is thirty-five miles west of downtown Cleveland, and about two miles east of the Lorain-Erie County border at the south entrance to the Mill Hollow-Bacon Woods Park. The south entrance is off North Ridge Road, itself off Vermilion Road. Vermilion Road can be reached via OH 2. Exit 8 of the I-80/I-90 turnpike provides access to OH 2.

0.0   At the Stop sign, turn LEFT out of the parking lot onto unmarked North Ridge Road.

The Mill Hollow House Museum, a two-and-a-half-story Greek Revival residence that is probably the oldest in Lorain County, is located at this entrance. It was built by Benjamin Bacon, a businessman and justice of the peace who came here from Stockbridge, Massachusetts, in 1817. The home, which was placed on the National Register in 1976, is open Sundays, May through October, from 1 PM to 5 PM. This section of Mill Hollow-Bacon Woods Park has pit toilets, picnic facilities, and water coolers.

Across from the house is the Shale Cliff Trail, a short walk leading to the red cliffs of the Vermilion River. The cliffs are actually composed of a sixty-five-foot base of hard black shale, overlain by fifteen to thirty feet of soft red shale. It is this smaller layer that accounts for the red coloring of the cliffs, for rains wash red-colored mud over the lower black shale.

Just west of the park entrance on North Ridge Road you'll see the remains of Bacon's mill race. A narrow gully to your left leads to a pipe that carries the water, when any is present, under the park. Immediately opposite the mill race, among the woods and poison ivy on the right side of the road, are a few foundation stones of the mill itself.

North Ridge Road climbs out of the Vermilion River Valley for about a quarter mile before leveling off in pleasant farm country. Located atop ancient lakeshore lines, ridge roads are usually level and slightly elevated above the surrounding countryside.

0.8   Turn RIGHT onto Gore Orphanage Road.

For about three-quarters of a mile, Gore Orphanage Road travels along the west perimeter of Mill Hollow-Bacon Woods Park; the tree-filled gorge formed by the Vermilion River is along the right side of the road. In another quarter mile, Gore Orphanage makes a turn to the left and becomes Darrow Road. Darrow is an excellent road for biking, largely level with small dips and rises and virtually traffic free.

2.5   Turn RIGHT onto West River Road.

West River Road remains rural and beautiful for biking even after crossing the Vermilion Corporation limit after one mile. In another mile, you'll begin to see, on the right, parts of the expansive small boat docking area for which Vermilion is famous. Shortly you'll reach the Vermilion Public Boat Facility, which affords good views of the harbor boat dock area, seasonal home to some two thousand pleasure boats.

4.8   At the Stop sign, turn LEFT onto Ohio Street, just opposite the north entrance to the boat ramp.

Ohio Street, developed somewhat later than those closer to the lake, has homes dating from the1880s.

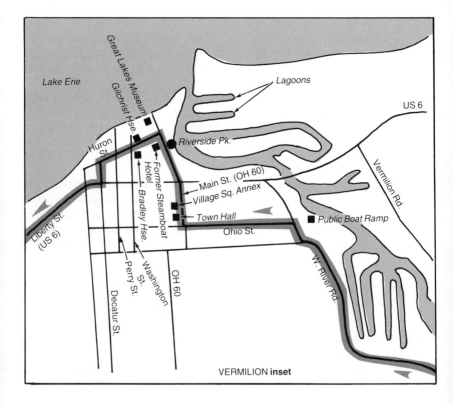

VERMILION **inset**

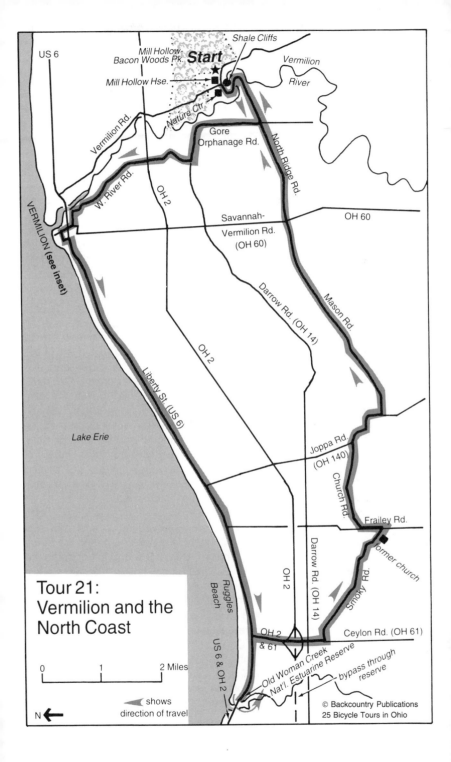

US 6

Mill Hollow-
Bacon Woods Pk. **Start**

Shale Cliffs

Vermilion
River

Mill Hollow Hse.

Vermilion Rd.

Nature Ctr.

Gore
Orphanage Rd.

North Bridge Rd.

W. River Rd.

OH 2

OH 60

Savannah-
Vermilion Rd.
(OH 60)

VERMILION (see inset)

Darrow Rd. (OH 14)

Mason Rd.

Liberty St. (US 6)

OH 2

Lake Erie

Joppa Rd.
(OH 140)

Church Rd.

Frailey Rd.

former church

Darrow Rd. (OH 14)

Smoky Rd.

Tour 21:
Vermilion and the
North Coast

Ruggles
Beach

OH 2

Ceylon Rd. (OH 61)

OH 2
& 61

0   1   2 Miles

US 6 & OH 2

Old Woman Creek
Nat'l. Estuarine Reserve

bypass through
reserve

© Backcountry Publications
25 Bicycle Tours in Ohio

N ◀

◀ shows
direction of travel

5.2   At the Stop sign, turn RIGHT onto Main Street (OH 60).

At this intersection are the 1883 Victorian Gothic Town Hall and the old Opera House, bordering the town square. Main Street bisects the square, on the northwest corner of which is the Village Square Annex. Formerly two private homes, the Annex, at 720 North Main Street, is now a restaurant and bed and breakfast establishment. Call owners Ron and Elizabeth Millett at (216) 967–8636 for reservations.

5.3   At the light, continue STRAIGHT on Main Street, crossing Liberty Street.

This intersection marks the heart of Harbor Town 1837, a shopping area renovated to recall the year of the town's incorporation. A walking map of Vermilion is available from the Chamber of Commerce on Liberty Street between Main and Exchange streets.

5.5   Turn LEFT onto Huron Street.

A right turn at this intersection will take you to a small riverside park with outstanding views of Vermilion's remarkable harbor.

Straight ahead you'll notice that Main Street continues directly to the municipal deck that overlooks Lake Erie. To the left of this deck are the buildings belonging to the Great Lakes Museum and Historical Society. The society was moved here from the Cleveland Public Library in 1953 when the Wakefield family donated the lakeside mansion at 480 Main Street. One wing of the museum has been built along the lines of a ship, with its "bridge" overlooking the lake, complete with navigation equipment and an engine room console. Great Lakes memorabilia include everything from the timbers of Commodore Perry's flagship *Niagara* to a life ring from the *Edmund Fitzgerald.* The museum is open daily from 10 AM to 5 PM and is only open weekends in winter. Admission is charged.

The home on the southwest corner of this intersection, portions of which date from 1838, formerly served as a hotel and was variously known as the Steamboat Hotel, Well's Inn, and the Stage Coach Inn. Continuing further on Huron Street, you'll come to the beautiful Italianate Captain Gilchrist House, built in 1885. Formerly a major shipping and shipbuilding center, Vermilion has been the home port for forty-two ship captains. The abundance of white oak in the area forests made Vermilion a premium center for ship construction, with the first vessel launched from the Vermilion River in 1812. In 1837 the Army Corps of Engineers built permanent harbor facilities in Vermilion, enhancing its commercial opportunities.

In 1841, Captain Alva Bradley began building ships in Vermilion. As his fame and fortune grew, the pull of Cleveland became too strong and he moved there in 1859, bringing his shipyards nine years later. When he died in 1885 he was the most powerful man on the lakes. A benefactor of the Samuel Edison family, Alva Bradley was paid tribute for his generosity when the Edisons' youngest son, born in nearby Milan, Ohio, was named Thomas Alva in his honor. Bradley's first house, a small Greek Revival built in 1840, is on the south side of Huron Street at number 5679. Several of the other outstanding houses on Huron Street date from the 1840s during the period of Vermilion's greatest prosperity.

5.7   At the Stop sign, continue STRAIGHT on Huron Street, crossing Washington Street.
The next cross street is Perry Street, named for Oliver Hazard Perry, hero of the Battle of Lake Erie. Details of his story are included in tour 24.

5.8   Turn LEFT onto Decatur Street.

5.9   At the Stop sign, turn RIGHT onto Liberty Street, US 6.
US 6 begins here as a divided highway with moderate traffic, although there is often a bit of a berm. The road affords fine glimpses of the lake beyond charming lakefront homes. In a little over half a mile, the road narrows to two lanes and has a few gentle slopes.

In five and a half miles, you'll reach Ruggles Beach, just before the Cranberry Creek Marina. The southwesterly direction of the Lake Erie coastline places Ruggles Beach at the southernmost point in all the Great Lakes. When the Connecticut Land Company was planning the sales of its Western Reserve holdings, it misjudged the degree to which Erie tilts on a northeast-southwest axis. Studying the inaccurate maps of the day, the speculators optimistically determined that there was considerably more land in the Western Reserve than the three million acres it had purchased from the State of Connecticut. Some of the speculators formed an "Excess Company," planning to buy all the additional land they expected would be revealed once the land was surveyed. Surveyor Augustus Porter had the unhappy task of reporting to the Company that the land they were expecting to acquire was under the waters of a lake that dipped much further south than they had thought.

The beach is named for another surveyor, Almon Ruggles, who was hired in 1807 to survey the Firelands — present-day Erie and Huron counties. As a bonus for his work, Ruggles was promised a one-mile tract anywhere along the lakeshore, and he selected this point in Berlin Township, a spot historian Harlan Hatcher considered "in some respects certainly the fairest location in the Firelands." For more on the surveying of the Firelands, see tour 23.

12.8   At the light, continue STRAIGHT on US 6, which at this point is joined by OH 2.

In three-quarters of a mile is the entrance to the Old Woman Creek Nature Preserve and the National Estuarine Research Reserve. The entrance is on the left side of the road, so the turn can be tricky if there is much traffic. Be prepared to walk across if necessary.

The waters of the lake and the river mix at Old Woman Creek to form a third mixture chemically different from the other two, therefore creating a rare habitat worthy of closer study. The Sanctuary's comfortable visitor's center, open Wednesday through Sunday from 1 to 5 PM, has extensive explanatory displays, an aquarium, and nature artworks. This building also houses the offices of the Ohio Center for Coastal Wetland Studies. Restrooms and drinking fountains are available. A nature trail leads from the parking area to an observation deck, where shorebirds and waterfowl are frequently seen.

13.4   Reverse your direction along US 6 to return toward Vermilion.

14.1   Turn right onto OH 2 East and OH 61 South.

The farm markets and greenhouses seen along this route owe their existence to the proximity of Lake Erie, which tempers the climate here. Erie County's frost-free season stretches for some 175 to 200 days, over a month longer than Huron County directly to the south. Consequently, Erie County adds apple, peach, and grape production to its list of agricultural accomplishments.

14.7   Go STRAIGHT onto the overpass over OH 2, staying on OH 61, Ceylon Road. OH 2 formerly ended abruptly at OH 61.

15.3   Turn LEFT onto Smoky Road.

Smoky Road runs between vast fields of soybeans, corn, and market garden crops. The road curves occasionally but is quite flat and excellent for biking, save for a very steeply banked railroad crossing after about three-quarters of a mile. In another mile, the road begins some gentle twists and climbs through picturesque woodland.

17.4   At the T-junction and Stop sign, take the LEFT arm onto unmarked Frailey Road.

On the right at this intersection is a former church, now renovated into a private home.

17.6   At the Y-junction, take the RIGHT arm—Church Road—as Frailey Road continues straight.

19.1   At the three-way Stop sign, continue STRAIGHT where Church Road becomes Joppa Road. (Joppa comes in from the left.)

The Lake Erie shoreline, such as this portion outside the Great Lakes Museum in Vermilion, attracts bicyclists of all sizes.

19.8   At the Stop sign, turn LEFT onto Mason Road.
Mason Road is flat and surrounded by fruit tree orchards and fields of corn and soybeans.

23.3   At the Stop sign, continue STRAIGHT on Mason Road, crossing OH 60.
In one mile you'll enter Lorain County, where Mason becomes North Ridge Road.

25.1   Continue STRAIGHT on North Ridge Road, crossing Gore Orphanage Road.
In three-quarters of a mile, the road begins a curving downhill to the Mill Hollow Park entrance.

26.0   Turn RIGHT into the south entrance parking lot.
A tenth of a mile past this entrance, you'll cross the Vermilion gorge. Immediately to the left after the bridge is another picnic area with a nature center.

Bicycle Repair Services
Bill's Wheel Shoppe, 5523 South Street, Vermilion, OH 44089 (216) 967–2453.

22

Firelands—Erie County

24 miles; moderate cycling
Level to rolling terrain
County maps: Erie and Huron

"Agriculture throughout Ohio," wrote local historian James A. Ryan, "was at a discouraging low ebb prior to 1830." The problem was not due to the soil and climate, which were considerably better than what the settlers had left behind in New England. Nor was there a lack of skill or effort on the part of the pioneer farmers who quickly began to produce more grain, cattle, lumber, potash, and whiskey than they could consume. Nor was there a lack of enterprising spirit, for the newcomers were eager to exchange their produce for the eastern manufactured goods unobtainable on the undeveloped Reserve. The problem was the prohibitive cost of transporting produce from farms scattered about a vast wilderness, in a land totally devoid of serviceable roads and largely without navigable waterways. The Firelands, in particular, had widely dispersed settlements, because the land had been distributed by lottery to those whose Connecticut property had been burned by the British during the Revolutionary War. According to Ohio historian Harlan Hatcher, "Each family, or each little party, fought its way through the wilderness until it came to its assigned spot; and there, in the vast loneliness, perhaps fifteen or twenty miles from the nearest neighbor . . . it chopped out its own hole in the forest."

One such hole in the forest developed into the small village of Milan (pron. *My-lin*), an energetic and resourceful community situated in the central range of the Firelands. Milan was surrounded by highly productive forest and farmland but, like other settlements on the Reserve, was largely sequestered from its equally isolated neighbors. In the early 1820s, the Firelands' transplanted New Englanders, many of them with seafaring skills, conceived the notion of a canal to carry produce the eight miles north to Lake Erie. Unlike the Erie Canal then under construction or the proposed Ohio Canal, they wanted one that would admit actual Great Lakes vessels, not barges. Since the Huron River could handle large ship traffic as far as Abbot's Bridge five miles inland, the canal itself would only need to be three miles long. In 1824, the Ohio legislature passed an act allowing the construction of a ship canal from

Huron to Milan. Due to delays in selling stock in the proposed canal, construction did not begin until 1833, and by the time it was completed the total cost was $23,392, four times the original estimate. Despite this underestimate, five years after the optimistic opening of the canal on the Fourth of July 1839, $102,000 had been gathered in tolls, and stockholders had received $20,000 in dividends. By 1847, Milan found itself second only to the Russian port of Odessa in world shipment of wheat. Thirty-five thousand bushels of wheat were handled in a single day that year, and wagons waiting to unload at the canal basin formed a line six miles long. Fourteen warehouses crowded the basin area, and shipyards were built, drawing on the resources of the vast white oak forest in the vicinity. By 1848, however, shipments had dropped to one-quarter of the previous year, much of the trade having been absorbed by the advancing railroad. That same year, Milan refused to allow a railroad right-of-way through town, and the Cleveland to Sandusky line was routed through Norwalk four miles to the south. Canal trade limped along until 1868, when the dam that fed the Milan canal basin was destroyed.

For the modern tourist, the vestigial remains offer a tantalizing reminder of Milan in its banner years. Impressive Greek Revival homes, a single warehouse, hints of the old towpath, and the birthplace of Thomas Alva Edison, whose formative years were during Milan's heyday, are a charming backdrop to the peaceful present-day village. This route continues on to Huron, which, though eclipsed by Milan in the 1840s, continues today as an active Lake Erie port.

The tour begins in the parking lot of Edison Park on Berlin Street in Milan. Berlin Street can be reached via OH 113, about 1 mile east of the center of Milan. Milan is at the junction of US 250 and OH 113, about 12 miles southeast of Sandusky and 4 miles north of Norwalk. Exit 7 of the Ohio turnpike (about 50 miles west of Cleveland) takes you to US 250.

Much of this tour follows the route of the official Milan Canal Bikeway, sponsored by the Firelands Wheels Bicycle Club. You will see bikeway signs much of the time.

0.0   Turn RIGHT out of the Edison Park parking lot onto Berlin Street.
Restrooms and water are available at Edison Park, which also has picnic tables, shelters, tennis courts, and other recreational amenities. You'll begin on a slight uphill on Berlin Street.

On your left, toward the east end of the Milan cemetery (behind you as you ride), is the Fries family mausoleum. Valentine Fries located in Milan in 1849. He opened shipyards first in Milan, then at Abbott's Bridge on the Huron River. Located just opposite the canal entrance, the spot became known as Fries' Landing. Here Fries built a number of schooners, among them the *Golden Age,* the largest schooner ever built on the Great Lakes.

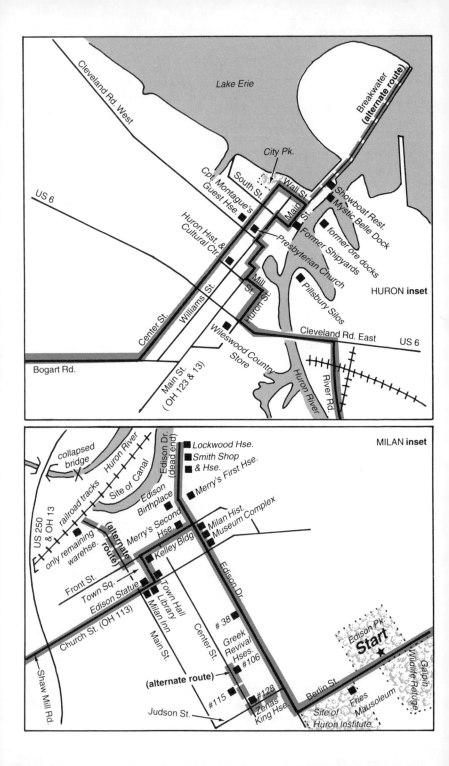

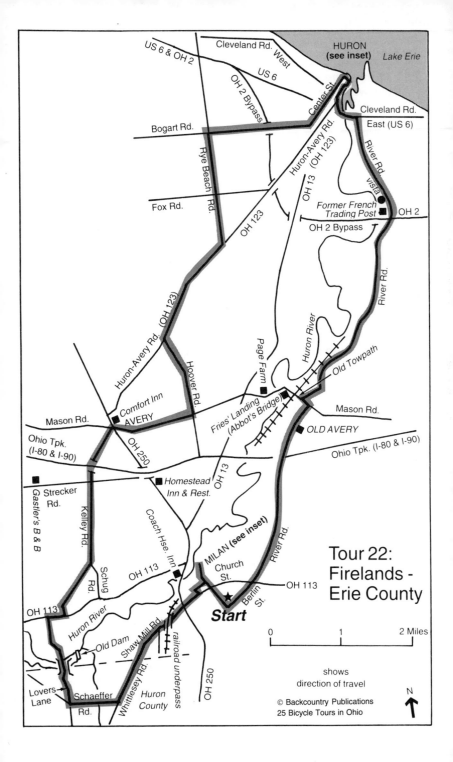

HURON
(see inset)

Lake Erie

Cleveland Rd. West

US 6 & OH 2

US 6

OH 2 Bypass

Center St.

Cleveland Rd.
East (US 6)

Bogart Rd.

Rye Beach Rd.

Huron-Avery Rd. (OH 123)

OH 13

River Rd.

vista

Former French
Trading Post

OH 2

Fox Rd.

OH 123

OH 2 Bypass

Huron-Avery Rd. (OH 123)

Hoover Rd.

Page Farm

Huron River

River Rd.

Old Towpath

Comfort Inn
AVERY

Fries' Landing
(Abbot's Bridge)

Mason Rd.

Mason Rd.

OLD AVERY

Ohio Tpk.
(I-80 & I-90)

OH 250

Ohio Tpk. (I-80 & I-90)

Strecker Rd.

Homestead
Inn & Rest.

OH 13

Gastler's B & B

Kelley Rd.

Coach Hse. Inn

MILAN (see inset)

Tour 22:
Firelands -
Erie County

Schug Rd.

OH 113

Church St.

OH 113

OH 113

Huron River

Old Dam

Shaw Mill Rd.

railroad underpass

Berlin St.

Start

0   1   2 Miles

Lovers Lane

Schaeffer Rd.

Whittlesey Rd.

Huron County

OH 250

HO

shows
direction of travel

© Backcountry Publications
25 Bicycle Tours in Ohio

N

0.2   At the Stop sign, turn right onto South Edison Drive (there is a bikeway sign).

At the corner, the large, grassy area that forms a westward extension on the cemetery was the site of the Huron Institute, which began operation in 1832 a year before Oberlin College opened. Sometime after its closing in 1889, the large brick building was dismantled and the bricks used for private homes.

Those interested in seeing more of Milan's architecture may want to turn left on Judson Street, then right onto Center Street. Among the striking Greek Revival homes on this thoroughfare is the Zenas King House at 128 Center. A brochure available at the Milan Historical Museum describes these houses in detail. As one might guess from this and other streets, the popularity of the Greek Revival style coincided with the period of Milan's greatest prosperity.

For those continuing straight on Edison Drive, note the curvilinear artistry of the Gothic Revival house at 38 Edison. It was built around 1838, when Milan's canal-based fortune was on the threshold of realization.

0.5   At the Stop sign, continue STRAIGHT onto North Edison Drive, crossing Church Street and following signs to the Edison birthplace.

On your right is the complex that makes up the Milan Historical Museum. The main museum in Galpin House is open April through October from 1 to 5 PM, with hours extended from 10 AM to 5 PM June through August. Several architectural walking tour brochures of the town are available at the main museum.

0.6   At the four-way Stop sign, continue STRAIGHT on North Edison, crossing Front Street and ignoring the bike route sign that indicates a left turn.

The Thomas Edison birthplace is on your left, overlooking the former Milan Canal Basin. The house was built in 1842 by the inventor's father, Samuel, who immigrated here from Canada in 1839, attracted by the shipping boom. The home and the adjoining museum contain numerous Edison memorabilia including some of his inventions, which number over one thousand.

Edison was born here in 1847, at the height of Milan's canal-generated commerce. Although his family moved in 1854, Thomas remembered the place as home and later purchased the homestead from his niece. He brought his friends, Henry Ford and Harvey Firestone, here when he made a nostalgic trip back in 1923. Years after introducing the incandescent bulb to the world, he returned to find the place still lit by candle power. The birthplace is open February through November from 1 to 5 PM daily except on

Mondays. On Tuesdays through Saturdays in the summer it opens at 10 AM. Admission is $2.00 for adults, $1.00 for children.

Edison Drive dead-ends a bit beyond the Edison birthplace, where more exemplary Greek Revival houses line up on the right. The first two were the shop and residence of cabinetmaker John Smith, both built around 1820. The last building on Edison Drive is the impressive Lockwood House, built in the Italianate style around 1850. The third story with its distinctive mansard roof and ornate tower were added around 1875.

0.7   Turn around and return to the four-way Stop sign, where you will turn RIGHT onto Front Street.

As you pass the Edison Birthplace again, look to your left at the house at 14 Edison Drive. The rear portion was built in 1817 by Ebenezer Merry, who came here from West Hartford, Connecticut. In 1817 he laid out the village, to be called Beatty for the land's original owner. Others favored the name Merry's Mills, before Milan was officially chosen in 1820.

When you make the right turn, the first house on your right at 21 East Front is Ebenezer Merry's second house, built around 1823 in the Federal style. Merry became a prominent citizen and a major promoter of and stockholder in the canal. After the canal had given an impetus to shipbuilding, Merry joined for a time with builder J. P. Gay to form the Merry and Gay shipyards. Several other houses on this block of Front Street are included on the Historical Museum's walking tour maps.

0.8   Turn LEFT on the east side of the square onto Park Street.

On the left side is the Italianate Kelley Building, built in 1869–1870 by shipbuilder Captain Henry Kelley. On the right is the town square, laid out by Ebenezer Merry and used as a hitching lot for horses until grass and trees were planted in 1868. A gazebo, a Civil War memorial, and a "Young Edison" statue depicting the budding inventor and his mother now grace the former hitching grounds. Off the southeast corner of the square is the 1888 Town Hall, with a clock donated by Captain Kelley. Across from the Town Hall on Church Street is the public library, a lovely brick, stone, and terra cotta building with a red-glazed tile roof.

0.9   Turn RIGHT onto Church Street (OH 113) at the south side of the square; at the light, continue STRAIGHT on Church Street, crossing North Main Street.

In the center of Church Street, facing the town square, is the Milan Inn. Built as a stagecoach stop in 1845, the building suffered major damage in the fire of 1888 and was rebuilt and remodeled that same

The modest birthplace of Thomas Edison was still without electric lights when he returned there with friends Henry Ford and Harvey Firestone in 1923.

year. It now serves excellent meals from 11 AM to 9 PM Tuesday through Saturday and Sundays from 8 AM to 8 PM.

If you turn right at the light on North Main Street and continue down the hill, you'll reach the canal basin and see the only warehouse that remains of the fourteen that once stood here. North Main Street used to continue across the river here on a bridge built by Zenas King. It was never rebuilt after it collapsed when struck by a truck in 1935.

1.1 At the Stop sign, continue STRAIGHT on Church Street, which becomes unmarked Shaw Mill Road, crossing US 250 and OH 13.

The Coach House Inn, a bed and breakfast, is a half mile north on the left where OH 113 turns east. The inn overlooks the Huron River and has canoes available for guests. Bicyclists are especially welcome. For reservations, call (419) 499–2435.

Although you are on the Milan Canal Bikeway here, speedy traffic makes this intersection one that should be negotiated with care. Shaw Mill Road goes gently downhill, then flattens out to go under a railroad underpass where you'll see another bike route sign.

1.5 At the three-way Stop sign, which comes as a bit of a surprise after the underpass, continue STRAIGHT on unmarked Shaw Mill Road.

Shaw Mill goes uphill after the railroad bridge, then becomes a level and excellent biking road through very pretty farm country. Shaw Mill changes to Whittlesey Road as you dip briefly into Huron County.

3.1   At the Stop sign, turn RIGHT onto Schaeffer Road.

You'll immediately cross a bridge from which there is a good view of the Huron River. Schaeffer soon begins a twisting and steep uphill for about a quarter mile.

3.5   At the four-way Stop sign, turn RIGHT onto Lovers Lane.

After half a mile, this road begins a curving downhill into the valley of the west branch of the Huron River. Just after the one-lane bridge, a sign to the right points to the Milan dam, built to provide water for the canal's capacious turning basin. A flat, paved road leads to what remained of the dam after it was destroyed by flood in 1868.

4.8   At the Stop sign, follow the bike route sign to the RIGHT onto OH 113.

5.0   Turn LEFT onto Kelley Road at the bike route and "Welcome to Milan" signs.

5.9   At the Y-junction, follow Kelley Road to the LEFT, avoiding Schug Road.

6.9   At the Stop sign, continue STRAIGHT on Kelley Road, crossing Strecker Road.

About a mile to the left on Strecker is Gastier's Farm Bed and Breakfast, which has been in the same family for over a hundred years. Call Ted and Donna Gastier at (419) 499–2985. A mile to the right on Strecker will bring you to the Homestead Inn Motel and Restaurant, set amid the acres of the Homestead farm. The restaurant is in an 1883 country mansion. For room reservations, call (419) 499–2990.

7.7   At the Stop sign, turn RIGHT onto Mason Road; at the immediate traffic light, continue STRAIGHT on Mason Road, crossing US 250—the Sandusky-Norwalk Road.

This busy intersection is the center of the village of Avery, not to be confused with Old Avery, on the east side of the river.

8.9   Turn LEFT onto Hoover Road.

10.0   At the Stop sign, turn RIGHT onto Huron-Avery Road.

11.6   Turn LEFT onto Rye Beach Road.

12.3   At the Stop sign, continue STRAIGHT on Rye Beach Road, crossing Fox Road.

Although you're within a mile of the city of Huron, Rye Beach Road runs through seemingly endless acres of corn fields on a beautifully flat stretch of land.

13.4   At the Stop sign, turn RIGHT onto Bogart Road.
Bogart continues like Rye Beach Road, flat and very straight.

14.8   Turn LEFT onto Center Street.

15.0   At the light, continue STRAIGHT on Center Street, crossing US 6 and OH 2, which is a major divided highway at this point.

15.2   At the Stop sign, continue STRAIGHT on Center Street, crossing Cleveland Road West.
At the northwest corner of this intersection is Captain Montague's Guest House, a comely Southern Colonial-style home built in 1876. A lavishly appointed bed and breakfast establishment, it has an in-ground swimming pool amid gardens with fountain and gazebo. For reservations, call (419) 433–2045.

15.4   At the four-way Stop sign, continue STRAIGHT on Center Street, crossing South Street.
On your left is the pleasant Huron City Park, first laid out in 1824 as the town commons. This charming green has playground equipment, shelters, picnic tables, restrooms, gazebo, and a comfortable beach facing the breakwater.

15.5   Turn RIGHT onto Wall Street, as Center Street continues toward the lake.

15.7   At the Stop sign, turn RIGHT onto Main Street.
To the left here is the breakwater, locally referred to as the Mile Long Pier. Work on the breakwater was begun as early as 1826 by the Army Corps of Engineers, with the latest addition done in 1906. Huron had a good natural harbor and grew quickly as a port after the Firelands became legally open to settlement. However, many ships refused to stop at Huron, preferring instead the protected port in neighboring Sandusky. During the first quarter of the nineteenth century, it was anyone's guess as to which of the Lake Erie ports would emerge the leader, with few betting on Cleveland, situated on the insect-infested flatlands at the mouth of the Cuyahoga. However, a cholera epidemic in 1834 killed a number of Huron residents and hastened the departure of many others. The construction of the Milan Canal shortly afterward siphoned off what was left of Huron's influence. It was not until the coming of the railroad and the building of coal and ore docks that Huron became a transfer point for ore from Lake Superior and coal from southern Ohio. This commerce, combined with a growing tourist trade, helped revitalize the city. The ore docks just closed a few years ago, and the Pillsbury silos are now run by a Minnesota firm that imports durum wheat from the northern Great Lakes states to process it for use in pasta products.

This and the Huron Lime Plant, whose piles of crushed stone are visible across the river from the pier, testify to Huron's reawakening, while its formerly energetic neighbor to the south slumbers amid the mementos of its short-lived affluence.

On the pier itself is the Showboat Restaurant and Waterfront Saloon, formerly a fish house. The *Mystic Belle,* an old-fashioned paddlewheeler, offers cruises of the lake and river in season. Information is posted at the boat's docking area outside the Showboat Restaurant.

15.9 Turn RIGHT onto South Street.

To the right at this intersection was the shipyard that built the lake steamer, *Great Western,* in 1832. This site was also the terminus of the Huron and Oxford Railroad from 1852 to 1863.

16.0 At the four-way Stop sign, turn LEFT onto Williams Street.

16.1 At the Stop sign and the red blinking light, turn LEFT onto Cleveland Road and immediately turn RIGHT onto Main Street.

At the northwest corner of this intersection is the Presbyterian Church, built in the Greek Revival style around 1848. The octagonal tower and spire are unusual in combination with the Greek temple facade.

16.2 After Main Street makes a sharp turn to the left and then to the right, turn LEFT onto Mill Street.

The Huron Historical and Cultural Center is housed in an 1874 Methodist Church one block to the right here.

16.3 Turn RIGHT onto Huron Street.

16.4 At the Stop sign, continue STRAIGHT, crossing the first two lanes of Cleveland Road East; at the next Stop sign, turn LEFT onto the eastbound lanes of Cleveland Road.

On the southwest corner of this quite busy intersection is the Wileswood Country Store, renowned for its old-fashioned candy counter and popcorn. Use the sidewalk along the right side as you cross the bridge over the Huron River.

16.8 Shortly after the bridge, turn RIGHT onto River Road.

There are two railroad crossings near the beginning of River Road. In about a mile, River Road veers slightly to the left, affording a panoramic tableau of the Huron River Valley. At the point where OH 2 spans River Road, the railroad, and the Huron River, Frenchman Jean Baptiste Flemmond set up a trading post in 1805.

21.1 At the T-junction, make a LEFT onto Mason Road, and an immediate RIGHT back onto River Road.

If you go to the right here on Mason for a quarter mile, you'll reach the Norfolk and Western Railroad, which runs along the old towpath of the Milan Canal. Another quarter mile west, as you go up the hill, you'll see a road on the left leading down to a private campground. This was the location of Abbot's Bridge, where the canal joined the Huron River and the first, or lower, lock was located.

A half mile further on River Road, a historical marker commemorates the site of Fort Avery, built by General Simon Perkins in 1811 to protect the early Firelands settlers from the British and Indian raids that helped precipitate the War of 1812. As the first settlement of any size in the Firelands, Avery was designated the county seat, with a log house serving as the courthouse and jail.

23.8   Continue STRAIGHT on River Road, crossing OH 113; the continuation is just slightly to the right on the south side of OH 113. (There is a bike route marker.)

After crossing OH 113, River Road becomes Berlin Road and goes downhill. The Galpin Wildlife Refuge on your left here was donated by William Galpin, whose father had been the town physician from 1839 to 1874.

24.1   Return to Edison Park parking lot.

Bicycle Repair Services

Arnie's Cycle Shop, 44 East Main Street, Norwalk, OH 44857 (419) 668–3027.
Bike Rack, 3005 West Monroe Street, Sandusky, OH 44870 (419) 652–3399.
A & B Hobbies and Cycles, 1048 Cleveland Avenue, Sandusky, OH 44870 (419) 652–4242.

23

Firelands—Huron County

39 miles; moderate cycling
Generally level terrain
County maps: Huron, with small portions of Seneca, Sandusky, and Erie

When the Connecticut General Assembly sold the land in its Western Reserve to investors after the Revolutionary War, it saved a half million acres in the westernmost section for the "fire sufferers." These fire sufferers were the over eighteen hundred residents of several towns along the Connecticut coast who had been petitioning the assembly since 1777 for relief due to the disproportionate share of enemy fire they had borne during the War for Independence. The British in 1779 had issued to the citizenry of New Haven a proclamation declaring that "the existence of a single habitation on your defenseless coast ought to be a subject of constant reproof of your ingratitude." The British attacked on July 5, 1779, killing over two dozen and taking many more prisoner, among them the president of Yale. More attacks followed on Fairfield and Norwalk. Danbury had experienced the same brutality two years earlier. The worst punishment of the war went to New London in 1781, the attack led by none other than former patriot Benedict Arnold.

By war's end, the assembly had received nearly two thousand petitions from the residents of New Haven, Greenwich, Norwalk, New London, Fairfield, Danbury, Groton, Ridgefield, and East Haven. On May 10, 1792, fifteen years after the first raid on Danbury, the assembly "released and quit-claimed to the Sufferers hereafter named . . . five hundred thousand acres belonging to this State."

It was another four years before the sufferers were incorporated under the name "The Proprietors of the Half Million Acres of Land Lying South of Lake Erie," and almost another ten years before, at the 1805 Treaty of Fort Industry, the Connecticut Land Company bought supposed title to the lands from Indians. The purchase price was less than $20,000, approximately one-tenth the amount at which the Connecticut Land Company had valued the land in 1792.

Still the sufferers waited, this time for the Connecticut Land Company surveyors to mark out the area into five-mile-square townships, which were then subdivided into four quadrants to be distributed by lottery. Another hold-up occurred when an error in setting the southwest

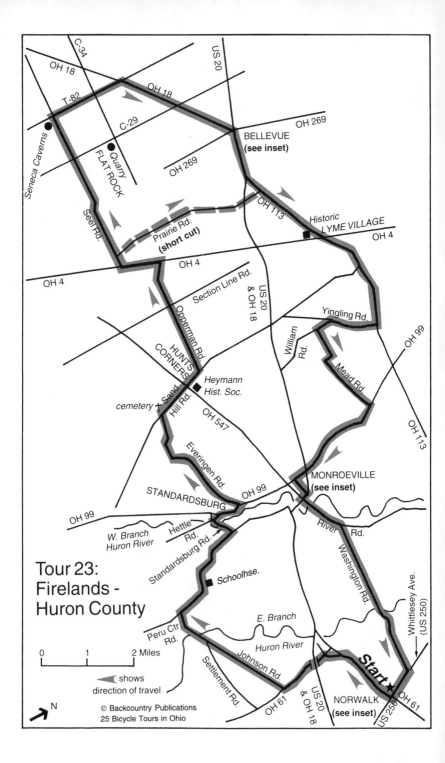

C-34

OH 18

US 20

T-82

OH 18

C-29

OH 269

BELLEVUE
(see inset)

Seneca Caverns

Quarry
FLAT ROCK

OH 269

OH 113

Historic
LYME VILLAGE

OH 4

Seel Rd.

Prairie Rd.
(short cut)

OH 4

Section Line Rd.

US 20
& OH 18

Yingling Rd.

OH 99

Opperman Rd.

HUNTS
CORNERS

William
Rd.

Mead Rd.

OH 113

Heymann
Hist. Soc.

cemetery

Sand
Hill Rd.

OH 547

Everingen Rd.

OH 99

MONROEVILLE
(see inset)

STANDARDSBURG

OH 99

River
Rd.

W. Branch
Huron River

Hettle
Rd.

Standardsburg Rd.

Schoolhse.

Washington
Rd.

Tour 23:
Firelands -
Huron County

E. Branch

Huron River

Whittlesey Ave.
(US 250)

Peru Ctr
Rd.

0   1   2 Miles

Settlement Rd.

Johnson Rd.

US 20
& OH 18

Start

OH 61

shows
direction of travel

OH 61

NORWALK
(see inset)

US 250

N

© Backcountry Publications
25 Bicycle Tours in Ohio

boundary of the Reserve required the recruitment of surveyor Almon Ruggles from Danbury, Connecticut, to redo the survey. Working along the southern boundary in what became New Haven township, Ruggles lettered the words "Great Marsh" on his map and recorded the following observations: "117th milepost west: We are in danger of our lives. 118th milepost west: Sat a post in Hell. I've travelled the woods for seven years, but never saw so hideous a place as this." Ruggles was generously rewarded for his efforts (see tour 21).

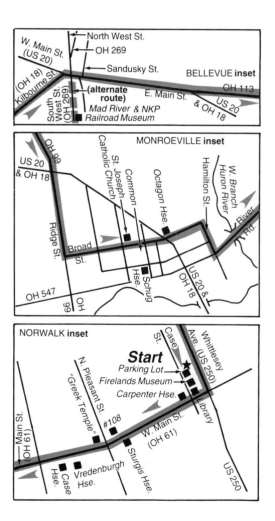

By 1807, when the sufferers were finally free to rush west and claim their allocation, many had been dead for nearly a quarter century, and most who had been in their prime during the Revolution were too infirm for the rigorous trip west. Many of the descendants who did undertake the adventure were forced to return due to the oncoming War of 1812.

Despite its unpropitious beginnings, the Firelands eventually was not only developed but enjoyed considerable prosperity, as the remaining number of fine, mid-nineteenth-century homes indicates. This tour begins at one of the most significant of these homes, which today houses the Firelands Museum, located just off Main Street in the city of Norwalk, the Huron County seat and the "capital" of the Firelands.

Main Street in Norwalk follows OH 61. The center of Norwalk can be reached by taking exit 7 from the Ohio turnpike (about 50 miles west of Cleveland) and following US 250 south. US 250 intersects OH 61 in the center of Norwalk, which is about 7 miles south of Milan.

The parking lot next to the Firelands Museum is shared by the public library, which is on the northeast corner of Case and Main streets. It's best to report your plans to someone in the library or the museum if you intend to leave your car there and bicycle this tour.

0.0   Leave the Firelands Museum parking lot and go STRAIGHT on Case Street to Main Street; turn RIGHT onto Main Street (OH 61).

The Greek Revival Preston-Wickham House, which now houses the Firelands Museum, was built in 1835 by the editor of the local newspaper, *The Norwalk Reflector.* In the museum, you'll find Ruggles' links and chains from his survey of the Firelands, plus a photostatic copy of the Treaty of Fort Industry, complete with Indian signatures.

The museum is open in July and August from 10 AM to 5 PM (on Sundays, noon to 5 PM). In May, June, September, and October, it's open daily except Monday from noon to 5 PM and is open weekends only in April and November. Admission is adults $2, seniors $1.50, youths $1, children free with adult.

As you pass the library on your left, a historic marker indicates that you are entering the Norwalk Historic District, placed on the National Register in 1974. Evidence of this history lines both sides of the street. Just after your right turn, at 54 West Main, is the Carpenter House. The careful restoration of this 1833–1835 Federal-style mansion earned it an architectural award. At 99 West Main, on the left, is the Sturgis-Kennan-Fulstow House. This 1834 Classic Revival-Federal mansion has a two-story portico, rarely seen in the Reserve. Octagonal columns occur on only one other Western Reserve building. Back on the right, at 108 West Main, is the oldest house in the district, built as a trading post with the Indians.

0.3   At the light at the intersection of North Pleasant and West Main streets, continue STRAIGHT.

> On the northwest corner of this intersection, at 114 West Main, is "The Greek Temple." Originally built as a girls' school in 1848, this Greek Revival building has been a private home since 1858. Note the large doorway and massive Ionic columns that give the place its monumental proportions. On the left, set far back from the street at 133 West Main, is the Vredenburgh-Gardiner House. Built some time before 1840, it has a Greek doorway with Federal elements in the second story. Right next door is the F. B. Case House at 141 West Main. Case, first president of the Humane Society, maintained a watering trough for animals on the sidewalk. Tombstones for beloved dogs dot the front yard.

0.8   At the light at the intersection of North West Street and West Main Street, continue STRAIGHT.

1.4   Turn LEFT onto the unmarked street just beyond the Marathon station with the convenience store; making this turn actually keeps you on West Main Street.

1.7   At the Stop sign, turn LEFT onto OH 61 (you'll see a dead-end sign ahead, indicating that West Main ends at the American Legion Hall).

> In about a quarter mile, you'll go under OH 18 and US 20 and begin climbing a hill. Although you are now out in the countryside, this highway has a narrow berm, so caution is advised.

2.8   Turn RIGHT onto Johnson Road as it comes in suddenly from the right.

> Fields of corn and soybeans surround you on this generally flat road. In about 2 miles, you'll pass a goat farm just before Settlement Road comes in from the left. Shortly afterwards, you'll cross the East Branch of the Huron River.

5.4   At the T-junction, turn RIGHT onto Peru Center Road.

> In less than half a mile, you'll dip into the valley of the West Branch of the Huron River, where you'll see the Monroeville Rod and Gun Club housed in a former schoolhouse.

7.3   Turn LEFT onto unmarked Standardsburg Road.

> In just over a quarter mile, a gentle downhill will carry you to a one-lane bridge and the hamlet of Standardsburg, a crossroads of four or five houses in the township of Ridgefield. This township was named for one of the nine Connecticut towns devastated by the British.

7.8   At the Stop sign, turn RIGHT on Hettle Road.

7.9   At the Stop sign, turn RIGHT onto OH 99.

8.5   Just after the bridge, turn LEFT onto Everingen Road.
Everingen is basically a one-lane road, surrounded by beautiful farmland dotted with farmhouses.

11.1   At the Stop sign, turn RIGHT onto Sand Hill Road.
In about a quarter mile on the left, note the nicely preserved local cemetery, largely devoted to the Heymann family.

11.8   At the Stop sign at the intersection with OH 547, continue STRAIGHT.
This lovely corner with its few houses and quaint-looking church is called Hunt's Corners for Heil Hunt, who lived here until his death at age one hundred. The church, now the Heymann Historical Society founded in 1982, was formerly the Hunt's Corners United Church of Christ.

12.4   Turn LEFT onto Opperman Road, which comes as something of a surprise in the middle of fields.
Opperman is an uphill road amidst rich farm country.

13.9   At the Stop sign, continue STRAIGHT, crossing Section Line Road.
After the intersection with Section Line, Opperman becomes flat, providing a swift ride if you have no headwind.

There are several "section line" roads in this county, refering to roads that follow the surveyor lines that cut each of the townships into four quadrants or sections.

14.8   Turn LEFT onto unmarked OH 4.

15.7   Turn RIGHT onto Seel Road. (A sign points to Seneca Caverns.) (Those wishing to cut the tour by about 4.5 miles can make an immediate right here onto Prairie Road; you will miss Seneca Caverns and Bellevue but will pick up OH 113 near mileage point 24.1, just before Old Lyme Village.)

17.0   At the Stop sign and T-junction, turn RIGHT onto OH 269, then make an immediate LEFT onto Township Road 178. (A large sign indicates that Seneca Caverns is reached in 2 miles.)
You are now in Seneca County and temporarily outside the westernmost boundary of the Reserve.

18.1   At the Stop sign, continue STRAIGHT, crossing Seneca County Road 29.

Northwest at this intersection is a vast limestone and gravel quarry located in the village of Flat Rock.

A quarter mile past the tracks is the entrance to Seneca Caverns on the left. Called the "Earth Crack," it actually is a fracture or fault in the earth's surface that accesses ten "rooms" on seven levels and a subterranean stream. The caverns are open seven days a week Memorial Day through Labor Day from 9 AM to 7 PM. They're open in May, September, and October just on weekends from 10 AM to 5 PM.

19.1   Turn RIGHT onto Township Road 82.

Seneca County roads have numbers, not names, and most of them lie on a grid cutting the county into well over a hundred one-mile squares.

20.0   At the four-way Stop sign, continue STRAIGHT on Township Road 82, crossing County Road 34.

20.7   At the Stop sign, turn RIGHT onto OH 18.

In about half a mile, you'll enter Sandusky County. In another three-quarter mile, you'll enter Bellevue, where OH 18 is called Kilbourne Street.

23.2   At the light, make a RIGHT onto OH 18 and US 20; this is West Main Street.

23.3   At the light at the intersection with South West Street, continue STRAIGHT.

A right turn onto South West Street will bring you to the Mad River and NKP (Nickel Plate) Railroad Museum in less than a quarter mile. Adopted as a bicentennial project by the city of Bellevue in 1976, the museum contains everything from Pullman sleepers to Fruit Growers refrigerator cars. The museum is open from 1 to 5 PM daily from Memorial Day to Labor Day, on Saturdays and Sundays in May and September, and on Sundays only in October. No admission is charged.

23.4   At the light at the intersection of Main Street and Sandusky Street, continue STRAIGHT on Main Street.

24.1   When you see the sign for East 113, get into the left lane; there is no light, so make this maneuver with care. Follow OH 113, avoiding the continuation of OH 18 and US 20, which goes off to the right.

Even though you are still on a state highway, most of the busy traffic will follow OH 18 and US 20. While in Bellevue, you crossed back into Huron County and thus back into the Western Reserve. If you

The Firelands Counties have remained predominantly rural with many small-scale agricultural operations from peach orchards to turkey farms.

took the Prairie Road cut-off mentioned earlier, this is the point at which you rejoin the tour.

In 2 miles on your right, you will see the 1882 Wright House, the landmark for the Historic Lyme Village. The Wright House is one of the dozen buildings restored to recreate a typical Ohio village of the mid-nineteenth century. The Wright mansion was unusual in that it was a relatively isolated farmhouse; most Second Empire homes, especially those as substantial and stately as Wright's, were found in urban settings. The home featured some rare modern conveniences. At a time when most people were using chamber pots, Wright pumped water by windmill to a third-floor tank to provide the two bathrooms with running water and flush toilets. In addition, he routed gas to his chandeliers from a small brick gas "plant" in his front yard and heated water in the basement, sending it to hot water radiators throughout the house.

Lyme Village also houses the world's largest postmark collection, in the building that once served as the Lyme, Ohio, post office. Tours of Lyme Village are conducted daily except Mondays, June through August from 1 to 5 PM, and in May and September on Sundays only. Admission is $4.00 for adults, $3.50 for seniors, and $2.50 for children over twelve. Snack food is available, as are picnic tables and restrooms.

26.3 At the light at the intersection of OH 4 and 113, continue STRAIGHT on East 113.

This is a busy corner. Shortly you'll cross out of Huron County to travel a couple of miles in Erie County's Groton Township.

28.5 Suddenly, in the midst of open farmland, turn RIGHT onto Yingling Road.

Soon you'll reenter Huron County, Lyme Township, named for Old Lyme, Connecticut.

29.5 At the Y-junction, turn LEFT onto William Road, avoiding the continuation of Yingling.

29.8 Turn LEFT onto Mead Road.

In a little over a quarter mile, Mead makes a right/left dog leg turn. These last three roads are excellent, flat, and narrow farm-access roads. Only one-car wide, they seem designed more for the bicyclist than the motorist.

31.8 At the T-junction and Stop sign, turn RIGHT onto OH 99.

33.8 At the Stop sign, continue STRAIGHT, crossing OH 18 and US 20.

Now in the village of Monroeville, OH 99 is called Ridge Street.

34.1 Turn LEFT onto Broad Street.

Broad Street goes downhill gently. In a little over a quarter mile, you'll reach the charming village common, with the beautiful St. Joseph Catholic Church and school on the left. On the far right side of the square is the diminutive Schug House, built about 1820. Architectural historian Richard Campen finds it "astonishing to see such a fine expression of the Greek mode at the western edge of the Reserve at such an early date."

34.5 At the Stop sign, continue STRAIGHT, crossing OH 18 and US 20.

On the corner opposite the Stop sign is the Hosford-Menard octagon house, built in 1856. Considered the finest octagon house in the Western Reserve, its four-sided rooms on each floor surround a circular staircase, which ascends to the cupola. The portions between the quadrilateral rooms are used for storage. The exterior is done in brick, laid in a variation of the Flemish bond pattern.

34.7 **At the three-way Stop sign, turn RIGHT onto unmarked Hamilton Street.**

34.8 **At the four-way Stop sign, turn LEFT onto River Road.**
You'll cross the West Branch of the Huron River.

35.3 **Turn RIGHT onto Washington Road.**
Washington is perfectly straight and flat for the first mile, after which you'll encounter a few small hills. In 2 miles, you'll cross the Huron River's East Branch.

38.6 **At the four-way Stop sign and red warning light, turn RIGHT onto Whittlesey Avenue (US 250).**

38.7 **At the traffic light, continue STRAIGHT on Whittlesey, crossing West League Street.**

39.1 **At the traffic light, continue STRAIGHT, crossing Monroe Street; at the light immediately following, turn RIGHT onto West Main Street.**

39.2 **At the light, continue STRAIGHT on West Main, crossing Hester Street; make an immediate RIGHT onto Case to return to the Firelands Museum parking lot.**

Bicycle Repair Services
Arnie's Cycle Shop, 44 East Main Street, Norwalk, OH 44857 (419) 668–3027.
Plymouth Schwinn Cyclery, 19 East Main Street, Plymouth, OH 44865 (419) 687–6404.

24

Lake Erie Islands: Put-in Bay

6 miles; easy bicycling
Generally flat terrain
County map: Ottawa

Lake Erie's unique aspects do not necessarily enhance its reputation. The oldest and shallowest of the Great Lakes, Erie has also been the busiest, the dirtiest, and the meanest, with more ships on its bottom, writes local historian Jessie A. Martin, "than any other similar body of water in the new world." A positive feature, however, is the archipelago at its western end, the only such island formation in the Great Lakes. Of the twenty islands large enough to have names, thirteen are south of the US-Canadian border. Most famous among them for the role it played in establishing that border and in determining the history of the New World is South Bass Island, generally known by the name of its single village, Put-in-Bay.

Designated as part of the Western Reserve, the Bass Islands were sold by the Connecticut Land Company to Alfred Pierpont Edwards, whose agent came with workers in 1811 to clear land and begin settlement. Not everyone agreed, however, that Connecticut had uncontested claim to the lands they were selling. At the onset of the War of 1812, the British and their Indian allies drove the new settlers off South Bass Island and destroyed the fledgling settlement. The raid was part of a program of harassment supported by the British in Canada to challenge the American government's claim to the rights of unquestioned northwest expansion.

During the war, it became clear to General William Henry Harrison that Lake Erie was the key to control of the northwest. The youthful Oliver Hazard Perry was sent with hastily built ships to assist Harrison in wresting control of Lake Erie from the British. Making his headquarters at the harbor of South Bass Island, Commodore Perry confronted the British naval squadron on September 10, 1813. After two hours, Perry's flagship, the *Lawrence*, was nearly blasted to pieces, and four-fifths of his men were dead or wounded.

Mysteriously, Perry's second brig, *the Niagara,* was held back from the fray by second-in-command Jesse Elliott, who, some speculate, delayed intentionally in an attempt to be the hero after Perry went down with his ship. In an audacious move that earned him his fame, Perry crossed through the gunfire in an open rowboat and boarded the undamaged *Niagara*. Met with Elliott's disingenuous inquiry, "How goes the day?" Perry took over the ship and headed for the British line, where he raked the enemy brigs with thirty-two-pound iron shot. Within fifteen minutes, the British had surrendered.

"We have met the enemy and they are ours," Perry wrote Harrison from his cabin on the *Niagara,* with a succinctness that has made it one of the most famous lines in American naval history. His modesty notwithstanding, Perry became an immediate and enduring hero. "More than any other battle of the time," wrote historian Henry Adams, "the victory on Lake Erie was won by the courage and obstinacy of a single man."

Commemorative celebrations for the victory began almost at once at South Bass Island, and by midcentury fifteen thousand people were coming yearly for the Fourth of July celebrations at which raising money

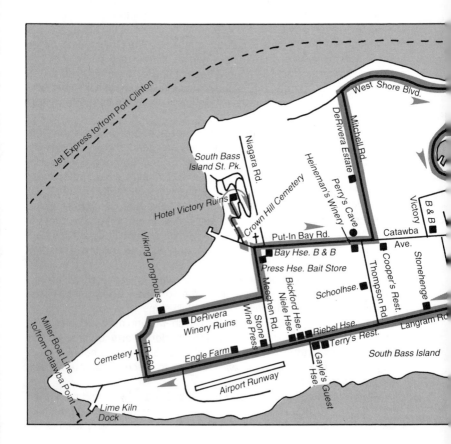

for a fitting battle memorial was always an agenda item. In 1908, nine states joined together to build a victory monument in time for the centennial of the battle. In 1972 it was renamed the Perry's Victory and International Peace Memorial National Monument, to indicate, explains the park service, that it memorializes not only Perry's victory but also the "principle of maintaining peace among nations by arbitration and disarmament, a principle now long symbolized by the unfortified boundary between two great North American neighbors."

This tour of the entire island begins at the ferry dock in the village of Put-in-Bay. Visitors can reach Put-in-Bay via Island Airlines (419–285–3371, or 734–3149) or one of three ferries. The Miller Boat Line (419–285–2421) car ferry leaves from Catawba Point on the mainland and reaches the Lime Kiln Dock at the south end of the island in eighteen minutes. From there a bus takes you to the village. The Jet Express (1–800–245–1JET), a high-speed, passenger-only catamaran, leaves

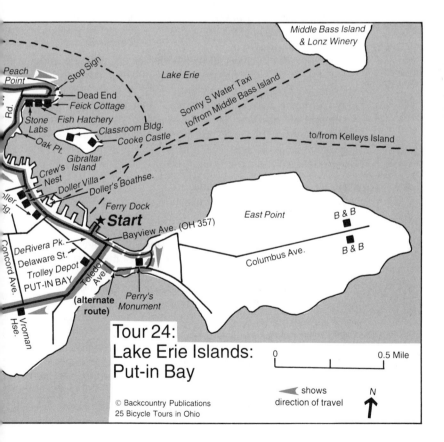

from Port Clinton on the mainland and goes directly to the village ferry dock. For those who plan to visit Kelleys Island, a third ferry comes and goes from there twice a day. Catawba Point is on OH 53 off OH 2. A little further west, Port Clinton is on OH 163, also off OH 2. OH 2 can be reached via exit 7 of the I-90 turnpike about 75 miles west of Cleveland.

Bicycles are permitted on the Miller Boat Line ferry for an extra charge, although there are concessions renting comfortable bikes, mopeds, and/or golf carts at five island locations. If you bring your bike via the Miller ferry, begin the tour at mileage point 1.9.

0.0   Turn LEFT off the ferry dock onto OH 357 (Bayview Avenue), heading toward the monument.

A glance to the right from this point affords a fine panorama of the village of Put-in-Bay surrounding the expanse of De Rivera Park, named for Señor Rivera de San Jargo (Americanized to Mr. J. D. Rivera), a wealthy Puerto Rican who bought the islands from the Edwards family for $44,000 in 1854. Given the initial settlement problems on the eve of the War of 1812, the island lay undeveloped until de Rivera divided much of the island into five- to ten-acre plots and sold them to settlers for a few dollars an acre. He imported sheep for his growing group of New England pioneers, but soon abandoned sheep for grapes and recruited German winemakers from Cincinnati and the Old Country. The Yankees were soon outnumbered by the Ruhs, Muellers, Wehrles, Vromans, Heinemans, Dollers, Fuchses, Burgraffs and Ingolds, whose success as vintners sent land prices soaring to $1500 an acre after the Civil War. De Rivera donated the land for the park in 1866.

0.1   Turn RIGHT onto Toledo Avenue.

If you continue straight for two hundred yards you'll reach Perry's Monument. The 352-foot granite tower is a Doric column, one of the tallest of its kind in the world. The observation promenade, which can be reached by elevator for a small fee, affords views of the Ohio mainland, Michigan, Canada, and several of the other islands, as well as South Bass.

This memorial to the soldiers killed in the Battle of Lake Erie is also a symbol of the end of British rule south of the Canadian border, for it was this battle that enabled the United States to lay claim to the entire Northwest Territory at the Treaty of Ghent in 1815. "The last roar of cannon which died along the shores of Erie," wrote Washington Irving, "was the expiring note of British domination."

The land on which the monument is located was formerly a sand bar and marsh. Filled in and protected by sea walls, it now forms a twenty-one-acre park connecting the two loaves of South Bass Island.

Circle the monument and go back on Delaware Street to Toledo Avenue, where you turn left.

0.2   At the four-way Stop sign, continue STRAIGHT on Toledo Avenue, crossing Delaware Street.

On the northwest corner of this intersection is the depot for the trolley to the south end of the island, where the Miller Boat Line ferry terminal is located. The Chamber of Commerce is also located here. Lockers are available at the trolley depot.

0.4   At the Y-junction, take the RIGHT arm, which is Langram Road, as Toledo Avenue continues straight.

Langram is a well-paved road traveled mostly by bicycles and golf carts.

In a little over half a mile, at the intersection of Concord and Langram, is the Gothic-style Daniel Vroman House, built around 1870. A quarter mile further is the Foster Farm, now called Stonehenge, consisting of a farmhouse and a press house, used for crushing grapes for the island's wine industry. Built of dolomite and grout rubble stone, both buildings were built around 1855 and are typical of nineteenth-century island farms. Currently under restoration, the farm is open to visitors on Saturday and Sunday from 11 AM to 5 PM. Admission is charged.

Just past Stonehenge is a sign to the right indicating Heineman's Winery and Crystal Cave; however, this tour will pass the winery at a more convenient point on the way back. Along this road to the right, which is unmarked Thompson Road, is the island's original schoolhouse built in 1855.

On the left after Thompson Road is Terry's Skyway Restaurant and Lounge, and beyond that is Gayle's Island Guest House (419–285–7181) complete with swimming pool and conveniently located next to the island airport. The airport maintains a bike and cart rental service (419–285–3371).

On the right is the former Riebel House Hotel, once a ranging, forty-room inn amidst vineyards. The house beyond the hotel, set far back from the road, is the Italianate George Bickford House, built around 1868. Beyond that is the Niele House, a rare brick structure built around 1870. Just past Meechen Road, still on the right, is the Stone Wine Press, now renovated as a private residence. The vineyards that once supplied the press are now runways for the airport. The L-shaped Italianate house beyond the Stone Wine Press is the Engle Farm. Built in 1872, it is still occupied by the original family. The frame wine-press house is behind the farmhouse.

1.9   Turn RIGHT onto unmarked Town Road 260 (Put-in-Bay Road).

Those coming to the island via the Miller Boat Line ferry should pick up the tour at this point.

Going straight here will take you to the Miller ferry terminal, often called Lime Kiln Dock for the limestone furnace that operated for a short time here in the 1860s.

The turn onto Put-in-Bay Road takes you up a slight hill, which crests at the Maple Leaf Cemetery. About a quarter mile past the cemetery, the road jogs right, then left, then right again. You're now heading northeast, back toward the village along Put-in-Bay Road.

A quarter mile past the jogs, on your left, are the earth-covered remains of the gateway to the Viking Longhouse. Built in 1980 using the techniques of the ancient Vikings, it used to serve as workshop and museum for the sculptor Eadwerd Hyl. About a quarter mile further, just past the entrance to the Island Club Estates on the right, are the unassuming remains of the De Rivera Wine facilities. The board and batten barn was built around 1874.

3.0   At the Stop sign, turn LEFT onto unmarked Meechen Road.

Meechen begins with a pleasant descent and ends with a short rise at the next intersection. As you approach the T-junction, on the right you'll see the Press House Bait Store built in 1865 by German immigrant and winemaker Max van Dohren. Perhaps the finest remaining example of an island press house, it still contains some of the original pressing equipment. The Press House sells groceries as well as bait, and also rents bicycles.

3.2   At the Stop sign, turn RIGHT onto Catawba Avenue.

To the left at this intersection, after a short downhill, is the entrance to South Bass Island State Park, with thirty-six acres and 134 campsites, many overlooking the lake. The park has an attractive beach and fishing pier, but its most fascinating feature is the remnants of the Hotel Victory. Opened in 1892, the Hotel Victory was once the largest hotel in the world, a spectacular multitowered Queen Anne building accommodating fifteen hundred guests and boasting the visits of several United States presidents. Never a financial success, it burned to the ground in 1919.

As you make the right turn onto Catawba, the Crown Hill Cemetery is on your left. Entering by way of the gate around the corner on Niagara Road, you'll see the modest tombstone of José de Rivera to the left of the entrance. In the center of the cemetery is the impressive Romanesque mausoleum of Valentine Doller, the German entrepreneur to whom de Rivera sold much of his island holdings after he went bankrupt in 1886. Also buried here is John Brown, Jr., son of the notorious abolitionist. John, Jr., settled here after his father's execution in 1859, becoming a grape-grower and highly respected resident of thirty-three years.

On the right at the junction of Niagara and Catawba is the attractive Bay House Bed and Breakfast. For reservations, call (419) 285–2822.

In half a mile on the right is the visitor's building for Heineman's Winery, founded in 1886. Now operated by third- and fourth-generation Heinemans, the winery offers tours of its facilities from mid-May to mid-September from 11 AM to 5 PM. Included in the price of the winery tour ($2.50 for adults, $1.00 for children) is a tour of the Crystal Cave. Discovered in 1897, the cave is actually a vastly oversized geode lined with strontium crystal formations and located forty feet below ground level.

Across Catawba Avenue from Heineman's is Perry's Cave. Larger than the Crystal Cave, it was, according to tradition, used by Perry's men to store ammunition prior to the Battle of Lake Erie. It is open weekends in May and September and daily in the summer months from 11 AM to 6 PM. Admission is $2.00 for adults, $1.00 for children.

3.8 Turn LEFT onto Mitchell Road (unposted).

If you continue straight here for a few hundred yards, you'll reach Cooper's Restaurant, built over the former Put-in-Bay Wine Company's wine cellar. Continuing straight on Catawba will bring you back to Put-in-Bay Village and cut off about a mile and a half of this route.

Mitchell begins with a beautiful, cool downhill. In a half mile, you'll see the former de Rivera estate on the left, which stayed in the family until 1912.

4.5 Turn RIGHT at the Stop sign onto West Shore Boulevard.

5.0 As the unmarked Bayview Road comes in from the right, continue STRAIGHT toward the "Children Playing" sign; at the Stop sign with the "Dead End" sign just beyond it, turn right onto East 357, which will bring you to another Stop sign; turn LEFT here onto Bayview Avenue.

As you make the turn after the first Stop sign, you'll see the Feick Cottage, a Colonial Revival-style cottage built in 1901. Next to the cottage is the State Fish Hatchery, also built by Feick. Established in 1893, the Put-in-Bay hatchery is one of the oldest in the United States and was used to hatch walleye for all of Ohio's lakes. In the 1960s, the hatchery switched to coho salmon, using eggs shipped from Michigan. Since salmon do not reproduce naturally in Ohio waters, the fish are used to stock many of the waterways in the

Western Reserve, including the Huron, Chagrin, Vermilion, Rocky, Grand, and Conneaut rivers. The hatchery is open to visitors weekdays from 1 to 4 PM and has displays of hatchery operations, fish communities, and Lake Erie fishing.

Next to the hatchery is the Stone Laboratory Research Station, a biological research center belonging to Ohio State University. Built in 1889, this building was the former Federal Fish Hatchery.

All of these buildings are located on Peach Point, selected by de Rivera as an ideal site for his orchards. After the turn of the century, the point attracted a number of artists and writers who set up small cottages here. The location affords some of the best views of Perry's Monument to the southeast.

Follow Bayview as it curves to the right, then heads downhill to the left, where you'll have great views of the bay itself. The origin of the name Put-in-Bay is generally thought to come from the navigational term meaning to land a vessel. Some cite a 1798 ship's logbook, however, which calls it "Puden Bay," thought to refer to the shape of the harbor—round like a pudding bag and soft on the bottom.

Bayview continues next to the water and passes the Oak Point Picnic Area maintained by the state park. Water and public restrooms are available here. From Oak Point one has a fine view of Gibraltar Island, six acres of solid limestone now owned by Ohio State's Stone Laboratory. Jay Cooke, the Philadelphia banker and financier, bought the island from de Rivera in 1864 for $3,001.

Born in 1821 in Sandusky, Cooke was a religious zealot who was continually at odds with the German immigrants, whose beer-drinking Sunday picnics grossly conflicted with his views on intoxicating beverages and the Sabbath observance. His ornate, fifteen-room mansion, built shortly after the Civil War, "was largely devoted to the comfort and rest of broken-down clergymen," according to historian Harriet Taylor Upton. "Each year," she continued, "he invited eight or ten exhausted ministers to this beautiful place for rest and relaxation." Cooke Castle, as it is now called, is the building at the eastern tip of the island with the four-story crenelated tower. The institutional building, the one most clearly visible from Put-in-Bay, was built in 1927 and houses the main classrooms of the Stone Lab. Cooke's former boathouse, built around 1865, houses the Invertebrate, Ichthyology, and Ecology Labs.

Gibraltar Island is also referred to as Perry's Lookout. Tradition states that the commodore stationed his sentries here to assess the activities of the British fleet. Cooke placed the first monument to Perry's victory here shortly after he purchased the island.

About a quarter mile past Oak Point, on the right, is the Crew's

Nest, built about 1875. Formerly the Eagle Cottage Hotel, it was remodeled as a private inn in 1971. Beyond the Crew's Nest is the Doller Villa. Built about 1870, this impressive private residence was built in the Italian villa style, characterized by the octagonal corner tower and the wrap-around veranda. The Dollers had six daughters, several of whom built the Colonial Revival house next door to the villa in 1932. Just beyond that, facing the park, is the Doller Building, originally built as a post office, store, and saloon in 1873. Across the street on the waterfront, the frame portion of the shopping complex was part of Doller's boathouse and dock.

As you pass in front of De Rivera Park, you'll see the pyramid of cannonballs that mark the former gravesite of the British and American officers who are now interred under Perry's Monument. Water and public restrooms are located in the park. Surrounding the park are a number of historic buildings, including the 1873 Round House, the Park Hotel constructed in 1887, the Kimberley Carousel built in 1917, and the Colonial, a sprawling entertainment center built in 1905 that included a bowling alley, restaurant, bar, and an eighteen thousand-square-foot dance floor. Details on these and other buildings of interest are found in the guide book *Island Heritage* by Ted Ligibel and Richard Wright. Additional information on the history of all the islands is available at the Lake Erie Islands Historical Museum on Catawba Street. It is open daily, June through September, from 11 AM to 5 PM.

The Sonny S water taxi leaves from De Rivera Park for Middle Bass Island. Middle Bass was sold by de Rivera to three German immigrants who quickly established vineyards. Andrew Wehrle opened the Golden Eagle Winery in 1870, and by 1875 it was the largest wine producer in the nation. The present Lonz Winery is built atop the original Golden Eagle cellars and is open for tours.

6.2   Turn LEFT into the village ferry terminal.

In addition to the Bay House mentioned on this route, there are usually at least a half dozen other bed and breakfast establishments on Put-in-Bay. For an up-to-date listing, contact the Put-in-Bay Chamber of Commerce at P.O. Box 250, Put-in-Bay, Ohio 43456.

Bicycle Repair Services

There are no bicycle sales and repair shops on the Erie Islands; the following are nearby on the mainland:

The Bike Rack, 3005 West Monroe Street, Sandusky, OH 44870 (419) 652–3399.
A&B Hobbies and Cycles, 1048 Cleveland Avenue, Sandusky OH 44870 (419) 652–4242.

25

Lake Erie Islands: Kelleys Island

8 miles; easy cycling
Level terrain
County map: Erie

"They rise up out of the water like huge green steppingstones for some legendary Indian god to stride over from one hunting and fishing ground to another," writes Great Lakes historian Harlan Hatcher about the twelve-mile Lake Erie archipelago. Fanciful as it sounds, Hatcher's observations have some geological accuracy. The islands are the remnants of a great bridge made of resistant limestone bedrock that spanned the area now Lake Erie. When the glacier dug into the limestone, scooping out the Lake Erie basin, certain pieces were more resistant than others, although the massive glacial grooves still visible on some of the islands indicate that the glacier did not give up without a struggle.

On Kelleys Island, the biggest of the fifteen Ohio islands, are the largest and most spectacular glacial grooves in the world. For the pioneering Yankees, however, it was not the geologic but the economic importance of the limestone that attracted their attention. When Irad and Datus Kelley, sons of Judge Daniel Kelley of Middletown, Connecticut, bought most of the island in 1833, there was already a fledgling quarry on the north shore. Before expanding the quarry business, however, the Kelleys focused temporarily on timbering, receiving revenue through the sale of fine red cedar cordwood and clearing the forest for the sixty-eight settlers the Kelleys had attracted by 1840. The timber supply was depleted, but the rich limestone soil and a growing season extended by the Lake Erie climate combined to provide ideal growing conditions for grapes. Vintners had considerable success, and by 1872 the Kelleys Island Wine Company, organized in 1860, owned the largest wine cellar on the island, with a 500,000 gallon capacity.

In the meantime, small-scale entrepreneurs continued to hack away at the limestone, selling it for building stone and flux stone for use in the iron and steel foundries. In 1891, the Kelleys Island Lime and Transport Company (KILT) consolidated most of the island's quarry business. As the wine industry declined with increasing competition from California, the limestone business grew along with the steel mills. Southern and Eastern European immigrant workers were recruited to join the Germans who had come for the wine business. When KILT ceased operation in

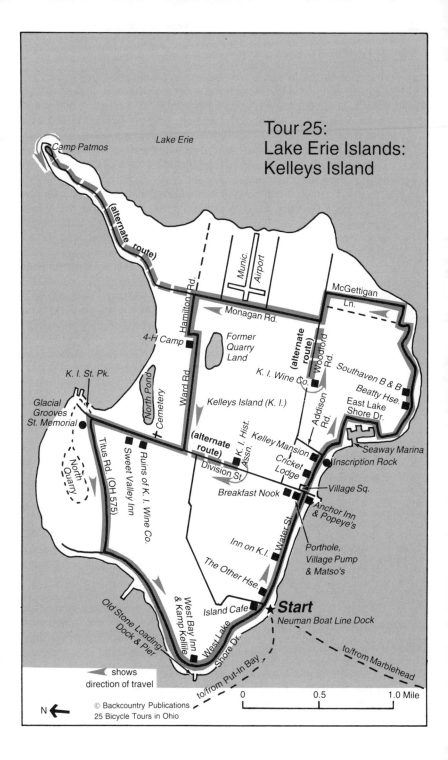

Tour 25:
Lake Erie Islands:
Kelleys Island

Lake Erie

Camp Patmos

(alternate route)

Munic.
Airport

McGettigan
Ln.

Monagan Rd.

Hamilton Rd.

4-H Camp

Former
Quarry
Land

(alternate route)

Woodford Rd.

K. I. Wine Co.

Southaven B & B

Beatty Hse.

K. I. St. Pk.

Glacial
Grooves
St. Memorial

North Pond

Cemetery

Ward Rd.

Kelleys Island (K. I.)

Addison Rd.

East Lake
Shore Dr.

North
Quarry

Titus Rd. (OH 575)

Sweet Valley Inn

Ruins of K. I. Wine Co.

K. I. Hist. Assn.

(alternate route)

Division St

Kelley Mansion

Cricket
Lodge

Seaway Marina

Inscription Rock

Village Sq.

Breakfast Nook

Anchor Inn
& Popeye's

Inn on K. I.

Water St.

Porthole,
Village Pump
& Matso's

The Other Hse.

Old Stone Loading
Dock & Pier

West Bay Inn
& Kamp Kelille

Island Cafe

West Lake Shore Dr.

★ **Start**
Neuman Boat Line Dock

to/from Put-In Bay

to/from Marblehead

← shows
direction of travel

N ←

0   0.5   1.0 Mile

© Backcountry Publications
25 Bicycle Tours in Ohio

1940 due to the effects of the Depression, outdated equipment, and shipping costs, the immigrants were jobless. The quarry business on Kelley's Island has been revived several times in the second half of this century and, in fact, just began operation again in 1990 on the west side of the island.

With such an industrial past, one may be surprised to find that Kelleys is now "the quiet island." Many of the twenty-four former wineries are now homes or businesses. The old quarries, which occupy a vast area in the center of the island, are maintained by the state park service as refuges for wildlife. And the portion of the quarry where the glacial grooves were rescued from demolition is now a state park and a registered National Natural Landmark. In 1989 the entire island was placed on the National Register of Historic Places.

This tour, which circles the whole island, begins at the Neuman Boat Line ferry dock on the southwest corner of the island. You can reach Kelleys Island via the Island Airlines (419–285–3371 or 734–3149) from Port Clinton or the Griffing Airlines (419–626–5161) from Sandusky. The Neuman Boat Line car ferry (419–626–5557) leaves regularly from Marblehead on the Ohio mainland, and the Inter-Island Ferry Service (419–285–2221) comes and goes from Put-in-Bay twice a day. Marblehead is on OH 163, which can be reach from OH 2 via OH 269. Sandusky can be reached via OH 2. OH 2 can be reached via exit 7 of the I-90 turnpike, about 50 miles west of Cleveland.

You can bring your bike on the Neuman Boat Line ferry for an additional charge; however, there are concessions renting bikes, mopeds, and/or golf carts at six island locations, one of which is right at the ferry dock.

0.0   Turn RIGHT out of the ferry terminal onto Water Street.

For bicycle rentals, try First Place Rentals (419–746–2314) just to the left on Water Street, or the Other House (419–746–2236), a tenth of a mile to the right on Water Street.

As you near Division Street, which is "downtown Kelleys Island," you'll pass the Porthole on your left, justifiably famous for its outstanding clam chowder. Directly across the street is the Anchor Inn (419–746–2366) and Popeye's (419–746–2551), both of which also rent bikes and carts. Next to the Porthole is the Village Pump, famous for its Lake Erie perch and Brandy Alexanders. And at the corner of Water and Division is Matso's—the locals' bar—which was originally a grocery store and post office. The oldest business establishment on the island, it was operated by Datus' son Addison Kelley.

0.7   At the four-way Stop sign, continue STRAIGHT on Water Street, which is now called East Lake Shore Drive.

Several other restaurants and places to rent bicycles line both sides of Division Street. On the northeast corner of this intersection is the typical Western Reserve/New England village square. Two houses up from the square is Cricket Lodge, a spacious and charming bed and breakfast. For reservations, call (419) 746–2263. Cricket Lodge is on the National Register of Historic Places.

Six houses down from Cricket Lodge is a massive blue and white frame home called Himmelein House, built in 1849, and originally intended as a family homestead for John and Johanna Himmelein. Their son John was an advance agent for repertoire acting companies, which he brought to the island during the summer. To house the actors, he added a third story and more rooms in the central portion of the family home and opened it formally as a hotel in 1890. Both Presidents Cleveland and Taft were guests here. It returned to private ownership in 1920.

Where Addison Road makes a junction with Lake Shore Drive, you are surrounded by ghosts of Kelleys Island prehistory and history. To your right, near the waters edge, is Inscription Rock, covered with Indian pictographs. The pictographs were discovered in 1834 and thought to have been carved by Erie Indians. Fortunately, when Connecticut visitor Charles Olmstead first discovered the partially buried rock, he reported it to the government. Captain Seth Eastman of the U.S. Army was sent to make drawings of the rock as well as the island, marking out Indian villages and mounds for the Bureau of Indian Affairs. The drawings were published in a six-volume work in 1852. A relief based on Eastman's drawings is provided at the site. The rock has had a protective covering placed over it by the Ohio Historical Society.

Across Lake Shore Drive on the corner of unmarked Addison Road is the Kelley Mansion, built by Datus Kelley during the Civil War years as a gift for his son Addison and his bride. With its tulip and oak hardwood floors, red Italian glass skylight, and Italian marble fireplaces, it was an Ohio showplace for half a century. Most intriguing is the central circular staircase, built of a solid piece of oak without the use of a single nail. The self-supporting staircase was constructed in London and hauled to the island in pieces. The stairs lead to the widow's walk and rotunda, under which is the skylight, placed in the attic floor. The two hundred-pound solid wood doors are complemented by cedar and mahogany shutters that fold back into a recess when opened. Purchased in 1933 by the Dominican sisters, the mansion served as a retreat and education center until 1945, when they turned it into a prestigious camp for girls aged six to fourteen. In 1974 it was sold to a private family.

The present owners rent guest rooms in the mansion from May

through September and offer tours of the premises from 11 AM to 6 PM for an admission of $1.00 per person. For reservations, call (419) 746-2273 or, off-season, (304) 525-1919.

Apparently, the environs surrounding the Kelley Mansion have been considered prime real estate for centuries. In 1975 an archaeological expedition, sponsored jointly by the Cleveland Museum of Natural History and Case Western Reserve University, excavated a prehistoric village of the Late Woodland Indians near the mansion. Of all the Erie Islands, Kelleys has yielded the most in the way of Indian artifacts, including tomahawks, arrowheads, pipes, pottery, needles, and fishhooks.

1.1 Follow the road as it bears left past the Kelleys Island Seaway Marina on the right.

With 186 boat slips, the Seaway Marina caters to the needs of lake sailors, in general an affable group, who may invite you aboard for a detailed look at their pride and joy should you take a detour along the gravel road going into the slip area. The marina road does not have an exit at the west end, however, and you will need to return to Lake Shore Drive to continue this tour. The marina also rents bikes and carts.

1.6 At this point, Lake Shore Drive makes a sharp curve to the LEFT.

At this southeastern portion of the island, newer A-frame and chalet-style homes alternate with houses redolent of Kelleys Island history. About a quarter mile from the left-hand curve is Beatty House, formerly a winery and now a bed and breakfast, the first one on the island. The oldest known stone residence on Kelleys Island, Beatty House was built in the 1850s by Ukrainian Ludwig Bette. Anglicizing his name to Louis Beatty, the enterprising immigrant planted twenty acres of vineyards behind the house and built a 75,000-gallon-capacity wine cellar beneath it. According to island records, his was a flourishing business. The fourteen-room limestone house still has the original floor plan, and hosts Jim and Martha Seaman keep the cellar doors open so that guests can view the vaulted ceilings and watertight construction. Continental breakfast is served on the porch. For reservations, call (419) 746-2379.

Two doors further down is Southaven Bed and Breakfast, also located in a former winery. Reservations can be made by calling (419) 746-2784.

2.4 Here you must make a sharp LEFT onto a hard-packed dirt road, which is unmarked McGettigan Lane.

On this east side of the island is the vacation home of former Ohio Governor Richard Celeste.

**3.0   At the Stop sign and T-junction, turn LEFT onto unmarked Wood-
ford Road.**

If you continue straight here instead of making the next right turn
onto Monagan, you'll reach the Kelleys Island Wine Company in a
little over a quarter mile. Today the company, which began in 1860,
is located in a renovated stone farmhouse-cum-winery run by the
Zettler family. The winery is open daily from 10 AM to 7 PM during the
summer and from noon to 5 PM in May and September.

3.1   Turn RIGHT onto unmarked Monagan Road.

In less than half a mile on Monagan, take note of the sign warning
"Caution: Low Flying Planes," followed by what appears to be a
misplaced Stop sign. Island Airline planes land from the west (your
left), skimming close to the road as they approach the runways.

3.9   Turn LEFT onto unmarked Hamilton Road.

If you continue straight on Monagan Road, you'll reach Camp Patmos, formerly a Roman Catholic camp for troubled boys, but purchased by the Baptist church in 1952. With a new cabin built each
year, the retreat now serves thousands of young campers.

Half a mile after the turn onto Hamilton, you'll come to a dog-leg
in the road, at which point the name changes to Ward Road. The
property on your right has been a 4-H camp since 1945. To your
left, occupying the entire central portion of the island, is East Quarry.
Maintained by Kelleys Island State Park, the former quarries are
now lakes, providing homes for numerous waterfowl and other birds
and mammals. Here it is easy to see that Kelleys Island is actually a
huge mass of limestone with a few inches of soil spread on top.

5.0   At the T-junction, turn RIGHT onto Division Street.

A half mile to the left is the Kelleys Island Historical Association,
located in the old German Reformed Church. Built in 1867, the
church was built on limestone quarried on its own property. The
Historical Association Museum is open to visitors on weekends.

As you head north on Division Street, you'll have a brief downhill
before reaching the Kelley's Island Cemetery on the right, where the
original Kelleys, Himmeleins, and Louis Beatty family members are
buried. The number of tombstones displaying Germanic surnames
like Diefenbach, Schlesselman, Schelb, Bauman, Schaedler, Rem-
linger, Bartsche, Zehringer, and Ploeger, are a testament to the
influx of German-speaking immigrants attracted by the island's flourishing wineries.

Just after the cemetery, on you left, are the ruins of the original
Kelleys Island Wine Company, hidden behind hedgerow trees and
on private property. The winery, completed in 1872, caught fire in
1876, 1915, and, finally, in 1933.

The Kelley's Island Glacial Grooves, the most remarkable in the world, were even more expansive before destruction by quarrying operations.

Beyond the ruins, also on the left, is the Sweet Valley Inn, a bed and breakfast in an attractive, restored Victorian home. For reservations, call (419) 746–2750.

5.5   Toward the end of Division Street is the entrance to Kelley's Island State Park on the right.

The park maintains 120 campsites and 661 acres of park land, including the central quarry lands. There are facilities for boat launching, fishing, swimming, and picnicking, and a bus shuttles campers from the ferry to the park. For camper-bicyclists who like to travel light, the park rents a camping package that includes a tent with dining fly, cots, sleeping pads, a cooler, fire extinguisher, picnic table, gas stove, and lantern.

5.7   Turn LEFT onto Titus Road, which here says simply "575" for OH 575, the only state route on the island.

Just beyond the intersection of Division Street and Titus Road is the entrance to the Glacial Grooves State Memorial on the left. Discovered over a century ago, these glacial grooves were initially visible for only about thirty-five feet. It was not until the early 1970s that the whole length of 396 feet was excavated and finally surrounded by fencing to protect it from visitors, who had been in the habit of chipping away sections for souvenirs. The fencing is accompanied by a stairway that permits excellent views of the grooves and the North Quarry beyond them. The park service has provided detailed interpretive signs at frequent intervals along the stairway.

Some twenty-five thousand years ago the weight of the moving Wisconsin glacier caused the rock debris at its base to gouge these seventeen-foot-deep grooves into the underlying limestone. The glacier's retreat ten thousand years ago left the gouged limestone covered with glacial till, and assiduous quarrymen added to the camouflage by dumping quarry waste atop the grooves. Although this section of glacial grooves was successfully excavated and preserved, some even more spectacular grooves extending for two thousand feet were destroyed by quarry operations.

Evidence of quarrying can be discerned by the long, vertical marks on the quarry walls, which were made by the quarrymen's drills. Before the use of mechanized drills and explosives, holes in the limestone bedrock were drilled by hand and then packed with green wood followed by water. As the wood expanded, large pieces of rock would break from the quarry walls. The same technique was used to obtain the long, narrow shafts of stone needed to fashion obelisks in ancient Egypt.

OH 575 begins with a slight uphill, followed by a cool and tree-shaded downhill with the North Quarry on your right. Titus Road continues as a slow and easy descent as it curves to the south.

In a little over a mile, you'll reach the West Bay Inn and Kamp Kellile, a fishing camp. A spacious and informal bar and restaurant, the West Bay Inn is an excellent place to stop for refreshments, restroom facilities, and Kelleys Island lore dispensed by the amiable bartenders. A former winery built of local limestone, the inn is said to be the oldest winery on the island.

Until 1990, as you approached this point in the tour you would have seen the Old Stone Loading Dock jutting out into the West Bay. Here barges and steamers loaded up with fifty to sixty cords of limestone at five and a half tons per cord. The dock was built in 1910, near the peak of the limestone business on Kelleys Island. By 1891 most of the stone business had been absorbed by the Kelleys Island Lime and Transport Company, who owned their own kilns, railcars, docks, and loading facilities. By 1924, wrote island historian Jessie A. Martin, KILT owned everything except the North Quarry near the glacial grooves and had merged all its quarries "into one immense opening extending from the west bay to the east for over a mile." But by 1937, the loading dock ceased operation, and in 1940 KILT moved its operations to the mainland, largely due to competition from Michigan quarries. Unsuccessful efforts were made to reopen the quarries in 1965 and again in the 1970s, and today the new owner of the West Bay Inn has reopened the Kelleys Island limestone quarries for yet another try. As you cross the bridge just past the West Bay Inn, you can see both the new tunnel conveyor and the remains of the old loading system on your left. In the village, post cards can still be found of the Old Stone Loading Dock, noting its importance as a fishing spot and boaters' landmark.

Shortly after passing the West Bay area, Titus Road curves to the east and becomes West Lake Shore Drive.

8.2   Turn RIGHT into the Neuman Boat Line Dock parking area.
For those who wish to stay on Kelley's Island, contact the Kelleys Island Chamber of Commerce, P.O. Box 783-F9, Kelleys Island, Ohio 43438, or call (419)-746 2360 for a list of accommodations.

Bicycle Repair Services
There are no bicycle sales and repair shops on the Erie Islands; the following are nearby on the mainland:

The Bike Rack, 3005 West Monroe Street, Sandusky, OH 44870 (419) 652–3399.
A&B Hobbies and Cycles, 1048 Cleveland Avenue, Sandusky OH 44870 (419) 652–4242.

Appendix A

Cleveland Area Bike Shops Not Listed in Tours

Broadway Cycle
7924 Broadway
Cleveland, OH 44105
(216) 341-6666

City Bike
1392 West Sixth Street
Cleveland, OH
(216) 771-2489

Euclid Bicycle Co.
22721 Shore Center Drive
Cleveland, OH 44123
(216) 731-1206

Fridrich Bicycle Inc.
3800 Lorain Road
Cleveland, OH 44113
(216) 651-3800

Hi-Tech Cycles
1904 Lee Road
Cleveland, OH 44118
(216) 321-0500

Jaye & Jaye Co.
22550 Lake Shore Drive
Cleveland, OH 44123
(216) 289-1880

LBS Bicycles
2211 Broadview Road
Cleveland, OH 44109
(216) 398-4823

Madison Cycle Center
13743 Madison Avenue
Cleveland, OH 44107
(216) 228-7865

Taylor Road Cycle Co.
2184 South Taylor Road
Cleveland, OH 44118
(216) 321-4977

Al's Bicycle Company
1789 Lee Road
Euclid, OH 44112
(216) 371-4438

Legend Creek Products
22721 Shore Center Drive
Euclid, OH 44123
(216) 731-2211

Parma Schwin
5758 Ridge Road
Parma, OH 44129
(216) 845-1711

The Bike Station
14755 Pearl Road
Strongsville, OH 44136
(216) 572-3680

Appendix B

Western Reserve Bibliography

Butler, Margaret Manor. *A Pictorial History of the Western Reserve.* Early Settlers Association of the Western Reserve and the Western Reserve Historical Society, 1963.

Campen, Richard N. *Architecture of the Western Reserve 1800–1900.* The Press of Case Western Reserve University, 1971.

Cantor, George. *The Great Lakes Guidebook: Lakes Ontario and Erie.* The University of Michigan Press, 1985.

Ellis, William D. *The Cuyahoga.* Landfall Press, Inc., 1966.

Geick, Jack. *A Photo Album of Ohio's Canal Era, 1825–1913.*

Godbey, Marty. *Dining in Historic Ohio.* McClanahan Publishing, 1987.

Hatcher, Harlan. *The Western Reserve: The Story of New Connecticut in Ohio.* Bobbs-Merrill, 1949.

Lindsay, David. *Ohio's Western Reserve: The Story of Its Place Names.* The Press of Western Reserve University, 1955.

Lupold, Harry F., and Gladys Haddad, eds. *Ohio's Western Reserve: A Regional Reader.* The Kent State University Press, 1988.

McCaig, Barbara, and Margie McCaig. *Ohio State Parks and Forests.* Affordable Adventures, 1987.

Noble, Allen G., and Albert J. Korsok. *Ohio—An American Heartland.* Ohio Department of Natural Resources Division of Geological Survey, 1975.

Ohio Atlas and Gazetteer. DeLorme Mapping Co., 1987.

Ramey, Ralph. *Fifty Hikes in Ohio: Walks, Hikes, and Backpacking Trips Throughout the Buckeye State.* Backcountry Publications, 1990.

Smith, Thomas H. *The Mapping of Ohio.* The Kent State University Press, 1977.

Traylor, Jeff, and Nadean D. Traylor. *Life in the Slow Lane: Fifty Backroad Tours of Ohio.* Backroad Chronicles, 1989.

Upton, Harriet Taylor. *History of the Western Reserve.* Lewis Publishing Co., 1910.

Undiscovered Ohio. 6th ed. B & F Publishing Co., n.d.

Zimmerman, George. *Ohio Off the Beaten Path,* 3d ed. The Globe Pequot Press, 1988.

Also from The Countryman Press and Backcountry Publications

The Countryman Press and Backcountry Publications, long known for fine books on travel and outdoor recreation, offer a range of practical and readable manuals.

Bicycling

Keep on Pedaling: The Complete Guide to Adult Bicycling,
by Norman D. Ford, $12.95

Bicycle Touring Guides

25 Bicycle Tours on Delmarva, $9.95
25 Mountain Bike Tours in Massachusetts: From the Connecticut River to the Atlantic, $9.95
25 Bicycle Tours in Eastern Pennsylvania, $8.95
20 Bicycle Tours in the Finger Lakes, $8.95
20 Bicycle Tours in the Five Boroughs (NYC), $8.95
25 Bicycle Tours in the Hudson Valley, $9.95
25 Bicycle Tours in Maine, $9.95
30 Bicycle Tours In New Hampshire, $10.95
25 Bicycle Tours in New Jersey, $9.95
20 Bicycle Tours in and around New York City, $7.95
25 Bicycle Tours in Vermont, $8.95
25 Mountain Bike Tours in Vermont, $9.95
25 Bicycle Tours in and around Washington, D.C., $9.95

Other Books for Ohio residents and visitors:

Fifty Hikes in Ohio, $12.95
Fifty Hikes in West Virginia, $9.95
Fifty Hikes in Western Pennsylvania, $11.95
Fifty Hikes in Western New York, $12.95
Pennsylvania Trout Streams and Their Hatches, $14.95

We offer many more books on hiking, walking, skiing, fishing and canoeing in New England, New York State, the Mid-Atlantic states, and the Midwest--plus books on travel, nature, and many other subjects.

Our titles are available in bookshops and in many sporting goods stores, or they may be ordered directly from the publisher. When ordering by mail, please add $2.50 per order for shipping and handling. To order or obtain a complete catalog, please write The Countryman Press, Inc., P.O. Box 175, Woodstock, Vermont 05091.